DYNAMIC JUDAISM

The Essential Writings of Mordecai M. Kaplan

Edited and with Introductions by
Emanuel S. Goldsmith
and Mel Scult

FORDHAM UNIVERSITY PRESS / *New York*
THE RECONSTRUCTIONIST PRESS

Acknowledgments

The editors wish to express their heartfelt gratitude to Kay and Jack Wolofsky of Montreal, to Rabbi David Teutsch of the Federation of Reconstructionist Congregations and Havurot in New York, and to Bonny Fetterman, our editor at Schocken Books, for their interest, encouragement, and assistance.

First edition 1985
Fordham University Press corrected reprint 1991
7   9   10   8
Copyright © 1985 by The Federation of Reconstructionist Congregations
and Havurot, Emanuel S. Goldsmith and Mel Scult

Library of Congress Cataloging in Publication Data
Kaplan, Mordecai Menahem, 1881–1983
Dynamic Judaism.
Bibliography: p.
Includes index.
1. Judaism—Addresses, essays, lectures.
2. Reconstructionist Judaism—Addresses, essays, lectures.
I. Goldsmith, Emanuel S., 1935–. II. Scult, Mel.
III. Title.
BM45.K3824   1985   296.8'344   85-2391

Designed by Richard Oriolo

Manufactured in the United States of America
ISBN 0-8232-1310-2

Grateful acknowledgment is made for permission to reprint excerpts from:

The Jews: Their History, Culture and Religion (3d ed.), ed. Louis Finkelstein, pp. 1012–1014, 1017, 1019. Copyright © 1949, 1955, 1960 by Louis Finkelstein. Reprinted by permission of Harper & Row, Publishers, Inc.

The Purpose and Meaning of Jewish Existence by M. M. Kaplan, pp. 10, 318–319. Copyright © 1964 by The Jewish Publication Society of America. This material is copyrighted by and used through the courtesy of The Jewish Publication Society.

"Reconstructionism Is Ecumenical" by M. M. Kaplan. Reprinted from *The Jewish Spectator* (February 1965), pp. 13–14.

For
Barbara Rochelle Gish
and
Shirley Zebberman Goldsmith
with
Love

Contents

DYNAMIC JUDAISM

Mordecai M. Kaplan: His Life
by Mel Scult

Mordecai M. Kaplan began his life's journey within the confines of a small Lithuanian town on the outskirts of Vilna. He was born on a Friday evening in June of 1881. Kaplan's submergence in a total Jewish atmosphere is illustrated by the fact that he knew his day of birth only by the Jewish calendar until he went to the New York Public Library as a young man to look up the corresponding date. Kaplan's family was a traditional one in every respect, and his father, Israel Kaplan, was a learned man. When Kaplan was a young boy he did not see much of his father because Reb Israel was travelling from one yeshivah to another. Israel Kaplan eventually received rabbinical ordination from the greatest rabbis of the day, Rabbi Isaac Elhanan Spektor of Kovno and Rabbi Naphtali Tzevi Judah Berlin (*Ha-Netziv*) of the Volozhin Yeshivah. He also studied with and received ordination from Rabbi Isaac Jacob Reines. Reines was the rabbi in the town of Swenziany where the Kaplans lived. Later Reines became head of a famous innovative yeshivah and the key figure in the founding of the religious Zionist group known as Mizrachi. In 1908 when Mordecai Kaplan was on his honeymoon in Europe, he visited Rabbi Reines, was examined by him, and received rabbinical ordination.

In 1888, Israel Kaplan came to New York to serve in the Rabbinical Court set up by Rabbi Jacob Joseph, who had been appointed Chief Rabbi of the city. During that year of the great storm, Anna Kaplan and her two children, Mottel (called Maurice, then Max, then Mark, then Mordecai) and Sprinza (later called Sophie), stayed with relatives in Paris, where Kaplan remembers playing near the Eiffel Tower, which was in the process of being built for the Paris Exposition of 1889. In July, the family came to New York to join Israel and settled on the Lower East Side. Israel Kaplan soon left the services of the Chief Rabbi, who had become embroiled in controversy, and served as a rabbinical supervisor at a number of local slaughtering houses.

The most important teacher of Mordecai Kaplan, with respect to his fine grounding in traditional Jewish sources, was his father. After the family came to America, Israel Kaplan was at home and studied Talmud and other rabbinic texts with young Mordecai. This continued on and off for many years. Kaplan also attended a yeshivah (Etz Chayim) and eventually a public school. About a half a year before his bar mitzvah, he was admitted to the Jewish Theological Seminary of New York, a school for training rabbis. The Seminary, which was founded by forerunners of the Conservative movement, had a curriculum quite different from a regular yeshivah. Students studied Jewish history, books of the Bible, Hebrew grammar, archeology, Talmud, and medieval Jewish philosophy. Kaplan's teachers, most of whom were local rabbis, were what we would refer to as modern Orthodox. Although they were observant of the Commandments, all of them had good secular educations. For a while, Kaplan lived at the Seminary, which was then located on Lexington Avenue opposite Bloomingdale's Department Store. When the family moved uptown to the East Fifties, Kaplan moved back home. Because the Kaplan household was close to the Seminary, the rabbinical students frequently came to visit on Friday evenings. Old Rabbi Kaplan was a tolerant man and frequently the boys were stimulated (entertained) by the conversation of a rather heretical Bible scholar named Arnold Ehrlich. Ehrlich visited the Kaplans because he wanted to use Rabbi Israel as a source to find out how certain key biblical words were used in the Talmud. Ehrlich for his part shared his ideas with the family and thus, at an early age, young Mordecai was exposed to biblical criticism and to the problems raised by a scientific study of the Bible. After a certain point, Rabbi Israel became annoyed with Ehrlich and hired a local savant (a *maskil*—enlightened Jew) by the name of Joseph Sossnitz to study Maimonides' *Guide for the Perplexed* with Mordecai.

At the same time that Kaplan attended the Seminary in the afternoon, he was attending the City College of New York in the morning. He studied the classical curriculum rather than the scientific and thus had a heavy dose of Greek and Latin. He received his B.A. from City College in 1900, whereupon he began to take courses toward his M.A. at Columbia University. Kaplan's courses were mainly in philosophy and sociology. He studied philosophy with Nicholas Murray Butler, who became the head of the institution; with Frederick Woodbridge, the famous teacher of philosophy; and with Felix Adler, the founder of the Ethical Culture movement. He studied the classical philosophers, along with Spinoza and Kant, and wrote his master's thesis on a nineteenth-century utilitarian philosopher named Henry Sidgwick.[1]

1. Kaplan's master's thesis may be found at Columbia University. It runs to some ninety pages and is written in Kaplan's hand. It is entitled "The Ethical System of Henry Sidgwick" and was submitted on February 28, 1902.

The course with Felix Adler was entitled "Political and Social Ethics." Adler's lecture notes for this course are to be found among the Adler papers at Columbia University, Box 100–1900E–1904 B, "Lectures for a Course at Columbia." The lecture notes are typed and dated.

Kaplan's philosophy has a strong pragmatic bent, and his thinking tends to be heavily sociological. Later in his life he was always talking about the way religious beliefs functioned and about the primary value of group life insofar as religion was concerned. It seems clear that the sociological bent was heavily influenced by his teacher at Columbia, Professor Franklyn H. Giddings. Kaplan took almost half his courses with Giddings, who was the first appointee in sociology in the United States. Giddings' own approach to sociology emphasized a concept which later became central to Kaplan—the idea of like-mindedness, or consciousness of kind as Giddings called it. Kaplan later referred to this idea as that of the collective mind. Kaplan came to believe in group consciousness as a source of values in general and religious matters in particular, long before this idea received its classical formulation in the works of Emile Durkheim.

Kaplan's pragmatic emphasis may have been influenced by William James and his essays on pragmatism, which were published in 1907. His pragmatic tendency may also be traced to his involvement with the utilitarian philosophy of the nineteenth century, which looks to the results of an act in order to judge its ethical quality, and to the philosophy of Felix Adler. Although Kaplan had contempt for Adler because he had left the Jewish fold when he established Ethical Culture, he was drawn to Adler's thought, both in the classroom and through his publications. Adler emphasized a religion of obligation which is realistically related to the experience of those professing it. More than anything else, he felt that religion had to be in tune with the truths about the world as established by science. Adler's ethics centered on the notion of obligation or duty which he related to society as viewed organically. If each person is a part of a "living organism," he or she must be viewed as indispensable and irreplaceable and ought to be treated as such. Society viewed organically came to play a central part in Kaplan's thinking.

At the same time that Kaplan was studying at Columbia, he was also serving in one of the better-known Orthodox congregations in the city. He came to Kehilath Jeshurun in 1903 and was appointed "minister" because at this point he lacked traditional rabbinical ordination. He had been graduated from the Seminary in 1902 on the eve of the takeover of the Seminary by Solomon Schechter. Kaplan was the first Seminary graduate to take a large Orthodox pulpit in New York City, and some of the more extreme among the Orthodox protested strongly. A warning was issued by a group of rabbis against any congregation taking Seminary graduates. Thus Kaplan, through no fault of his own, became the center of controversy within a short time after he was ordained. He continued to be controversial throughout his life. Solomon Schechter, who liked Kaplan, is known to have said that Kaplan gained more from his own *apikorsut* (heresy) than anyone else.[2]

2. Kaplan's journal, December 13, 1928.

At this point in his life (in his early twenties), Kaplan's views were virtually unknown. His private diaries and papers reveal that he was tortured within because of his beliefs about the nature of religion and of Judaism at the same time that he had to function as the leader of an Orthodox congregation. The people he served, for their part, were very happy with him, and his salary increased significantly during his relatively short stay, from 1903 to 1909. He was, however, unhappy and looked for a way out of the rabbinate. He considered, at one time or another, a career as a lawyer or going into business with his brothers-in-law or going into insurance. Thus in 1909, when he was invited by Solomon Schechter to become principal of the newly created Teachers Institute of the Jewish Theological Seminary, he jumped at the chance.

The Seminary had instituted courses for teachers soon after Schechter's arrival. The first courses failed, however, because they were offered at the Seminary, which by then was located on 123rd Street, far from the centers of Jewish population. The Teachers Institute (T.I.), which began in 1909 as a consequence of a gift from Jacob Schiff, was directed by Kaplan from its inception until his retirement as dean in the 1940s, and until 1929 was located downtown at the Hebrew Technical Institute, in what is now called the East Village. Although students were few and standards were low at the beginning, Kaplan quickly became more selective as elementary Hebrew education improved.

His contribution to Jewish education in America is significant. He was responsible for bringing into the field many people who later became leaders and shapers. Men such as Alexander Dushkin came to serve the Jewish community because of Kaplan, and all those who held significant positions in Jewish education during the first half of the twentieth century were students of Kaplan's, including Leo Honor, Samuel Dinin, Isaac Berkson, and Israel Chipkin. During the first decade of his tenure as principal of the T.I., Kaplan created a curriculum which was taught largely in Hebrew by outstanding Hebraists (e.g., Zvi Scharfstein, Morris Levine, and Leo Honor, who all joined the T.I. in 1917; Hillel Bavli, who joined it in the early 1920s; and Abraham Halkin, who joined it in 1929).

Throughout this period, Kaplan was very active in the community at large. He served the New York kehillah (organized Jewish community) as a trustee of the Bureau of Jewish Education and worked closely with Samson Benderly, who was the director of the Bureau. He was quite active at the Y.M.H.A. on 92nd Street, and for a number of years he spoke regularly at the Y on Friday evenings and organized the religious activities. He strongly supported new educational ventures, such as the School for Jewish Communal Work and the Central Jewish Institute, an innovative educational institution located on Manhattan's Upper East Side. He also spoke widely before synagogues and organizations in the city and travelled to lecture to the Menorah Societies at Harvard and Yale.

In his speeches, but even more so in his published articles, Kaplan's growing radicalism was becoming apparent. At a rather early point (1914) he made it clear that he accepted the major assumptions of biblical criticism, although he believed strongly that the scientific study of the Torah need not undermine its place in Jewish life. ". . . Traditional belief as to the origin of the Torah is not the sole support of its supremacy. If this is found to give way, the one derived from its having rendered Israel the instrument of divine revelation is no less effective in maintaining its pre-eminence."[3] In 1915 and 1916 he published a series of articles in *The Menorah Journal* which clearly articulated his belief that religion in general and Judaism in particular can be understood best by the use of the new social sciences, especially sociology. He emphasized that religion must be linked to experience; otherwise it will wither and die. In his words, "a condition indispensable to a religion being an active force in human life is that it speaks to men in terms of their own experience," or ". . . But to those who want to find in Judaism a way of life and a higher ambition, it must address itself in the language of concrete and verifiable experience."[4] Because experience changes, religion changes, and it is important, Kaplan believed, to find ways in which beliefs and rituals can function today as they did in the past. To do this might mean changing a ritual, dropping it completely, or substituting something new.

It is important to note that Kaplan rejected Reform Judaism with as much vehemence as he rejected Orthodox Judaism. More than anything else, he perceived Reform as a radical break with the Jewish past. He decried its lack of appreciation (during this period) for ritual of any kind and its militant stand against Jewish nationalism. From his earliest years, Kaplan believed strongly in the Zionist cause. His growing sociological sophistication led him to have a strong feeling for the importance of group life. Judaism cannot survive, he believed, if it is perceived merely as a set of beliefs. Rather Judaism must be understood as the life energy of the Jewish people. When he looked around him, he perceived that this group energy was at an all-time low. Something new had to be done to foster group life in a way which would make sense in twentieth-century America. Kaplan's work at the Y.M.H.A. gave him the beginning of an answer. He saw the interest of the young men in all manner of activities including sports, dramatics, and the arts. If only a religious dimension could be added to all this activity, perhaps Jewish life could be renewed.

The opportunity came in 1915 when a group of men who wanted to organize a new synagogue on the Upper West Side approached Kaplan

3. Mordecai M. Kaplan, "The Supremacy of the Torah," in *Students Annual of the Jewish Theological Seminary* (New York, 1914), p. 186.

4. Mordecai M. Kaplan, "What Judaism Is Not," in *The Menorah Journal* 1:4 (Oct. 1915), p. 215.

for help. He told them of his ideas for a synagogue that would be the center of life for the community which it served. The founders were supportive, and Kaplan joined their initiative. A fine building was constructed which had not only a synagogue but the facilities for sports and all other kinds of social activities. The synagogue was to be known as the Jewish Center. The group wanted Kaplan as their rabbi, and he finally agreed, although he warned them that he was not Orthodox and did not follow strict Jewish law. He stipulated that his salary be given to the Teachers Institute so that he could be free to express his ideas. His service at the Center lasted until 1921, but the idea of the Jewish Center inspired a great many followers from that time on.

While Kaplan was at the Center, he continued his work at the Seminary. Not only was he principal of the T.I. (the title was changed to dean later), but he also taught in the Rabbinical School. He began teaching at the Rabbinical School in 1910 and continued there until his retirement in 1963. Although officially he was supposed to deal with homiletics, or the art of giving a sermon, it occurred to him from the beginning that he must deal not only with the mechanics of the sermon but also with the content. All of Kaplan's courses at the Rabbinical School, whether they dealt with philosophy or midrash or homiletics, attempted to focus on the fundamental religious questions which face the modern Jew. Not every student was willing to follow Kaplan in his philosophy, but every rabbi who studied with him was grateful for having been exposed to Kaplan and for Kaplan's having asked the right questions. Among his students may be counted all the leaders of Conservative Judaism in the twentieth century: Louis Finkelstein, Max Kadushin, Simon Greenberg, Max Arzt, Robert Gordis, Solomon Grayzel. All these men and many others were significantly influenced by Mordecai Kaplan.

Kaplan's energy always overflowed the classroom. He was forever forming one group or another which would meet at his house and would devote itself to the study of fundamental questions. In 1913 a group of rabbinical students met with Kaplan and studied the philosophies of William James and Josiah Royce; another was formed in 1915. A few years later (1919–20) Kaplan organized his rabbinical colleagues into the Society for Jewish Renascence. This group was to meet regularly with the following aims: "to interpret, in terms of present-day thought, the concepts of Judaism and the content of the authoritative Jewish literature. To revitalize the traditional Jewish practices, both within and without the synagogue, so as to make them the expression of the living spiritual experience of our people at the present time. . . ."[5] Among the members of this organization were Louis Finkelstein, Herman Rubenowitz, Solomon Goldman, Joshua Bloch, Jacob Kohn, and Israel Unterberg.

5. *The Society for Jewish Renascence*, n.d., p. 4.

At the same time that Kaplan was organizing the Society for Jewish Renascence, he published an article in *The Menorah Journal* which was highly critical of the Orthodox. "Nothing can be more repugnant to the thinking man of today," he wrote, "than the fundamental doctrine of Orthodoxy, which is that tradition is infallible."[6] The article, entitled "A Program for the Reconstruction of Judaism," stated that the only way to revitalize Judaism was to dispense with mythological ideas about God, to create a dynamic code that would guide Jewish behavior, and to establish a center for Jewish culture in the Land of Israel. The key to the whole program was a new way of thinking which Kaplan characterized as realistic rather than ideological, pragmatic rather than tradition-oriented.

The article was widely discussed throughout the Jewish community. Some of the more traditional Jewish Center leaders began to feel that they could no longer support Kaplan as their rabbi. After many meetings and negotiations, Kaplan, along with a sizable group of congregants, decided to leave the Center. They established a new organization which would more directly be a reflection of Kaplan's beliefs and philosophy. The new group, called the Society for the Advancement of Judaism (S.A.J.), eventually occupied a converted brownstone on West 86th Street in New York City, a block from the Jewish Center.

The S.A.J. allowed Kaplan free rein to explore his ideas and to implement his philosophy. At times he was boldly innovative in terms of changing long-established rituals. In 1922, for example, soon after the S.A.J. was established, he held a *bat mitzvah* ceremony for his eldest daughter, Judith. Kaplan always said that he had four good reasons for initiating the *bat mitzvah* ritual in the United States—his four daughters. It took a long time for American Jews to catch up with him in terms of bringing women into full equality with respect to ritual. Had he lived and written later, he would probably have modified his style and theological terminology to reflect his commitment to the equality of women. The other important innovation from this early period occurred in 1925 when Kaplan substituted Psalm 130 for the words of the Kol Nidre prayer.[7] The tune was kept. Both of these innovations beautifully illustrate Kaplan's desire not just to drop outmoded forms but to change them so that they become meaningful and functional.

Kaplan's growing radicalism made some of his Seminary colleagues uncomfortable. There is evidence that some supporters of the Seminary threatened to withdraw their funds unless Kaplan was terminated as a professor in the Rabbinical School and as head of the Teachers Institute. For his part, Kaplan was increasingly unhappy with the lack of support

6. Mordecai M. Kaplan, "A Program for the Reconstruction of Judaism," in *The Menorah Journal* 6:4 (Aug. 1920).

7. The Kol Nidre text was restored a number of years later.

for his ideas, from either colleagues or the administration. Thus, when Stephen Wise invited him to the newly organized Jewish Institute of Religion, he was very tempted to leave the Seminary. Wise extended the invitation a number of times. In 1927, Kaplan finally accepted and tendered his resignation. There was, however, such a great uproar from the rabbinical students and from the Seminary alumni that Kaplan decided to stay.[8]

Throughout the 1920s, Kaplan continued his activities at a vigorous pace. His diaries and journals reflect the fact that he travelled widely to speak to Jewish groups both within congregations and at colleges and universities. Before the age of easy air travel, Kaplan made frequent trips on the East Coast but also travelled to the South and the Middle West. In addition to his congregation, his teaching, his family life, and his speaking, he began to devote himself seriously to his writing. In 1926, he recorded his despair that he had reached the age of forty-five and had not yet produced a major published work.

By 1933, however, he had written what was destined to become a classic in American Jewish thought. He won a prize from the Rosenwald Fund for his manuscript and used the money to help defray the cost of publishing *Judaism as a Civilization*. The book was published in May 1934. Kaplan's views were well known before the publication of his book, but here was a forceful and complete statement of his ideas on a wide variety of subjects, and it raised him in the minds of many to the first rank among Jewish ideologues. In 1934 Kaplan was fifty-three years old.

As a direct result of his book and the attention it received, Kaplan and his followers launched a biweekly publication on topics of current interest to the Jewish community to serve as a forum for Kaplan to disseminate his views. The first number of the *Reconstructionist* appeared in January of 1935 under the editorship of Kaplan and with the aid of Ira Eisenstein. Eisenstein had been a student of Kaplan's at the Seminary, became his assistant at the S.A.J., and married Kaplan's daughter Judith. He continued to be Kaplan's most loyal disciple and assumed a primary role in the Reconstructionist movement.

During most of his life, Kaplan resisted the temptation to establish Reconstructionism as a separate denomination. He believed strongly that as a school of thought the movement could have significant impact on all types of Jews. He did not want to leave the Seminary nor did he want to contribute to divisiveness within the Jewish community. Kaplan's overriding concern was always the creation of greater unity among the Jewish people. His ideas, however, have consistently drawn significant criticism. Indeed, one might say that his most important contribu-

8. Regarding this incident in 1927, see this author's "Mordecai M. Kaplan: Challenges and Conflicts in the Twenties," in *American Jewish Historical Quarterly* 66:3 (March 1977), pp. 401–16.

tion has been to force others into defining their positions more precisely because they could not ignore the issues he raised.

Throughout his years at the S.A.J., Kaplan had always been impatient with traditional rituals and prayers. He felt that the prayers rarely reflected the deepest concerns of modern Jews. He was constantly trying new approaches. One lasting manifestation of his willingness to experiment is the Passover Haggadah which he, Rabbi Ira Eisenstein, and Rabbi Eugene Kohn published in 1941. It is hard for us in this age of freedom seders and feminist Haggadahs to realize the impact of the Reconstructionist Haggadah. Many were shocked because of what was left out (the Ten Plagues), because of what was changed (the language of the kiddush, where references to chosenness were removed), and because of what was inserted (historical portions on Moses, which are not in the traditional Haggadah). Kaplan's colleagues at the Seminary were outraged and wrote him a ten-page letter detailing their protests.

Kaplan was never deterred by opposition. The criticisms of the *New Haggadah* did not stop him from preparing the Reconstructionist *Sabbath Prayer Book*, which was published by the Reconstructionist Foundation in 1945. The introduction to the prayer book details the many beliefs of traditional Judaism which Kaplan felt were not accepted within the Jewish community. Again he and his disciples dropped, changed, and added material so that a new prayer book was created which reflected what Jews actually believed. The opposition to the *Sabbath Prayer Book* was loud and clear from many quarters. The senior professors at the Seminary (Professors Ginzberg, Marx, and Lieberman) criticized him strongly and publicly. The Union of Orthodox Rabbis of the United States and Canada, in June of 1945, issued a ban (*herem*) against Kaplan because of the prayer book. The *New York Times* recorded that his prayer book was burned during the *herem* ceremony which was held at the Hotel McAlpin in New York City.

Although Kaplan retired as dean of the Teachers Institute in the middle forties, he continued to teach at the Rabbinical School until 1963. As years passed, long past the point when most people begin to think about retirement, his energy seemed almost to increase. In the forties, he made a number of trips to the West Coast and was instrumental in both the ideological groundwork and the actual setting up of the University of Judaism in Los Angeles. He continued to be active within the Conservative movement, hoping that Reconstructionism would be officially declared as the left wing of Conservative Judaism.

In 1949, at the age of sixty-seven, Kaplan published *The Future of the American Jew*. This large work again stated his basic approach, but more importantly it spelled out his mature thinking on the chosen-people idea, the nature of religion, Jewish law, the status of women in Jewish law, and the way in which a reconstructed Judaism understood the basic moral and spiritual values. The fifties and sixties were years of great creativity for Kaplan. He continued to publish frequently and produced important works on Zionism, on Judaism in the modern age, and on ethical nationhood. His last book, *If Not Now, When?*, which is actually a record of his conversations with the theologian and novelist Arthur A. Cohen, appeared in 1973 when Kaplan was ninety-two years old.

Kaplan's goal of renewal led directly to the founding of the Reconstructionist movement. In Kaplan's determination not to be divisive, the movement remained loosely organized. The Society for the Advancement of Judaism was not only a congregation but also the focus for groups or even congregations who wanted to affiliate with the Reconstructionist philosophy. In 1954, the Federation of Reconstructionist Congregations and Havurot was organized.

As years passed, the number of affiliates grew, but it was not until the late sixties that the movement actually became a separate denomination. There were always people within the movement, particularly Rabbi Eisenstein, who wanted a separate and distinct identity rather than a group united by an ideology. In 1968, the Reconstructionist Rabbinical College opened its doors with Ira Eisenstein as its first president. The school was located in Philadelphia, and Kaplan, although in his late eighties, travelled regularly to lecture there. The structure of the curriculum reflected Kaplan's approach, with each successive year devoted to a different phase of Jewish civilization (biblical civilization, the first year; rabbinic, the second; and so on). The school also reflected Kaplan's commitment to the world of secular learning. Each graduate was required to have a graduate degree from a secular institution. Many of the students have taken degrees in religion, education, or social work, particularly at Temple University.

A rabbinical school meant a new denomination. The divisiveness associated with a new stream in Jewish life was a stumbling block to Kaplan but the success of the venture was not. The school flourished and in 1982 moved to a beautiful campus on the outskirts of Philadelphia in Wyncote, Pennsylvania. The Federation of Reconstructionist Congregations and Havurot likewise grew apace and in 1983 there were some fifty groups affiliated with the movement. One very striking feature of these institutions was that the leadership was young. It should not surprise us that innovative and experimental modes continue to be the hallmark of Reconstructionism. The ideology of Mordecai M. Kaplan has not yet become a tradition in need of reconstruction.

In a sense, Mordecai Kaplan's life embodies the American Jewish experience of the first half of the twentieth century. The fact that he died in 1983 at the age of 102 means that, in a literal sense, he lived through the whole saga of the American Jew in our times. Arriving here as a boy, growing up in New York City, becoming thoroughly Americanized, he struggled to find ways of making Judaism compatible with the American experience and the modern temper. As rabbi, teacher, writer, and lecturer, he spearheaded the founding of new institutions and stimulated the reconsideration of long-held assumptions. Kaplan's life is a model for all of us.

Mordecai M. Kaplan:
His Interpretation of Judaism
by Emanuel S. Goldsmith

Among the giants of twentieth-century Jewish thought, Rabbi Mordecai
M. Kaplan, with his Reconstructionist understanding of Judaism, and
his vision of a future reconstituted Jewish people and a greater Judaism,
figures prominently. Kaplan's interpretation continues to evoke broad
interest for a variety of reasons, including its religious modernism, Zionist radicalism, and application of America-inspired notions of pluralism
and democracy to the Jewish people. In addition to influencing virtually
every aspect of Jewish life in the United States and almost every organized non-Orthodox manifestation of Judaism the world over, Kaplan's
thought has given birth to Reconstructionism, an influential Jewish religious movement on the American scene, which has been accorded the
status of a fourth denomination in American Jewry. It is, however,
primarily the all-embracing nature of Mordecai Kaplan's interpretation
of Judaism that continues to make it a major force to be reckoned with in
Jewish life despite changing theological, philosophical, and sociological
fashions. Mordecai Kaplan remains the only nineteenth- or twentieth-
century Jewish thinker to have painstakingly constructed a comprehensive analysis of Judaism in terms of community and peoplehood; organization and structure; philosophy and theology; and history, culture,
ethics, and ritual; and to have charted a course for the Jewish future in
all these areas.

The unprecedented rapid acceleration of social change and the immer-
sion of the Jews in a wide variety of social and cultural milieus in the
twentieth century produced a rich panoply of interpretations of Judaism. In Eastern Europe, the Hebrew essayist and social critic Ahad
Ha'am developed his Cultural Zionism, the Yiddish and Hebrew writer
Y. L. Peretz his language and culture-centered humanistic Judaism, the
Hebrew novelist and essayist M. Y. Berdichevsky his Nietzschean view
of a transvaluated Judaism, and the historian Simon Dubnow his Dias-

pora Nationalism and Autonomism. In Central Europe, the neo-Kantian philosopher Hermann Cohen put forth his view of Judaism as the Religion of Reason *par excellence* while his disciples, Franz Rosenzweig and Martin Buber, produced a daring original translation of the Hebrew Bible into German and interpreted it, as well as other aspects of the Jewish experience, from an existentialist perspective. In the United States, theologian Kaufmann Kohler wrote his classical analysis of Judaism from a Reform point of view, while Yiddish essayist and philosopher Chaim Zhitlovsky conceived his secularist and nationalist interpretation, and Rabbis Abraham J. Heschel and Joseph Soloveichik their Conservative-Hassidic and Orthodox-halakic interpretations, respectively. In Palestine-Israel, the Zionist pioneer A. D. Gordon viewed Judaism from the dual perspective of kabbalistic mysticism and the return to the soil, Rabbi Abraham Isaac Kook effected a poetic synthesis of traditional Judaism and Zionist aspirations, and David Ben-Gurion, pioneer and prime minister, a synthesis of Israeli nationalism, secularism, and modern Hebrew culture.

Mordecai Kaplan's Reconstructionist Judaism is the only modern version of Judaism to have originated entirely in the United States. Its roots, however, may be sought in the *mussar* heritage which Kaplan inherited directly from his father; in the Jewish enlightenment movement or Haskalah, from which in the eighteenth and nineteenth centuries the modern "scientific" approach to Jewish scholarship, as well as Reform, modern Orthodoxy, Conservative Judaism, and, later, Zionism emerged; in modern developments in philosophy and theology, as well as in sociology, anthropology, psychology of religion, and comparative religion; and, finally, in the American Jewish experience and Kaplan's own career as an American rabbi.

Whereas the Hassidic movement, established in Poland and the Ukraine in the middle of the eighteenth century by Rabbi Israel Baal Shem Tov, stressed joyous piety and emotional ecstasy, the only slightly less influential *mussar* (ethics) movement, founded by Rabbi Israel Salanter of Lithuania in the nineteenth century, emphasized introspection, self-analysis, and the study of Hebrew ethical literature in a contrite and penitent mood. Its major themes were responsibility, conscience, and soul-searching. Mordecai Kaplan's father, Rabbi Israel Kaplan, was a follower of Rabbi Salanter, whose *mussar* convictions were so strong that he declined to serve in the practical rabbinate for fear that he might have to compromise them. Mordecai Kaplan always admitted that his father's influence on him had been great. An amateur sculptor, he treasured a small wood sculpture he once made of his father. The dedication of his first major book reads: "To the memory of my virtuous and noble father and teacher, Rabbi Israel Kaplan, who guided me as I wandered in the wilderness of doubt and confusion."

It was the Haskalah movement which opened the spiritual and cultural walls of the European ghettos to the larger society and fought Jewish insularity and isolationism. It was also out of the Haskalah that the modern, scholarly approach to Jewish studies and the new Hebrew and Yiddish literature emerged. The modern Jewish religious philosophies and movements, too, were practical and organized expressions of various trends in the Haskalah. Mordecai Kaplan, as his writings show, learned much from all of these developments. It was Zionism, however, which to him represented what was the essentially worthwhile and creative outgrowth of the Haskalah. Ahad Ha'am's cultural interpretation of Zionism, despite its negative attitude to institutional religion, always seemed to Kaplan to have particular relevance and significance because of its brilliant, ethical approach to Jewish collective identity.

The influence of modern philosophy, theology, comparative religion, and the social sciences on Mordecai Kaplan was also considerable. The major thrust of all of these disciplines for him was the conviction that religion could not exist apart from the total life and culture of a people and that economics, politics, and other environmental influences are crucial in the development and maintenance of a religion.

The unique character of the Jewish experience in America, the diversity of the American Jewish community in the 1920s and 1930s, the challenges of America and the "adventure in freedom" it offered its diverse peoples presented a particularly exciting challenge to Mordecai Kaplan in the development of his interpretation of the Jewish heritage. He was greatly aided by the instruction he received at the Jewish Theological Seminary of America, at New York's City College, and at Columbia University. His years in the American rabbinate, first in two Orthodox synagogues, and later in his own Reconstructionist congregation, rendered him particularly sensitive to the spiritual needs and aspirations of America's Jews. It came as no surprise to Rabbi Kaplan that, toward the end of his life, a sociologist discovered that what he had been saying about Judaism was actually what most American Jews had come to believe about it.[1]

Mordecai Kaplan's interpretation of Judaism is a modernistic and not simply a modern one. It proceeds from the hard-won, early realization he had as an American rabbi that "as long as Jews adhered to the traditional conception of Torah as supernaturally revealed, they would not be amenable to any constructive adjustment of Judaism that was needed to render it viable in a non-Jewish environment."[2] Religious modernism may be distinguished from traditionalism in that its point

1. Cf. Charles S. Liebman, "Reconstructionism in American Jewish Life," in *American Jewish Year Book:* 71 (1970) 3–99. New York, 1970.

2. Mordecai M. Kaplan, "The Way I Have Come," in *Mordecai M. Kaplan: An Evaluation,* ed. I. Eisenstein and E. Kohn (New York, 1952), p. 293.

of departure in religious life is the contemporary scene and present-day religious experience rather than the dictates of authority and the religious experience of past generations. Religious modernists are eclectic, selecting out of the garnered treasures of their forebears only those which they see as relevant and significant for their community's life today. Only those aspects of tradition which can be reconciled with what they regard as true and valid in their general world view and approach to life will be incorporated into their religious conceptions. For them, it is modernity, despite its flaws and failings, that is the judge and test of tradition rather than the reverse.[3]

Kaplan's principal teachings may be subsumed under three major categories: (1) transnaturalism or antisupernaturalism, (2) religio-culturalism or civilizationism, and (3) Diaspora Zionism or ethical peoplehood. As a religious modernist, Mordecai Kaplan viewed Jewish religion as the product of history and evolution, as a dynamic process subject to continuous growth and development. "The historical approach," he wrote, "implies that the Jewish tradition is a human phenomenon subject to the natural laws of human behavior and to the normal reaction between human life and the environment."[4] A religious naturalist and religious humanist, Kaplan saw the divine as immanent in universal human experience and therefore rejected the grounding of Jewish religion in the authoritarianism of past generations. Moreover, the Jewish religion was for him the product of the thought and experience of the Jewish people, and therefore all supernaturalism had to be rejected. Amid premodern cultural conditions the Jewish tradition's claim to supernatural origin may have been "entirely natural and normal," for it was simply "a way of expressing awareness of supreme worth and binding authority."[5] For modern Jewry, however, Kaplan developed the concept of a Judaism without supernaturalism, a "transnatural" Judaism which envisaged God in the "organicity" of the cosmos and in the fulfillment of human nature and destiny, rather than in the miraculous suspension of the laws of nature. "Transnaturalism," he wrote, "is that extension of naturalism which takes into account much that mechanistic or materialistic or positivist science is incapable of dealing with. Transnaturalism reaches out into the domain where mind, personality, purpose, ideals, values, and meanings dwell. It treats of the good and the true."[6]

In the tradition of American philosopher John Dewey, Kaplan was frankly more concerned with the ethical validity of the Jewish religion and its survival value for the Jewish people than with its factual veracity.

3. Cf. *Encyclopedia of Religion*, ed. V. Ferm (New York, 1945), p. 499, s.v. "modernist."
4. Mordecai M. Kaplan, *The Future of the American Jew* (New York, 1949), p. 377.
5. *The Future of the American Jew*, p. 377.
6. Mordecai M. Kaplan, *Judaism Without Supernaturalism* (New York, 1958), p. 10.

"Its validity must be judged by its effectiveness in securing the emergence of a warless world based on freedom and justice."[7] Surely no great religious tradition could afford to be without myth. Transnatural religion, Kaplan admitted, needed to utilize the language of simile and metaphor, symbol and myth, poetry and drama, "not to help man overcome the hazards of nature, but to enable him to bring under control his inhumanity to his fellow man."[8] Although many traditional beliefs might not be verifiable, they had served historically to help the Jewish people survive in the face of adversity. "Demythologizing, rather than discarding, such unenviable assumptions can help maintain their essential validity."[9]

The primary issue for Kaplan was never merely the rejection of belief in God as a supernatural being but rather the rejection of authoritarianism and supernaturalism (which always seeks validation in authority) in every aspect of Jewish religious life and thought. Kaplan did not simply reject the supernatural God-idea. He also and most emphatically rejected the supernatural people-idea commonly known as chosenness and the supernatural revelation-idea known as *Torah min hashamayim*.

For Kaplan, supernaturalism was a Pandora's box. If there was a supernatural God, a supernatural people, and a supernatural doctrine, mankind—let alone the Jewish people—was doomed because accommodation and mutual respect became impossible. If, on the other hand, there was a naturalistic, humanistic, or transnatural God (whom we experience in our efforts to control our impulses, better our lives, and improve our world), then there was hope because there could be tolerance, compromise, and mutual understanding between individuals and groups. Kaplan believed that nothing so threatened the future of humanity generally and of the Jewish people in particular as the dogmatism, chauvinism, fanaticism, and intolerance of supernatural religion. The Holocaust became for the Jewish people a particularly painful demonstration of the evils to which doctrines of chosenness, superiority, supernaturalism, and authoritarianism could be subject. Moreover, the religious establishment of the State of Israel, he felt, threatened the very survival of that country as a democratic republic at the same time that Orthodox intransigence in the Diaspora threatened the viability of any kind of multidenominational organized Jewish life there.

Despite Kaplan's great influence on Reform and Conservative Judaism, they could never accept his basic approach because although Reform rejects authoritarianism, both movements accept diluted forms of supernaturalism. Kaplan's Reconstructionism unequivocally rejected both authoritarianism and supernaturalism. It sought to have faith in democracy

7. Mordecai M. Kaplan, *The Religion of Ethical Nationhood* (New York, 1970), p. 1.
8. *Judaism Without Supernaturalism*, p. 10.
9. *The Religion of Ethical Nationhood*, p. 10.

replace authoritarianism, and religious naturalism (Kaplan's transnaturalism) and religious humanism (salvation in this world through the improvement of human character and conscience) replace supernaturalism. Kaplan's supporters viewed his position as consistent with the Judaism of the past because of its emphasis on the centrality of the Land of Israel and the primacy of Jewish peoplehood and because in Judaism God has always been seen primarily as the cosmic source of spiritual values and ethical purpose.

Mordecai Kaplan's interpretation of Judaism may be viewed as a Jewish synthesis of the empirical approach to religion, pragmatic philosophy, and pluralistic process theology found in the writings of such twentieth-century philosophers and theologians as William James, John Dewey, Alfred North Whitehead, Henry Nelson Wieman, Douglas Clyde Macintosh, Charles Hartshorne, Schubert M. Ogden, and John B. Cobb, Jr. This modernistic orientation to religion is characterized by openness and tentativeness. It begins with the question of what in the world may be pointed to as unambiguous manifestations of divinity. It establishes the hypothesis that there is a creative process bringing values into being, transforming humanity for the better, and thus making human life worthwhile and holy.[10]

Kaplan's approach may also be viewed as a Jewish version of what has been termed the "religion of quest" or the "quest orientation" to religion. Complexity, doubt, and tentativeness are terms that have been utilized to describe the religion of quest. An individual who approaches religion in this way surrenders the certainty of final answers without denying the importance of religious questions and without denying the religious dimension of human life. This orientation to religion is associated with a heightened love of humanity, tolerance, and sensitivity to others.[11]

In addition, Kaplan's approach may be seen as a Jewish version of the "religion of maturity" described by such students of religion as Erich Fromm, Erwin R. Goodenough, Gordon Allport, and H. Richard Niebuhr.[12] "The test of modern maturity," according to Goodenough, "is the ability to tolerate paradox and question marks, to accept the unknown as unknown, to adjust to the universe of flux and our apparently miniscule place in it."[13] Eager search and passionate quest for meaning characterize religious maturity. Though tentative, mature religion evokes feelings of wonder and awe and encourages responsible behavior in all areas of life.

10. Cf. Randolph C. Miller, *The American Spirit in Theology* (Philadelphia, 1974), p. 25.
11. Cf. C. Daniel Batson and W. Larry Ventis, *The Religious Experience* (New York, 1982), pp. 150, 298.
12. Cf. Orlo Strunk, Jr., *Mature Religion* (New York, 1965).
13. Erwin Goodenough, *The Psychology of Religious Experiences* (New York, 1965), p. 175.

Mordecai Kaplan's passionate commitment to the survival of the Jewish people, in a world of freedom, justice, and peace in which war has been abolished and democracy securely established, led to the development of his functional approach, which, while denying the traditional theological attempts to discover what God *is*, stressed what God *means* to mankind. "Since its main concern in understanding reality is to improve it, functionalism deals with the relation of means to ends and sheds light upon the purpose and meaning of human experience."[14]

"Judaism," Kaplan wrote, "is more than a specific philosophy of life; it is the ongoing life of a people intent upon keeping alive for the highest conceivable purpose, despite changes in the general climate of opinion."[15] The main function of Judaism as an evolving religious civilization is "to involve the individual in the social and spiritual heritage of a historic society and to commit him to the transmission of that heritage. . . . It expects its adherents to identify themselves with all the generations of their forebears who created that tradition and lived by it. Self-involvement in the social and spiritual heritage, and commitment to transmit it, are bound to transform the vicarious experience of the reality of God into a personal experience."[16] In other words, Judaism is a matter of both heart and head, of both celebration and cerebration, requiring both the love and understanding of the Jew. In Kaplan's view, it is as natural for a people to love its civilization and to want to see it grow as it is for children to love their parents and want them to be happy. A Jew raised in a healthy, self-accepting Jewish atmosphere and environment naturally develops a love for the Jewish people and all it holds dear. But, said Kaplan, it has never been enough for the Jews just to survive, just to remain alive as a people. The Jewish people has usually been "intent upon keeping alive for the highest conceivable purpose." "A people that is of minority status," he wrote, "must have great confidence in itself, great faith in its own *raison d'être*, if it is not to be intimidated by the handicaps that go with having minority status."[17]

What is that "highest conceivable purpose"? In biblical times, Jews believed that by keeping the ethical and ritual rules of the Torah, they were serving as witnesses to the one God of all the world and helping to establish God's Kingdom on earth. In talmudic times, the highest conceivable purpose was for the individual Jew to attain a share in the world to come by studying Torah and fulfilling the *mitzvot*. To Maimonides, in the twelfth century, the highest conceivable purpose was to

---

14. *The Religion of Ethical Nationhood*, p. 4.

15. Mordecai M. Kaplan, *The Purpose and Meaning of Jewish Existence* (Philadelphia, 1964), p. 40.

16. *The Purpose and Meaning of Jewish Existence*, p. 306.

17. *The Purpose and Meaning of Jewish Existence*, p. 288.

arrive at a philosophical understanding of God and God's law, while to Hermann Cohen, at the beginning of the twentieth century, it was to arrive at a conception of ethical living based on rational thought and philosophical idealism. Martin Buber, a great Jewish thinker of the twentieth century, believed that the highest conceivable purpose of human life is to help build an ideal community and a true society and that Jews should build such a society on the foundations of their ancient spiritual heritage.

Kaplan had his own view of the highest conceivable purpose of human existence, one which linked him with the ancient prophets and sages as well as with the leading philosophers and religious thinkers of his day. To him that purpose was to help create a society which would nurture persons whose lives were motivated by what he called a sense of active moral responsibility. "For us Jews," he wrote, "there can be no higher purpose than that of exemplifying the art of so living individually and collectively as to contribute to the intellectual, moral, and spiritual progress of mankind. . . . The type of religion which we Jews as a people, and which mankind as a whole, urgently needs as a means to *survival* has to consist, or take the form of *moral responsibility in action*."[18] That type of religion would help humanity rid itself of three illusions which threaten to destroy it in a nuclear age: (1) the illusion of collectivism, (2) the illusion of "rugged individualism," and (3) the illusion of the unchangeability of human nature. Moral responsibility in action is the modern equivalent of the dictum of Hillel the Elder, "If I am not for myself, who will be for me? And being for my own self, what am I? And if not now, when?" (*Avot* 1:14)

Kaplan believed in the law of polarity: everything that exists is both itself and more than itself, both individual and interactive, independent and interdependent. That law is divine, a law of God penetrating every nook and cranny of the universe. In human beings it takes the form of conscience, making us aware of our individual rights as well as of our responsibilities to others. To be human, people must both exercise their rights and fulfill their responsibilities. If they exercise their rights without accepting their responsibilities, they become brutes, savages. If they accept their responsibilities without exercising and enjoying their rights, they become slaves to others. It is the combination and balance of rights and duties that constitutes conscience, the human instrument of moral responsibility. Conscience is the divine law of polarity, independence and interdependence, action and interaction, as that divine law operates among people.

The purpose of Jewish existence, for Kaplan, was not that Jews survive as a relic of the past but that they take the old biblical idea of human-

18. *The Purpose and Meaning of Jewish Existence*, p. 294.

ity's being created in the likeness of God and apply it to human life, that they try to make themselves, in A. D. Gordon's brilliant expansion of a biblical phrase, "a *people* in the image of God." Kaplan always stressed that individuals with a sense of moral responsibility were not enough. If humanity is to survive, the total group must order its life in accord with the dictates of conscience and develop itself along the lines of active moral responsibility. The unique quality of the Jewish religion is that it is "the only religion of mankind which from its very inception has been based on the ongoing history of a people in its relation to mankind."[19]

The Jewish people, which always sought to make itself an instrument for the development of better human beings and a better world, now must take that goal and spell it out in greater detail. It must develop a kind of Jewish religion that views God not as a supernatural being up in the sky but as that power or force in the universe, in nature, and in the human heart and mind which impels us both to be ourselves and to be a part of something bigger than ourselves at one and the same time. God is the Power, Force, Process, Dimension, or Energy by means of which people are motivated to exercise their rights, pursue their responsibilities, and strive to be at peace with themselves, with nature, and with other people. The idea that religious truth is derived from a realm beyond natural experience and that it has to remain unaffected by natural experience is to be summarily rejected. "For a religious tradition to become part of our personal experience nowadays, it has to possess the authenticity we associate with scientific fact. It has to convey the kind of literal meaning which we can integrate into our normal experience."[20] No religious tradition could do that, said Kaplan, unless its supernaturalism was translated into naturalistic terms. That, however, was a small price to pay for the sense of historic continuity which confers meaning and zest upon a religious community. Kaplan believed that the Jewish tradition could without difficulty be translated into transnatural terminology and humanistic experience.

Why Jewish survival? Because, replied Kaplan, the striving and suffering of the Jewish people and the evolution of Judaism as a religious civilization during more than three thousand years should render contemporary Jewry committed to the type of religion which *humanity* urgently needs if *it* is to survive. "The Jewish people is committed *to the promulgation of that belief in God which can impel man to create a social order based on freedom, justice, peace, and love. . . . The purpose* of Jewish existence is to be a people in the image of God. The *meaning* of Jewish existence is to foster in ourselves as Jews, and to reawaken in the rest of the world, a sense of moral responsibility in action."[21] Kaplan hoped

19. *The Purpose and Meaning of Jewish Existence*, p. 310.
20. *The Purpose and Meaning of Jewish Existence*, p. 307.
21. *The Purpose and Meaning of Jewish Existence*, pp. 313, 318.

that such purpose and meaning would motivate Jews to rebuild the Jewish people, reinterpret and creatively expand their religious tradition, and reconstruct their historic way of life.

According to Kaplan, it is the application of functionalism (which he sometimes referred to as functional rationalism) to Jewish experience that led to his discovery of "Judaism as not merely a system of religious beliefs and practices, but as the sum of all those manifestations of the Jewish people's will to live creatively," and to his redefinition of Judaism as an *evolving religious civilization*.[22]

From its earliest full formulation (in 1934), Kaplan's definition of Judaism has been revolutionary, challenging virtually all accepted definitions in vogue since the emancipation of Western Jewry in the nineteenth century, when questions such as What is a Jew? and What is Judaism? had first begun to be raised. It challenged both the original Reform concept of Judaism as only a religion of ethical monotheism and the Orthodox view of Judaism as a set of divine rules. Nor could it accept totally the Conservative concept of Judaism as a "positive-historical" religion. To Kaplan, Judaism is a civilization—dynamic and evolving, with religion at its core, but containing other integral elements such as language, secular history, music, art, literature, customs and folkways, and love of the Land. "To choose to remain a Jew," he wrote, "is a three-dimensional affair. It involves choosing to belong to the Jewish people, to believe in Jewish religion, and to practice the Jewish way of life. In terms of contemporary philosophy, Judaism as an evolving religious civilization is *existentially* Jewish peoplehood, *essentially* Jewish religion, and *functionally* the Jewish way of life."[23]

Kaplan also disagreed with the methods which the various Jewish denominations were using to make Judaism viable in the modern world. He was as opposed to the Reform method of changing Jewish religion to suit the external pressures of the current culture as to the Orthodox method of unquestioningly preserving the traditions of the past, and to the Conservative approach of analyzing and explaining practices in order to preserve the past while assenting to change only when absolutely necessary. Kaplan sought to refashion the whole of Judaism to meet what he called the "spiritual needs" of the Jewish people, brought on by the rapidly expanding dimensions of modern science, philosophy, and political life in a global culture in which the Jewish people now participated.

Kaplan also taught that as an organic civilization Judaism is not static; it has always been in a state of flux—developing, growing, changing. In opposition to the notion that what is static is authentic and that what

22. *The Religion of Ethical Nationhood,* pp. 4f.
23. *The Purpose and Meaning of Jewish Existence,* p. 30.

always remains the same should rightfully command our respect and allegiance, Kaplan's view was that only that which is dynamic, which evolves and changes without losing its identity or continuity, is authentic. He agreed with the statement of the seminal Jewish philosopher Hermann Cohen that "true progress depends on continuity in change, not on the preservation of dogmatic principles."[24]

Since Judaism is more than a religion, it cannot be limited to a particular philosophy. In the past it welcomed, and today it continues to harbor, different and even conflicting philosophies. This is so because Judaism involves the life of a whole people, with different individuals and groups embracing every conceivable viewpoint and approach to life. "The dogmatism that would rule out more than one absolutely true rationale for Jewish existence ignores the intellectual freedom which has come to be a *sine qua non* of being human. Jewish existence will henceforth have to be compatible with the inevitable variety of human minds."[25]

According to traditional Judaism, that is, Judaism as it existed before Jewry's contact with the modern world, the return of the Jewish people to the Land of Israel, the restoration of its national sovereignty, and the reinstitution of the Davidic monarchy were divine promises as certain of fulfillment as the recurrence of the seasons and the shining of the sun, moon, and stars. But that return and restoration were to be achieved by a series of supernatural divine miracles to be performed by God. The Jew's role was to hope and wait, to pray and believe. "Even though the Messiah tarry, I still believe with perfect faith. I await his coming every day." For Jews themselves to initiate the redemption, to "force God's hand," would constitute a sign of little faith in God's miraculous power and an act of betrayal.

Zionism represents the continuation of the Jewish people's love and longing for Zion but it rejects the passivity, supernaturalism, and authoritarianism of a bygone age. For these it substitutes a dynamism, naturalism, and commitment to democracy that was inconceivable before Theodor Herzl's classic, *The Jewish State*, and before his proclamation to the First Zionist Congress in Basel, Switzerland, in 1897 that "we are a people, one people." Zionism is Judaism transformed, modernized, radicalized. Zionism is dynamic, naturalistic, and democratic. It replaces passivity, reliance on miracles, and authoritarianism with a call for action. Herzl said, "If you will it, it is no dream." If you seek the restoration and redemption, go to the Land—rebuild it. Clear the swamps, plant the trees, build the cities, revive your ancient tongue, and create a modern democratic commonwealth where rulers are not appointed by God but chosen by, and responsible to, the will of the people.

24. Quoted in *The Purpose and Meaning of Jewish Existence*, p. 148.
25. *The Purpose and Meaning of Jewish Existence*, p. 285.

Zionism achieved what it achieved and became synonymous with Judaism for the overwhelming majority of the world's Jews precisely because it adjusted itself to modern ways of thinking and doing. It had more far-reaching implications for Judaism than any of the modern theologies or religious denominations. It meant for millions of Jews that God works through people rather than for them, that God is in us, not only above us, that doing is prayer in action and that conscious striving is hope realized. That is why, according to Kaplan, the task of Zionism is not over. For him the fulfillment of the Zionist vision has only begun. Zionism means the translation of the concepts of Judaism into the language of the twentieth century and the transformation of the Jewish people into a modern people.

Zionism signifies the effort to preserve both the life and the distinctiveness of the Jewish people the world over. Without a vibrant State of Israel, there is no hope for Jewish life anywhere. At the same time, however, the goal of Zionism is the survival and enhancement of the life of the Jewish people. The survival of the Jewish people is the end, the State of Israel the means. As there is no future for Israel as a Jewish state without the Jewish people, so there can be no future for the Jewish people without a strong, secure, democratic, and spiritually and culturally Jewish Israel.

According to Kaplan, the Zionism of an Ahad Ha'am and the Diaspora Nationalism of a Simon Dubnow must be fused into a new synthesis of striving for the reconstitution of the Jewish people and for Jewish continuity and dynamic growth throughout the world. "To be a Jew today means nothing less than to aid in the rebuilding of the House and in the reconstituting of the Household of Israel." In order to survive as a corporate entity in the modern world, Jews would have to transform themselves into a new kind of society, "partly as a commonwealth developing in its own historic landscape, and partly as a people which can integrate itself with other nations in other lands, without losing its own individuality."[26]

Diaspora Zionism, which Kaplan called "Greater Zionism" and "New Zionism," is Zionist because it affirms both the essence of Zionism—the need to preserve the life and distinctiveness of the Jewish people—and an awareness of the indispensable role of the State of Israel in fostering that aim today. But it is Diaspora Nationalist because it affirms the mutual interdependence of Israel and the Diaspora and rejects the Zionist negation or debunking of the Diaspora which has given Jews outside Israel an inferiority complex and the role of second-class citizens in Jewish life.

Diaspora Zionism, or the striving to reconstitute the Jewish people, is

26. *The Future of the American Jew*, p. 105.

the reaffirmation of the sense of Jewish peoplehood, the unity of Jewry throughout the world, and the equality of Israeli and Diaspora Jewry in Jewish life. Diaspora Zionism rejects the lachrymose conception of Jewish history as exclusively a tale of sorrow and suffering. It views both modern Israel and the modern Diaspora as products of two thousand years of exilic existence which must be viewed in a positive light.

Diaspora Zionism is primarily the attempt to recover Jewish ethnic consciousness, the sense of Jewish peoplehood. Kaplan has described ethnic consciousness as a group soul "the body of which is the particular civilization through which it functions." Kaplan saw ethnic consciousness and civilization as concrete realities. He noted that "in that they can outlive many generations of human beings, they are of infinitely greater worth, and the essence of the greatest worth which those who live by them attain."[27]

For generations of Jews down through the ages, the Jewish people has not been an abstraction. It has been as real a unit of life as any individual human being. That is why it could elicit loyalty and respect, responsibility and love. *Bat-ami* (the daughter of my people), *Bat-Zion* (the daughter of Zion), *Beyt Yisrael* (the Household of Israel), *Dos Yidishe Folk* (the Jewish people) were for Jews in all times and places names of a reality more real than themselves. They point to the fact that the Jewish people has in the course of four millennia managed to evolve a personality and conscience as authentic as the personality and conscience of any individual human being.

According to modern process philosophy, which greatly influenced Kaplan, what accounts for the sense of identity of the human personality (despite the fact that every second we actually undergo a whole variety of distinct experiences and that we ourselves thus actually constitute a different set of experiences every second) is the fact that in every occasion or experience, there are sympathetic feelings of memory and anticipation.[28] Memory and anticipation, which constitute personal identity, may also be said to constitute group identity. Diaspora Zionism would have us perpetuate Jewish identity by fostering Jewish memory, Jewish creativity, and hope for the Jewish future in the heart and mind of every Jew.

Diaspora Zionism means existentially recalling the Jewish past, living creatively as a Jew in Israel or the Diaspora in the present, and actively anticipating the Jewish future. Diaspora Zionism takes advantage of the current approach to history as more than a cataloguing of facts. The meaning of history, it is now believed, lies in "interpretation and living-

27. *The Future of the American Jew*, p. 83.
28. Cf. Charles Hartshorne, *Reality as Social Process* (Glencoe, Ill., 1953), p. 102, and Alan Gragg, *Charles Hartshorne* (Waco, Tex., 1973), p. 58.

experience of facts in a community."[29] Real history is a living-out of the past in the present, a vivid awareness of the past as it contributes to the creation of modern social existence in the present and the future.

Diaspora Zionism encourages finding new ways of spelling out the interdependence of Israeli and Diaspora Jewry; encourages an experimental approach to Jewish community, education, and worship; and fosters deliberate planning for the future in every phase of Jewish endeavor. Mordecai Kaplan referred to Diaspora Zionism as "if-ist." It heeds the biblical admonition *vehaya im shamoa*—"it shall come to pass *if* Jews harken" to the call of the hour and affirm the peoplehood of the Household of Israel and the unity of Jewry in Israel and the Diaspora in thought and deed by fostering ethnic consciousness and Jewish civilization everywhere.

Mordecai Kaplan's modernistic interpretation of Judaism constitutes a highly original synthesis of concerns and concepts responsive to the inner spiritual and cultural needs of the Jewish people in the period following the tragedy of the Holocaust and the rebirth of Jewish national sovereignty in the ancestral homeland of the Jewish people. He viewed antisupernaturalism as just as significant in the contemporary world as anti-idolatrism was in ancient Israel and anti-anthropomorphism was in medieval Judaism. Most people can no longer conceive of God as a being out there telling humanity what to do. But they do feel the need to conceive of God coursing throughout nature as well as inside their own hearts and minds, goading them to be and to do their best, and helping them overcome life's frustrations and tragedies. Similarly, the Jewish people's contribution to humanity must be sought not in its being superior to others but in its being itself. As Y. L. Peretz, the distinguished Yiddish and Hebrew writer, put it: Judaism is simply seeing the world through Jewish eyes, that is, from the perspective of universal unity and mutual responsibility.[30]

In Mordecai Kaplan's view, the Torah (which for him meant the Five Books of Moses as well as the later classical works of Judaism) should be seen as the product of the Jewish people's never-ending quest for purpose, meaning, and value and, therefore, as in no way finished or complete. His view of Torah was inclusive rather than exclusive, and he spoke of its "creative expansion" to include the best products of Jewish culture and universal ethical teachings. Torah has to embrace all the worthwhile products of the Jewish spirit and of the universal spirit for the never-ending task of civilizing religious and national bodies and

29. W. Norman Pittenger, "Process Thought: A Contemporary Trend in Theology," in *Process Theology*, ed. Ewert H. Cousins (New York, 1971), pp. 29f.

30. Cf. Emanuel S. Goldsmith, "Yitzkhok Leybush Peretz on His Sixtieth *Yortsayt*," in *The Jewish Frontier* 42:6 (June–July 1975), p. 23.

heightening the sensitivity of people everywhere to the higher needs and destiny of all living beings.

Religio-culturalism or Judaism as a civilization meant to Mordecai Kaplan that without Jewish culture—literature, history, art, music, drama, dance, customs, folkways, and folklore—there can be no Jewish religion that will emotionally affect Jews for the better. It meant, moreover, that through their culture, Jews can discover the God who makes life beautiful and meaningful. It meant that Jewish life has to be built primarily on the foundation of strong historical and cultural ties among Jews and only secondarily on ideology. It meant that cultural unity is possible among Jews today despite ideological diversity, that continuity is possible despite new growth and development.

Modern Jewish culture has, in the main, been associated with formal secularism because organized Jewish religion considers it superfluous and godless. In the State of Israel today, cultural creativity flourishes primarily in the secularist rather than in the religious camp. The same is true of the Diaspora, where living Jewish culture, to the extent that it exists, is found primarily among the secularist advocates of Yiddish culture. Kaplan's Reconstructionism is the only movement that promises to reconcile modern Jewish culture with modern Jewish religion, and Jewish secularism with the religious heritage of past generations. It can do so because it replaces Jewish law with the concept of folkways and emphasizes Jewish *sancta* (sacred texts, seasons, events, persons, places, customs, etc.) as the indispensable, unchanging vehicles of an ever-changing, dynamic, quest-oriented religion.

"The primary *mitzvah* of Jewish peoplehood," wrote Kaplan, "is rebuilding the House and reconstituting the Household of Israel."[31] Kaplan's Greater Zionism, which includes the international recognition of the Jewish people as a transnational people and the establishment of "organic" or united-despite-diversity Jewish communities the world over, seeks to place Jewish group existence on an equal footing with Jewish religion. In his view, Jewish peoplehood can never be less significant than Jewish religion because Zionism, or the eventual rebirth and reconstitution of the entire Jewish people as "a people in the image of God," has always been synonymous with the highest type of Jewish religion.

The God of Israel meant to Kaplan "the power of salvation which the collective self-consciousness generates by means of its organic function,"[32] the spirit of the Jewish people at its best—the Jewish people

---

31. Mordecai M. Kaplan, *The Greater Judaism in the Making* (New York, 1960), p. 484.

32. Mordecai M. Kaplan, "Our God as Our Collective Conscience," in *Reconstructionist* 41:1 (Feb. 1975), p. 14.

living true to its own character in both Israel and the Diaspora without exaggerated notions of self-grandeur or xenophobia. When Jews said "our God and God of our ancestors," Kaplan wanted them to mean the universal process making for world peace, ethical nationhood, and personal fulfillment: that aspect of the culture of past generations of the Jewish people in which modern Jews can perceive the seeds of Jewish spiritual growth in future generations. Such Jewish religion can never become self-worship because Jews are called upon to worship not themselves but the God in themselves and their ancestors who is "inherently akin to that which makes the cosmos or nature as a whole possible."[33] The God of Israel is "nature's God"—the spirit of freedom, justice, truth, loyalty, and compassion in Jewish history and in all of human civilization.

33. "Our God as Our Collective Conscience," p. 14.

I

The Modern Predicament

1. Judaism in the Past

To get to the root of Jewish survival in the past, it is necessary to take into account a highly significant leverage which the Jewish religion possessed during the pre-Enlightenment period, and which it has since lost. That leverage consisted in the fact that, before the Enlightenment,* the religion of the greater part of mankind was based on the same world outlook as was the religion of the Jews. Christians and Mohammedans accepted as axiomatic three such basic and far-reaching assumptions as the following: (1) the Old Testament account of the creation of the world and of the beginnings of the human race is not only authentic but constitutes the premise of all that man should believe in and strive for; (2) human life on this earth, being full of sin and travail and ending in death, can attain its fulfillment or achieve salvation only in that perfect world which is known as the world to come; and (3) the only way man can attain such salvation is by conducting himself in accordance with the supernaturally revealed will of God. It is, therefore, a mistake to assume that in the past the Jews were able to ignore or defy their environment. They were, on the whole, just as responsive to it then as they are now, though they lived entirely segregated from their neighbors. But to be responsive to environment formerly meant to be confirmed in one's adherence to Judaism. To be responsive to it now means to be perplexed by doubt and torn by inner conflict.

Judaism as a Civilization, pp. 5–6.

2. The Challenge of the Modern World

The Emancipation** . . . by no means put an end to the problem of Jewish status. The truth is that it created more problems for the Jew than

*Kaplan refers here to the general European Enlightenment of the eighteenth century which stressed rationalism, this-worldliness, and universalism.—eds.

**The granting of citizenship to Jews in their respective countries, beginning with the United States and France in the late eighteenth century.—eds.

it solved. This is the case because the secular conception of the state implies the principle that its function is to direct the cultural and economic activities of the nation, with a view to greater internal solidarity and to greater power in its relation to other states. These newly awakened needs gave rise to a new organization of society. In place of the heterogeneous mass of communities, classes, and other political groups, each with its own system of law and mores and its own type of cultural life during the medieval period, there emerged the modern homogeneously constituted and governed state. Whereas in the past a nation was a conglomerate of all kinds of groups and corporations, it now seeks to achieve as tightly integrated a unity as possible. To that end, the modern nation would have the state direct its energies. . . .

Since the state has become secularized, it has taken over three important functions from the various corporate groups which were formerly part of the state. These are the administration of civil law, the prerogative of validating marriage and divorce, and the education of the child. Under the premodern organization of society these functions could be exercised by a minority group, so long as its presence in the land was tolerated. The modern state, however, insists that its citizens submit to the laws enacted by it and that they resort to its courts for their litigation. Only courts for the arbitration of disputes may be established under private or voluntary jurisdiction. That situation presented itself as soon as Jews were given civil rights and has necessitated the suspension of all Jewish code law in civil matters. The shock which this administered to the organic unity of the Jewish people was felt only by the generation in whose lifetime the suspension of Jewish courts was decreed. Before long, Jews grew insensitive to the disintegrative influence of that decree on their life as a people. . . .

Most embarrassing of all has been the challenge of the modern state to that element of international Jewish unity inherent in Jewish religion which had found expression in the yearning of Jews for return to their ancient homeland. The modern State is jealous of all other loyalties. It definitely deprecates, even if it does not actually prohibit, loyalties that transcend its boundaries, whether they be to universal ideals or to historical memories. What was then to become of the Messianic hope and of the whole mind-set which traditional Judaism has fostered for centuries, and which pointed to Eretz Yisrael as the land of Jewish destiny? The lack of a clear answer has been the main source of many Jews' resistance to Zionism.

The Greater Judaism in the Making, pp. 159–62.

3. Secularization

With all the revolutionary changes in man's outer and inner life, the traditional cosmic orientation could not but grow obsolete, despite the fact that it took a long time for the Copernican revolution to penetrate the mind of the average person. The Roman Catholic Church did not officially permit the teaching of the heliocentric conception of the universe until 1843. But once started on its way, this conception was bound to destroy the traditional world outlook which was based on the biblical account of the creation of the world and of man.

The Greater Judaism in the Making, p. 167.

4. On Evolution and Darwin

The Darwinian conception of the descent of man from the lower animals . . . holds forth the promise of man's evolving into a much higher type of being than he now is. If we were to judge the potentialities of human nature solely by the way man, as we know him, behaves, we could easily despair of his ever developing into that reasonable, honest, just, and kind creature which he must become, if he is to fulfill the prophetic vision of the Kingdom of God.

When, however, we reflect, we note that man has so far transcended his original animal nature as to possess reason and spirit. He has the capacity to transform his environment and direct his own future to a degree that puts him in a category utterly distinct from that of the lower animals, in spite of his kinship with them. It is not difficult to conceive of his destiny as involving the eventual dominance of his rational and ethical sense over his sensual appetites and savage lusts.

Questions Jews Ask, pp. 107–108.

5. The Emancipation: A Mixed Blessing

The disillusioned Jew, who still possesses the will to live as a Jew, should sense the equivocal character of what has happened to his people during the last one hundred and fifty years. He should understand why it is necessary to revise the interpretation which has hitherto been given to the Jewish Emancipation. It can no longer be viewed as an unqualified blessing. It certainly was not the forerunner of the millennium. Since the Emancipation was in line with the general policy of the rising bourgeoisie to bring into play additional forces for the exploitation of the newly created commercial and industrial opportunities, it meant for the Jew nothing more than the freedom to join in the general scramble for wealth and power. It was part of the general tendency to repudiate other-worldly restraints, not for the sake of this-worldly salvation but for the sake of worldly prosperity. Worldly prosperity which may satisfy the personal ambitions of the few who come out on top in our competitive economic system is but a cheap caricature of this-worldly salvation and in the end leads to frustration. In the success which depends upon someone else's failure, man can never find a substitute for other-worldly salvation. Complete self-fulfillment in this world presupposes the maximum of individual self-realization through the maximum of social cooperation. But even the promise of success and prosperity which the Emancipation held out to the Jew has proved a snare and a delusion, tragically void of anything for which he might live at all, to say nothing of living as a Jew. This fact, however, should not lead the Jew to ignore the element of genuine human goodness and of sincere desire to increase the measure of happiness and self-fulfillment for all men, that was latent in the rise of democracy. That element might yield what he is so badly in need of—something to live for, something to strive for as a Jew. That element is the social idealism which at present finds an outlet in various movements for social reconstruction.

Judaism in Transition, pp. 29–30.

6. A Critique of Orthodoxy

Nineteenth-century Reform in Germany had aimed at the following three objectives: (1) the substitution of a rationalist attitude to tradition for the one based on unquestioning faith, (2) the elimination of those religious observances and prayers which emphasized the particularistic aspect of Judaism, and (3) the shifting of emphasis from the legalistic to the prophetic aspect of Judaism. To counteract that threefold program, Orthodoxy proposed a program of its own, which called for the following: (1) faith in the supernatural origin of the written and oral Torah, (2) maintenance of all traditional observances and forms of worship, and (3) the continuance of the study of Torah in the traditional spirit. This program was intended to rule out any possibility of compromising with modernism. In practice, however, Orthodoxy did not shut out completely all tendencies that conflicted with tradition.

The entire style of thought in Reform bears the imprint of Protestant theology and philosophy. Jewish Orthodoxy, on the other hand, clearly reflects the style of thought characteristic of Catholic theology. That may explain in part why Orthodoxy attained its greatest strength in the Catholic part of Germany. The reaction of the Orthodox Jews against the modernist emphasis upon reason and the spirit of the times was very similar to that displayed by the Catholics among whom they lived. The spokesmen of Orthodoxy maintained that to recognize the primacy of reason was to place oneself outside of Judaism. They maintained that the authoritative character of traditional Judaism should be sufficient to validate whatever demands it makes on the Jew. Those demands, they argued, are intrinsically meant to be a challenge to whatever happens to be the spirit of the times, rather than a concession to it. For Samson Raphael Hirsch,* the essence of modernity is the humanist assumption that salvation consists in the achievement of happiness and self-perfection. That assumption, according to him, is morally and spiritually untrue.

The Greater Judaism in the Making, pp. 318–19.

7. Orthodoxy and Modern Thought

The salvation of Judaism cannot come either from Orthodoxy or from Reform. Orthodoxy is altogether out of keeping with the march of human thought. It has no regard for the world view of the contemporary mind. Nothing can be more repugnant to the thinking man of today than the fundamental doctrine of Orthodoxy, which is that tradition is infallible. Such infallibility could be believed in as long as the human mind thought of God and revelation in semi-mythological terms. Then it was conceivable that a quasi-human being could hand down laws and histories in articulate form. Being derived from a supramundane source, these laws and histories, together with the ideas based upon them, could not but be regarded as free from all the errors and shortcomings of the human mind. Whenever a tradition contradicts some facts too patent

*Samson Raphael Hirsch (1808–88): rabbi and theologian; founder and principal spokesman of Orthodox (also called Modern Orthodox and Neo-Orthodox) Judaism in Germany.—eds.

to be denied, or falls below some accepted moral standard, resort is had to artificial interpretations that flout all canons of history and exegesis. The doctrine of infallibility rules out of court all research and criticism, and demands implicit faith in the truth of whatever has come down from the past. It precludes all conscious development in thought and practice and deprives Judaism of the power to survive in an environment that permits of free contact with non-Jewish civilizations.

There are, no doubt, a few who manage to acquire a high degree of modern culture and even to achieve distinction in some branches of modern knowledge without finding themselves intellectually at variance with Orthodoxy. They belong to those who see no need for welding tradition and experience into a unitary organized mental background. They willingly subscribe to the medieval principle that Torah and philosophy have nothing to do with each other, because it saves them a great deal of mental bother. But such religiosity is only a small eddy in the main current of Jewish life.

"A Program for the Reconstruction of Judaism,"
The Menorah Journal 6:4 (Aug. 1920), pp. 182–83.

8. A Critique of Conservative Judaism

The attitude of the Historical School* of thought has a paralyzing effect on any attempt to cope realistically with an unprecedented situation. This was amply demonstrated by what happened to the United Synagogue in 1918, when it was proposed to organize an authoritative council that would interpret Jewish law in accordance with the spirit of historical Judaism. Nothing came of that proposal. The reason for its failure may be traced to the statement which was intended to serve as a frame of reference. That statement was so ambiguous and inhibiting as to preclude helpful guidance in the functioning of an authoritative body.

On the one hand, the statement read: "We who stand on the firm ground of historical Judaism must insist on the immutability of the Torah." On the other hand, it said: "Neither the physical nor the spiritual world presents us with any instance of absolute fixities or absolute mobilities, and to eliminate human agency from the workings of Jewish law would lead to Karaism of the worst kind." This apparent paradox was by no means resolved by the following definition of Jewish law: "What constitutes Jewish Law is the interpretation and application of

*On the Historical School see p. 153.—eds.

the words of the Torah by an authoritative body." How does that coincide with the immutability of the Torah? But even if this seeming contradiction were to be ignored, who or what can determine what are the qualifications of a body needed to render it authoritative? What kind of law does the Historical School expect the Jews to live by if no one is qualified to interpret it? Such law must, indeed, be either "in heaven" or "beyond the sea."

The spokesmen of Conservative Judaism repudiate indignantly the charge of failing to reckon with the principle of development. They maintain that Jewish law has been developing since its very inception, and that it has always reckoned with changed conditions of life and thought. They keep on repeating [Abraham] Geiger's* discovery that Pharisaism represented the principle of development, in contrast with the attitude of the Sadducees, as Rabbinism did later in contrast with Karaism. Upon examination of those claims, however, it turns out that the conception of development of Jewish law which is thus read into the rabbinic tradition and held up by the Conservative movement as offering practical guidance in our day is virtually the same as that of which the Roman Catholic Church boasts. It is merely a mechanical process of defining and explicating in detailed terms what is implied in revealed doctrine, which is necessarily immutable and forever authoritative. There is in this conception no place for a living interaction of a tradition with advancing thought and experience, no room for criticism, modification, or amendment. In actual practice, the principle of "Catholic Israel" operates like the turnstile which, in *Mother Goose Rhymes*, says of itself: "I am in everyone's way, but no one I stop."

The Greater Judaism in the Making, pp. 377–78.

9. A Critique of Reform Judaism

Our dissent from Reform Judaism is even more pronounced than that from Orthodoxy. If we have been content to put up with much in Orthodoxy that we do not approve of, it is that we might not be classed with the "Reformers." The reason for this attitude of ours toward Reform is that we are emphatically opposed to the negation of Judaism. The principles and practices of Reform Judaism, to our mind, make inevitably for

*Abraham Geiger (1810–74): scholar and rabbi; a leading figure in the Reform movement in Germany.—eds.

the complete disappearance of Jewish life. Reform Judaism represents to us an absolute break with the Judaism of the past, rather than a development out of it. In abrogating the hope for a national restoration, it has shifted the center of spiritual interests from the Jewish people to the individual Jew. Reform Judaism has as little in common with historic Judaism as has Christianity or Ethical Culture. Although it insists that the Jews are a religious community and not a nation, it has never taken the trouble to develop the full implications either of the term "religious" or of the term "community." It overlooks the fact that a community implies living in common and not merely believing in common. A community is not merely a society. It is because we refuse to sublimate the Jewish people into a philosophical society that we object to the Reform movement. While the Reform movement gives free scope to the intellectual inquiry, it does not take full advantage of that freedom. Being opposed to ancient ideas is not the same as having acquired modern ideas. There is as much credulity in gulping down ill-understood modern slogans as in blindly accepting ancient dogmas. If the Reform movement had learned from the recent studies of the history and nature of religion, it would have abandoned its attempt to reduce Judaism to a few anemic platitudes.

The untenability of the Reform position is never so apparent as in its attempt to find in the mission idea a substitute for the national aspiration of the Jewish people. On the face of it the mission idea appears more absurd than the belief in the personal Messiah. The belief in the personal Messiah at least has an air of poetry and romanticism to it, and until recently no one thought of questioning its literalness; whereas the mission idea, as entertained by Reform Judaism, represents a half-hearted attempt at self-hypnotization. So far as making the Jews understood to the rest of the world is concerned, which is after all the avowed aim of the Reform movement, the so-called mission idea is certainly a failure, for it does more to accentuate the alleged megalomania of the Jews than the most extravagant Messianic doctrine.

"A Program for the Reconstruction of Judaism,"
The Menorah Journal 6:4 (Aug. 1920), pp. 183–84.

10. The Weaknesses of Reform Judaism

Deliberate and direct striving for certain objectives in human life is known to be self-defeating. One such objective is happiness. It is a well-known psychological fact that the more one makes happiness the only purpose in life, the more one fails to secure it. The same is, in a sense, true of religion. That may well be what is wrong with the Reform philosophy of the synagogue. It is based on the mistaken notion that the way to foster religion is to organize congregations for the sole purpose of cultivating it. It is interesting to note that when a Reform congregation wants to hold its own members or to increase its membership it has to reckon with the foregoing psychological principle. In some of the congregations, a plan had been devised whereby young married couples were invited to meet within the walls of the temple. The plan was called "Mr. and Mrs. Limited." Two rules were laid down by the inventors of that plan: (1) "discreet relationship between the temple and the group." That meant that those who were invited must not suspect that the motive was to get them to belong to the temple. "No proselytism, please!" (2) "Emphasis on sociability rather than religion and education." What that implies is indicated by the kind of activities in which the group was advised to engage. They were: a harvest party, a quiz show, truth-and-consequence show, dramatic production, magician's exhibition, with a few meetings "of a more serious nature," such as an address on the subject of "rent control."*

The foregoing travesty on the function of the synagogue is in a sense a *reductio ad absurdum* of the basic approach of the Reform movement to Judaism as nothing else than a religion and to the synagogue as the end-all and the be-all of organized Jewish life. . . .

What is wrong with Reform Judaism is perhaps best summed up in an article entitled "Liberal Judaism as a Living Faith," which appeared in the magazine *Commentary.*** In that article, Robert Langebaum, a member of the English Department at Cornell University, takes to task David Daiches, a well-known literary critic, for having assailed Reform Judaism for the wrong reasons. "The failure of spirituality ought to have been the main object of Mr. Daiches' attack. . . . Our reforms embarrass us because we know we have made them not to promote a higher

*"The Synagogue," in *Liberal Judaism* (Nov.–Dec. 1948), pp. 51f.
**July 1952.

spirituality, but in order to get by with as little spirituality as possible. . . . Worst of all is the danger of second-rateness which threatens liberal Judaism as it must any attempt to tailor a tradition to our needs. . . . That may be why so few intellectuals can make a place for themselves in liberal congregations. . . . There is really, as things now stand, no place in our liberal congregations for anyone who, whether by choice or necessity, cannot live according to the routine assumptions of the middle class. . . . The case for liberal Judaism must in the end stand upon the extent to which it has kept alive the religious need by institutionalizing and cultivating it, and the extent to which it will in the future realize the possibilities of religious development."

The Greater Judaism in the Making, pp. 312–15.

11. Why Moderns Reject Religion

The function of a religion is twofold: to foster the unity and cohesion of its adherents and to enable its adherents individually to achieve salvation, or the full and the good life. To achieve this twofold function each religion promulgates a specific conception of God. A religion fulfills its twofold function as long as the conception of the God it promulgates in its public or institutional manifestation is congruous and compatible with the conception of the God that figures in the religious experience of its individual adherents. A religion is most apt to be authentic when it is indigenous. It is indigenous when it exercises its cohesive influence through the *sancta* of the people, or civilization, of which it is the soul or conscience. Those *sancta* are the events, the heroes, the writings, and the occasions signalized by a people as giving concreteness to the values deemed essential by the people to its existence.

The present crisis in the traditional religions is due to their dualistic assumption that reality as a whole consists of a twofold order, a natural and a supernatural, and that salvation is not achievable in this world but only in a world "wholly other." Those assumptions are rejected by the overwhelming majority of modern thinking men and women. In consequence, they either reject religion altogether and dispense entirely with the belief in God, considering this belief to be a self-deceptive illusion, or they identify some emotional, numinous, or mystical experience—usually devoid of any ethical directives—as revealing an authentic presence of God.

"When Is a Religion Authentic?"
Reconstructionist 30:12 (Oct. 16, 1964), pp. 25–26.

12. Religion and Group Life

The study of any phase of human life, whether for theoretical or for practical purposes, must be based upon the recognition that man is not merely a social animal, as Aristotle put it, but that his being more than an animal is due entirely to his leading a social life. In opposition to the older point of view, which prevailed in the more materialistic schools of thought during the nineteenth century, social science has proved that the forces that operate in human life are not merely those that are derived from the physical environment but also those which are of a mental character. These psychical forces operate with a uniformity and power in no way inferior to those of the physical world. Social science is gradually accustoming us to regard human society not merely as an aggregate of individuals but as a physical entity, as a mind not less but more real than the mind of any of the individuals that constitute it. The perennial source of error has been the fallacy of considering the individual human mind as an entity apart from the social environment. Whatever significance the study of the mind, as detached from its social environment, may have for metaphysical inquiry, it can throw no light upon the practical problems with which the mind has to deal—problems that arise solely from the interaction of the individual with his fellows. The individual human being is as much the product of his social environment as the angle is of the sides that bound it.

This new method of studying mental life both in the race and in the individual has revealed not merely the true significance of religion but the way in which it functions and the conditions which affect its career. We now know that those phenomena in life which we call religious are primarily the expression of the collective life of a social group, after it has attained a degree of consciousness which is analogous to the self-consciousness of the individual. When a collective life becomes self-knowing we have a religion, which may therefore be considered the flowering stage in the organic growth of the tree of social life. The problem of religious adjustment is at bottom that of maintaining in a social group the psychical or spiritual energy which expresses itself in beliefs, ideals, customs, and standards of conduct. Accordingly, when a religion is passing through a crisis, what is really happening is not so much that certain accepted truths or traditional habits are threatened with obsolescence as that the social group with whose life it has been identified is on the point of dissolution. Whatever interest we have in the cultivation of the spiritual life must go toward conserving this kind of social energy. To have roses we must take care of the tree on which they grow and not content ourselves with having a bouquet of them to put into a vase filled with water. This newer conception of the religious life is fraught with far-reaching consequences.

"What Is Judaism?"
The Menorah Journal 1:5 (Dec. 1915), pp. 315–16.

13. The Function of Religion

As the consciousness of the group, the main function of religion has ever been to enable the group so to adjust itself to its environment as to make the most of its life. In the course of this adjustment there developed spiritual values, ideas, and beliefs by means of which it was able to overcome all dangers and to utilize to the best advantage whatever opportunities of growth the environment offered it. The analogical reasoning, the mystical interpretation of its social experiences in terms of God, represent the normal, healthy working of the group mind. But when analogical reasoning was transferred to the field of purely logical concepts and formulated into a theological system, religion developed an "incidental excess of function," which in time was mistaken as the chief purpose of religion. Thus arose the fatal aberration that religion was a sort of schoolmistress to instruct humanity in all things in the heaven above and on the earth beneath. Her curriculum included metaphysics, physics, history, politics, economics, and kindred subjects. Anyone who ventured to explore reality on his own initiative compromised the dignity of religion. And if he went so far as to assert any fact that contradicted tradition he was adjudged a heretic who deserved chastisement. All this has changed. The scientific spirit has invaded the entire domain of human thinking. Even theology is giving way to the science of religion to which it bears the same relation as alchemy to chemistry. Religion will be restored to its rights. It will once again react naturally to the supernatural* and will find truer and more apt analogies to answer to the deepening of the sense of mystery. Being drawn from different fields of experience, each religion will seek to express that mystery by means of analogy and ritual that will constitute its unique contribution to the spiritual life of mankind.

"The Future of Judaism," *The Menorah Journal* 2:3 (June 1916), p. 169.

---

*At a later time, Kaplan abandoned the term "supernatural" for the term "transcendent" and, still later, for the term "transnatural."—eds.

14. Judaism as a Civilization

The Jew's religion is but one element in his life that is challenged by the present environment. It is a mistake, therefore, to conceive the task of conserving Jewish life as essentially a task of saving the Jew's religion. When a person is about to abandon a house for fear that it might fall about his ears at any moment, it is folly to try to convince him that he ought to remain in it because of the beautiful frescoes on its walls. Jewish life is becoming uninhabitable because it is in danger of collapse. The problem is how to make it habitable. To drop the metaphor and return to the more abstract method of viewing the problem of Judaism, the task now before the Jew is to save the otherness of Jewish life; the element of unlikeness will take care of itself.

Put more specifically, this means that apart from the life which, as a citizen, the Jew shares with the non-Jews, his life should consist of certain social relationships to maintain, cultural interests to foster, activities to engage in, organizations to belong to, amenities to conform to, moral and social standards to live up to as a Jew. All this constitutes the element of otherness. Judaism as otherness is thus something far more comprehensive than Jewish religion. It includes that nexus of a history, literature, language, social organization, folk sanctions, standards of conduct, social and spiritual ideals, and esthetic values which in their totality form a civilization. It is not only Judaism the religion that is threatened, but Judaism the civilization. What endangers that civilization is not only the preoccupation with the civilizations of other peoples but also the irrelevance, remoteness, and vacuity of Jewish life. There is little at present in Jewish life that offers a field for self-expression to the average man and woman who is not engaged either as rabbi, educator, or social worker. If one does not have a taste for praying three times a day and studying the Bible and rabbinic writings, there is nothing in any of the current versions of Judaism to hold one's interest as a Jew. Activities that might hold one's interest, and through which one might express oneself as a Jew, have not been recognized as part of Jewish life because there has been found no concept which might integrate them into it. Lacking that integration, they are bound to remain sterile, and Jewish life is apt to become an empty shell. . . .

The categories under which it has been customary to subsume Judaism have proved inadequate. It can no longer be confined within the terms of revealed religion or ethical monotheism. Both its own nature and the temper of the time preclude its being classified with either the one or the other. We must, therefore, find for it a category which will do justice to the whole of it. Those who try to interpret Judaism to the outside world are in the habit of describing it in terms which they imagine would justify its existence in the opinion of their audience. This is why Philo and Josephus found it necessary to represent Judaism to the Gentiles of their day as a philosophy, and this is why modern Jewish apologists deem it necessary to represent Judaism as a religion. But what may reconcile non-Jews to the existence of Judaism does not necessarily help the Jews in solving the problems to which it gives rise. Now that it is in need of intelligent planning and direction Jews should learn Judaism's essential character so that they might know what to do with it in times of stress.

The term "civilization" is usually applied to the accumulation of knowledge, skills, tools, arts, literatures, laws, religions, and philosophies which stands between man and external nature and which serves as a bulwark against the hostility of forces that would otherwise destroy him. If we contemplate that accumulation as it works in the life process, we realize that it does not function as a whole, but in blocks. Each block of that accumulation is *a* civilization, which is sharply differentiated from every other. Each block or unit of civilization can exist and flourish, even if every other should become extinct. This fact indicates that a civilization is a complete and self-contained entity. Civilization is an abstract term. The actuality is civilizations; for example, the civilizations of Babylonia, of Egypt, of Palestine.

Not all elements of a civilization constitute its otherness. Each civilization possesses elements which it shares with other civilizations and which are transferable *in toto* to other civilizations. Among these would be included mechanical developments, inventions, the funded discoveries of science. But it would be wrong to assume that these improvements in the mechanics of living constitute a civilization. The elements which give it otherness and individuality are those which produce the human differentia in the individuals that are raised in it. The development of the human differentia is due mainly to nontransferable elements like language, literature, arts, religion, and laws. They are nontransferable in the sense that they cannot be adopted by other civilizations without essential changes in their character.

By placing Judaism within the category of civilizations we shall know how to fit it into the framework of the modern social order. That classification should help us identify, in the complex thing called Judaism, all of the elements and characteristics which go to make up its substance and which can be properly appraised in terms of present-day values and desiderata, because they can be studied as the reactions of human nature to social environment. Judaism is but one of a number of unique national civilizations guiding humanity toward its spiritual destiny. It has functioned as a civilization throughout its career, and it is only in that capacity that it can function in the future.

> If Judaism is to be preserved amidst the new conditions [said the late Israel Friedlaender], if, lacking as it does, all outward support, it is still to withstand the pressure of the surrounding influences, it must again break the narrow frame of a creed and resume its original function as a culture, as the expression of the Jewish spirit and the whole life of the Jews. It will not confine itself to a few metaphysical doctrines, which affect the head and not the heart, and a few official ceremonies which affect neither the head nor the heart, but will encircle the whole life of the Jew and give content and color to its highest functions and activities.*

A civilization is not a deliberate creation. It is as spontaneous a growth as any living organism. Once it exists it can be guided and directed, but its existence must be determined by the imperative of a national tradition and the will to live as a nation. Civilization arises not out of planned cooperation but out of centuries of inevitable living, working, and striving together. Its transmission takes place by the method of suggestion, imitation, and education of the young, sanctioned by public opinion and authority. The operation of these forces is postulated by the existence of the social institutions of the family, school, religious organization, and communal self-government. The process cannot wait until the child reaches the age of choice. Civilizations live by the inherent right to direct the child into their ways. It is only thus that the whole course of human development has been made possible.

Judaism as a Civilization,
pp. 177–81.

15. Living in Two Civilizations

The true significance of the separation of state from church is to be found in the changed status of the citizen. As far as his cultural life is concerned, he may be a hyphenate. Before that separation took place, he could live only by the civilization which was represented in the state; he may now live, in addition, by the civilization of whatever other group he chooses. As a matter of fact, that is how the average citizen does live. He derives his political values, his language, literature, and the arts from

*Israel Friedlaender, *Past and Present* (Cincinnati, 1919), pp. 269–70.

the civilization embodied in the state; his ethical and spiritual values from that embodied in the church.

The same confusion which prevails in the mind of the average person with regard to the status of the Jewish people and the nature of Judaism prevails also with regard to the status of the church and the nature of Christianity. The same clarification is needed in Christianity as in Judaism. The fact that Christendom is divided into many nations and that the collective term by which it is usually designated is "the church" has prevented most people from realizing that Christendom was to have constituted the one nation which was to embrace all mankind. As a world-nation, or Catholic nation, Christendom wanted to impose one language, one history, and one social structure upon all its adherents. During the Middle Ages, Christianity was a full-fledged civilization. The fact that religion permeated all its constituent elements and that other-worldliness was the characteristic of that religion in no way disproves the cultural character of Christianity. For the Catholic Church, Christianity is still more than a special department or phase of human life; it is synonymous with the whole of human life. The Catholic Church has never retreated from that position. It has consistently demanded of its adherents that in the education of their children they give priority to its doctrines, sanctions, laws, and authority over those of the civilization embodied in the state. It insists upon being regarded not as a voluntary organization but as "a structure of law and government." The Catholics take full advantage of the principle of religious freedom to live as cultural hyphenates.

The Protestants are all in a tangle. Their conception of Christianity as a "purely spiritual" institution is just as illogical and inconsistent as the Reformist conception of Judaism. Once in a while even a liberal Protestant, realizing that the Protestant churches are losing ground, and that Protestant Christianity is fast disintegrating, raises a warning voice to urge his fellow believers not to yield all prerogatives to the state. "Let the Churches reassert that the state is not a final moral authority for the citizen," writes George A. Coe. "This is an ancient doctrine, but it has fallen into disuse among Protestants. It is high time to recover the old position. . . . A super-political conscience must be developed in and through the church schools."*

All this indicates that for a long time to come citizenship in the Western world will take the form of hyphenism. Living in two civilizations which yield different types of values is not merely a necessity into which modern nations are driven by historical forces beyond their control; it is a means of warding off the danger of raising the state to a religion. Far from viewing the hyphenated cultural allegiance of the citizen of a mod-

*"Shifting the National Mind-Set," in *The World Tomorrow*, Feb. 1924.

ern state with alarm, we should rejoice that there is present in the body politic an influence counteracting the danger of chauvinism. Christianity, in whatever form, is so far the only cultural agency the occidental man has developed to broaden and spiritualize his outlook upon life. The English, the Germans, the French, and the Americans who are loyal to Christianity live in two civilizations. Simple justice requires that the same right be extended to the Jew. The only difference is that, since Christians are in the majority, they require no justification for their right to hyphenate. But since Jews are in the minority, they must define their status clearly. Since they can no longer claim the right to cultivate a corporate Jewish life on the traditional basis of being the sole possessors of supernatural revelation, they must be able to base that right on their interpretation of nationhood. To do that they must learn to interpret nationhood in conformity with the deepest intuitions of their own forebears, intuitions which harmonize with the tendencies to see in nationhood an expression, not of political separatism, but of cultural individuality and spiritual creativity.

The conception of Judaism as a civilization yields two corollaries by which Jews will have to be guided in their efforts to reconstruct Judaism in accordance with the spiritual needs and social conditions of the present time. They are as follows:

1. Only in a Jewish national home is it possible for Judaism to achieve those environmental conditions which are essential to its becoming a modern, creative, and spiritual civilization.

2. As long as the modern nations depend upon historic civilizations like Christianity or Mohammedanism for the moral and spiritual values which they cannot find in their own native civilization, the Jews must insist upon the right to cultivate their own historic civilization as a means to their spiritual life. Such cultivation necessarily takes on the twofold form of rebuilding Eretz Yisrael and endeavoring to maintain in the Diaspora as much social cohesion and organization and as much of each of the constituent elements of their historic civilization as are compatible with unqualified loyalty to the countries of which they are citizens.

Judaism as a Civilization,
pp. 249–52.

II

Jewish Peoplehood

1. Ethnic Consciousness a Human Value

In the past, no attempt was made to distinguish, except quantitatively, between the we-feeling of ethnic consciousness and the we-feeling of family consciousness. Both were regarded as due to blood kinship. What is actually the difference between the we-feeling which expresses itself as ethnic consciousness and the we-feeling which expresses itself in other types of collective consciousness? The difference should be sought mainly in the factors that contribute to ethnic consciousness. Moreover, it should be one which would account for all kinds of ethnic groups both ancient and modern.

Ethnic consciousness, or the sense of peoplehood, functions through the medium of a living civilization, which is an organic ensemble of the following cultural elements having their rootage in a specific territory: a common tradition, a common language and literature, history, laws, customs, and folkways, with religion as the integrating and soul-giving factor of those elements. To this ensemble must be added an active leadership which is concerned with translating that tradition into a means of serving the essential needs of all who are identified with the people. The foremost among those are: being wanted and having something to be proud of.

An ethnic consciousness is thus coextensive with a unit of civilization. An ethnic consciousness is a group soul, the body of which is the particular civilization through which it functions. Both the consciousness and its body, or vehicle, are distinctively human creations. They exist as two aspects of a manifold of specific living realities known as peoples. Neither ethnic consciousness nor civilization exists merely in the abstract. Each exists as a particular process, associated with concrete realities. Each is certainly as real a unit of life as is any individual human being, to say the least. Actually, in that they can outlive many generations of human beings, they are of infinitely greater worth, and the essence of the greatest worth which those who live by them attain. It is normally expected of the individual to prove his worth by sacrificing his life, in order that his civilization may live. According to Milton, "as good almost kill a man as kill a good book." By what standard then shall we measure the unnecessary death of a civilization? Nothing more tragic can happen than for a people and its civilization to disintegrate and die. To be in any way responsible for this tragedy is to be guilty of snuffing out life in its most human and sacred form.

These considerations should help us see each of the various elements of a civilization in a new light—as the highest manifestation of human life struggling to live. Among the earliest evidences of recognition of language as an element of ethnic consciousness and as a mark of peoplehood is the story of the Tower of Babel. It is also implied in the term "tongues" as a synonym for peoples, as in the following: "The time cometh, that I will gather all nations and tongues" (Isa. 66:18). Why differences of language should mark off one people from another is quite understandable. Those who speak the same language are in a position to be of one mind and to cooperate. A common language is, therefore, conducive to the we-feeling, whereas when we hear a different language, we become aware of the group-otherness of those who speak it. . . .

That the variety of languages is the primary factor in the division of mankind into peoples is of utmost significance. It implies that peoplehood and ethnic consciousness are not the product of any hereditary tendency or instinct, but of historical circumstances. The outcome of those circumstances constitutes the social heritage which is transmitted from generation to generation. Peoplehood does not originate in the hereditary instincts like those which make for the family. The very fact that it is not inherited biologically makes it a distinctively human value which has to justify itself by the good that it does. . . .

Language, which gives a people its sense of unity, brings in its train a whole complex of elements that go into the making of peoplehood. It brings into play the remembrance of past heroes and events of history, the customs to which every member of the people is expected to conform, laws which regulate conflicts of interests and help to maintain the peace, and folkways which include characteristic forms of esthetic self-expression. Besides enabling a people to carry on social intercourse, a common language is thus a vehicle for factors which give content and meaning to that social intercourse.

The Future of the American Jew, pp. 83–85.

2. Peoplehood and Immortality

Peoplehood is that social structure of a society from the most primitive
to the most advanced, including government, economy, culture, and
religion, which provides through those organizations and institutions
the necessary conditions for salvation, or the self-fulfillment of the
individual.

Insofar as the self-fulfillment of the human person is inconsistent with
total annihilation at death, it calls for some form of immortality. That
demand is satisfied through an organically constituted people, with a
common history and common destiny that is the sum of all the individual lives which have been and will be identified with it. A people thus
provides its individual lives a kind of continuing radiation or anonymous immortality.

The Greater Judaism in the Making, p. 480.

3. Jewish Peoplehood and
Jewish Religion

The problem presented by world Jewry is undoubtedly unique. Jews no
longer wish to accept common ancestry, or kinship, as the main unifying element [of the Jewish people]. That is too reminiscent of Nazism.
Language by itself is meaningless as a unifying element, unless it arises
out of shared day-to-day interests. That can be the case only in Israel.
But for Jewry as a whole only a common religion based on a long tradition like that of the Jewish people, and which can be made to include
language, culture, and day-to-day human interests growing out of involvement in the nuclear segment of the Jewish community in Israel,
can and should serve as a uniting bond.

Judaism will have to be conceived as a *noncreedal* religious civilization, centered in loyalty to the body of the Jewish people throughout
the world. Its religious articulation should take place through autonomous institutions of learning, congregations and societies, and hypo-
thetical rather than authoritative theologies. All Jewish group activities
should be conducted in conscious dedication to the solidarity of the
Jewish people and the growth of its ethical and spiritual consciousness.
If Jews are to have a mission, a purpose serving as criterion and mea-

sure of its endeavors, they can choose none more worthy than that of demonstrating the humanizing influence of a religion that encourages freedom of thought and unity in the diversity of democratic social structure.

A New Zionism, pp. 111–12.

4. The Implications of Jewish Peoplehood

What are the implications, social, political, cultural, and religious, of the status of the Jews as an international people with Israel as its cultural center?

The social implications of that status for Jews in their relation to one another are the sense of oneness and the mutual responsibility of Jews for their material and spiritual well-being. Its social implications for the relation of Jews to non-Jews are the affirmation of the right to group survival and the maintenance of group individuality, combined with the readiness to cooperate as Jews in all endeavors for the establishment of a free society based on justice and peace.

The political implication of Jewish peoplehood is the concern of Jews everywhere with the freedom, stability, and security of the State of Israel. For, only Eretz Yisrael, where Judaism is the civilization of the majority of its people, can serve as the cultural center of Jewry. That is entirely compatible with the recognition that the sole political allegiance of Jews in the Diaspora is to the state or nation in which they individually are citizens.

Culturally, Jewish peoplehood means the fostering of the Hebrew language and culture by Jews in the Diaspora and their interest in cultural developments in Israel; also, the interest of Israeli Jewry in the life experience of Jews in all lands. In relation to the non-Jewish world, it means the appropriation and integration into Jewish culture of values found in other cultures that are compatible with Judaism, and the translation and interpretation of Jewish cultural creations as a contribution to other cultures.

Religiously, Jewish peoplehood implies a change in the conception of the destiny of the Jewish people. The traditional Messianic ideal involved the return of all Jews to the Promised Land. That ideal implied that only in that land could Jews live in accord with the will of God. The status of the Jews as an international people with its cultural center in Eretz Yisrael, however, constitutes a departure from the traditional doctrine. It renders legitimate the Jews' remaining in the Diaspora, even when they have the opportunity to live in the homeland of Jewish civilization.

This conception of the Jewish future is not a retreat. It marks a higher stage in the development of Jewish religion. It places the basis of Jewish unity not in an authoritative traditional creed or code but in the common purpose of Jews to raise the moral and spiritual level of their group life. Within that purpose, different interpretations of the significance of Jewish experience must be regarded as legitimate. Thus, for the first time, freedom of conscience is fully accepted as a component of Jewish religion.

In relation to the non-Jewish world, the status of the Jews as a people sets an example to all other historic and religious bodies to affirm their right to make the most of their traditions in the face of trends to totalitarian cultural regimentation by the state, based on an idolatrous conception of the doctrine of national sovereignty.

Questions Jews Ask, pp. 33–35.

5. Jewish Peoplehood and Modern Nationalism

Four elements—homeland, self-government, culture, and mission—both are basic to the normal functioning of national life and must function in a mutually organic relationship: that is the sum and substance of modern nationalism. At first thought it might seem strange to think of the Jewish people, which has been without a land and a government of its own for almost nineteen hundred years, as having anything in common with modern nationalism. On second thought, however, we discover that actually both homeland and self-government played a greater role in the life of the Jewish people during those centuries of exile than the same elements did in the life of any other people in the world. . . .

So long as modern nationalism was confined to its promulgation by its first apostles, the possibility that it might clash with the nationalist character of historical Judaism was unthought of. When, however, modern nationalism began to be translated into practical politics in parliamentary debate and governmental policy, it became clear that, if Jews were consistently to adhere to traditional Judaism, its nationalist character would make them ineligible for citizenship. In the National Assembly of France the Girondist Clermont-Tonnerre drew a clear and sharp distinction between equality of rights for Jews as individuals and rights for them as part of a Jewish nation.

What alternatives had the Jews under those circumstances other than frankly and sincerely to renounce their historically national character or retain their solidarity under the guise of religion? That meant either abandoning the hope of renewing national life in Eretz Yisrael or stressing the supramundane character of that hope as part of an order of reality which was irrelevant to the practical issue of Jewish emancipation. Reform cut the Gordian knot by declaring that Jews in their dispersion had nothing in common but ethical monotheism. Orthodoxy was content to treat the prayers for return to Eretz Yisrael as awaiting God's answer in God's own time. And Conservatism, insofar as it had a chance to flourish in the Old World, was equally averse to viewing those prayers as an incentive to human initiative. What the synagogue movements propose in place of the traditional hope for a return to Zion is like amputating a broken leg and giving the patient a matchstick to hobble on.

Those synagogue movements did more than deactivate the hope for return to Eretz Yisrael. They surrendered the age-old group autonomy of the Jewish people and the authority of Jewish code law in all matters arising out of economic and social conflicts. Evidently they had no alternative, if they were to avert additional repressive measures against the Jews in the countries which harbored them. That, however, does not excuse the failure of the leaders of the Orthodox and Conservative movements to give formal notice to the world that the elimination from Jewish life of group autonomy and national code law was carried out under duress. They should have declared openly that, while emancipation from the medieval disabilities was a welcome relief, it was being carried out at the expense of the very substance of Judaism—its civilizational content—leaving only the shell. That no such declaration was issued was probably due in part to the fear of encouraging the opponents of Jewish emancipation. More largely, however, it proceeded from the assumption that Judaism was essentially a religion concerned with beliefs about God and salvation and with ritual practices as a means of keeping those beliefs alive.

The Greater Judaism in the Making, pp. 384, 386–87.

6. Zionism: Jewish Peoplehood Reborn

Zionism has been vindicated as the only movement capable of saving the historic nationhood of the Jewish people from the danger of being lost in modern nationalism's melting pot. Zionism is far from having arrived at a way of life whereby Jews who remain in the Diaspora might retain more than a nominal vestige of their historic nationhood. So far it has not contributed to the continuance and enhancement of Jewish life in the Diaspora. But there can be no question that the establishment of the State of Israel has given Jewish nationhood a new lease on life. That is an epoch-making achievement, the full significance of which will become apparent in time. . . .

The main weakness of the Zionist ideologies is that they fail to reckon with the future of the Jewish people as a whole. They do not take into account the consequences of the fact that a complete ingathering of world Jewry in Eretz Yisrael is inconceivable. Zionism has been narrowly pragmatic, without paying adequate regard to all its involvements in the contemporary world. It has succeeded in providing a precarious measure of physical security for about two million Jews, but it has augmented the spiritual insecurity of all Jews.

Zionism as a yearning for the return of the Jewish people to Eretz Yisrael and of Eretz Yisrael to the Jewish people was until a century ago an integral part of Judaism. But when the time came for that yearning to be translated into action it had to separate itself from Judaism with all its controversial issues and to concentrate on the achievement of its primary purpose: that of establishing a free and independent state. With the achievement of that purpose, the élan has gone out of Zionism. At the same time, insofar as the existing synagogue movements have become accustomed to treat the restoration of the Land of Israel as outside the purview of their religious activities, Judaism has been deprived of the main source of its vitality and viability, namely the generative and self-renewing potency of Jewish peoplehood.

The Greater Judaism in the Making,
pp. 394, 448–49.

7. Actions and Action-Symbols of Jewish Peoplehood

The primary *mitzvah** of Jewish peoplehood is the rehabilitation of Eretz Yisrael as the spiritual homeland of the Jewish people.

The Arabs contest the Jews' right to the Land and are biding their time to gather enough strength to invade it and drive the Jews into the sea.

---

*Literally commandment, traditionally understood as divine; in Kaplan's thought, religious imperative.—eds.

The State of Israel finds itself completely isolated. In the present world, where no great or small state considers itself secure unless it is part of some alliance, Israel is left out in the cold. The Western and the Soviet world compete with each other in wooing the Arab nations, whose only bond of unity is the determination to destroy Israel and who therefore dare not display any great friendship for Israel. Under these circumstances, for Jews in the free countries to justify their interest in the security and well-being of Israel merely on humanitarian and philanthropic grounds is to contribute to the growing belief among Western statesmen that the establishment of Israel was a mistake.

Both Jews and non-Jews have to be reoriented to the significance of the Zionist movement. Zionism must become known as the religious or spiritual revival of the Jewish people, whose belief in God is in need of being validated by means of the opportunity to build a full-fledged civilization based on social justice. In the light of this Greater Zionism, the basic *mitzvah* of Jewish peoplehood is to help build the Land— through *Aliyah* for those who can settle there, through economic aid and financial investment for those who cannot.

A series of duties pertaining to pilgrimages, cultural interchange, technical aid, etc., would grow out of the primary one of the rehabilitation of Eretz Yisrael.

Next in order of importance is the establishment of a permanent advisory body, be it in the form of parliament, conference, research institute, or forum, that would speak to the entire Jewish people in an advisory capacity concerning the meaning of the spiritual unity of the Jewish people and the most effective ways of translating it into various activities, communal, institutional, educational, cultural, etc.

Thus, a second series of actions as *mitzvot* of peoplehood would be the planning and executing of various techniques to arouse public interest and participation in all efforts leading to the establishment of such an advisory body. This body should develop a method whereby all who would be willing to commit themselves to the acceptance of its recommendations should formalize such commitment by covenanting themselves publicly. The aim should be to make of this ritual or action-symbol a means of Jewish identification.

A third series of actions as *mitzvot* of peoplehood is the reorganization of the present communal structure of Jews in the free countries of the world into organic communities. These communities would have to take on the same spiritual or religious character as world Jewry as a whole. Only they, and not individual congregations, should have the right to be designated by the name of *kehillah kedoshah* (holy community). That name may properly be borne only by such a segment of the Jewish people as embodies an entire gamut of civilizational functions, and thereby confers reality, even if in miniature form, upon the Jewish people as a whole.

Without going into an analysis of the present structure of American Jewish communities, we may affirm without fear of contradiction that it is inherently not calculated to sustain Jewish life, much less enhance it. Each generation is less Jewish than the preceding. The failure to hold those with a penchant for the reflective life, the self-alienation of the most creatively minded Jews, is a fatal omen for the future of American Judaism. Inherent in the very way in which independent congregations have to manage their economic affairs is their tendency to keep out both the very well-to-do and the lower middle class. That narrowing of the Jewish religious life to the upper middle class is as disruptive of Jewish life and values as the centrifugal pull of the gentile world.

Nothing but a properly devised organic structure of Jewish communal life may in part counteract those disintegrative forces. The criterion of its organic character would be the extent to which it would result in the kind of creative interaction among Jewish organizations which would eliminate the currently "rasping paradoxes" from Jewish life. Among the important communal activities would be keeping vital statistics, maintaining all-day Jewish schools wherever feasible, providing arbitration and other ways of dealing with problems of social justice, such as those involving unionism, the right to work or to strike, etc., sanctioning marriages and divorces, and being in charge of *kashrut*. Hence all activities leading to such an organic structure belong to the *mitzvot* of Jewish peoplehood.

A fourth series of actions which should be instituted pertains to spreading a knowledge of Hebrew. There is a definite psychological value to the knowledge of modern Hebrew and the ability to converse in it. For Jewish life in the Diaspora, however, the knowledge of biblical and liturgical Hebrew is of even greater importance, since it is more likely than vernacular Hebrew to communicate the basic values of Judaism. Without those basic values, Jewish peoplehood cannot constitute one of the three dimensions in the process of Jewish religion.

Though by far less potent a factor than Hebrew, the practice of adopting Hebraic personal names has a psychological influence from the standpoint of identification with the Jewish people. Considering it a *mitzvah* to bear a Hebraic name will help to spread the practice.

A fifth series of actions must concern itself with the revitalization of Sabbaths and festivals. The dimension of peoplehood which is built into the traditional motivation for their observance warrants a special effort to explore all possible ways and means of having them readopted by the masses of our people. A Sabbathless people cannot possibly cultivate the life of the spirit.

All of the foregoing courses of action naturally call for action-symbols. Most of the action-symbols take the form of ritual practices and worship or prayer. The revival of the observance of *kashrut* and Sabbaths and festivals would lead to the vitalization of the action-symbols associated with them.

There is one action-symbol, however, which has to be created for the purpose of developing an active awareness of the need of reconstituting and maintaining the spiritual unity of the Jewish people. This would be a ritual of conferring a higher degree upon those who arrive at maturity, just as the elementary degree of *bar* or *bat mitzvah* is conferred at present at the beginning of adolescence. However we may deplore the fact that congregational attendance at Sabbath services has come to depend on *bar* and *bat mitzvah* occasions, those occasions have become indispensable for the upkeep of Jewish life. A similar ritual enacted during the period of maturation would be even more effective in contributing to the intensification of Jewish consciousness and to a sense of responsibility for fostering the spiritual unity of the Jewish people by living a life of *kiddush ha-shem*, or spiritual dedication.

The Greater Judaism in the Making, pp. 484–87.

8. Peoplehood and *Mitzvot*

A pragmatic consequence of the fact that Jewish peoplehood is a dimension of the Jewish religion bears on the concept of *mitzvot*. It enables the Jew who can no longer accept his tradition in the form in which it has come down to him so to reinterpret that tradition as to render it viable. Literally understood, *mitzvot* means laws commanded by God. According to tradition, all the 613 *mitzvot* were actually dictated by God. That belief had the effect of rendering them immutable. When conditions of life and thought made them obsolete, as was true of the entire sacrificial cult, the traditionalists had to persuade themselves that those *mitzvot* were merely suspended for a time. When, as in the case of other *mitzvot*, the traditional version became restrictive, legal fictions or sophistries were resorted to as a means of overcoming their restrictive character. Neither solution could satisfy those for whom the *mitzvot* had the same kind of human history as the cult practices of all other religions.

On the other hand, to resort to the secularist solution of abolishing the *mitzvot* altogether is to perform a surgical operation that might kill the patient. A third alternative is to transfer them from the dimension of divinity to the dimension of peoplehood as an indispensable dimension of religion. The *mitzvot* would thus retain their imperative character, not merely because they are the product of collective Jewish life but because they point to the same cosmic or divine drive as that which impels man to transcend his animal heredity. So viewed, *mitzvot* have to be relevant to our spiritual needs. Some traditional *mitzvot* may become obsolete, some may have to be modified, and some may have to be created anew.

The Greater Judaism in the Making, pp. 488–89.

9. Peoplehood and Moral Responsibility

The fact that peoplehood is a dimension of Jewish religion implies that our vocation as a people coincides with the urgent need of contemporary mankind. The fact is that the world situation is currently fraught with dangers that might lead to the extinction of mankind, due for the most part to the explosive character which nationhood has assumed. The nature of modern warfare is such as to compel nations to form alliances and to limit their own political sovereignty. More nations, however, are coming into being, and each nation is getting to be more conscious of its individuality and intent upon fostering it. By resuming our peoplehood as a dimension of our religion, we Jews have the opportunity of articulating the imperative need of each nation to foster its national individuality as a gift from God and not as an acquisition of an earthly or demonic power. A nation must be subject to the same divine laws of social justice and moral responsibility in relation to its own citizens and to other nations as is the individual person.

The Greater Judaism in the Making, pp. 487–88.

10. Peoplehood and Divinity

Jewish identity demands of the individual Jew that he so come to know the Jewish people, its entire history, its civilization, and its destiny as to experience the reality of its God. This God, YHWH, is that aspect of the Jewish people which renders it more than the sum of its individuals, past, present, and future, and gives meaning to all its virtues, sins, successes, and failures.

If Not Now, When?, p. 68.

11. Jewish Peoplehood: The Mystical Element in Jewish Religion

The self-identification of the individual Jew with his Jewish people is the source of the mystical element in the Jewish religion. Why that is so becomes evident when we stop to consider what it is we characterize as mystical in any experience that we undergo.

In the first place, we characterize as mystical anything which we regard as indispensable to our life as human persons, without being able to explain why that is so, on logical or rational grounds. We accept our parents and our community with all their ways as the indispensable foundation of our lives. Why that is so is a mystery. Secondly, whatever experience gives us a feeling of direct personal contact or *rapport* with what we consider to be ultimate reality we refer to as mystical. If we have a perceptive eye for the beauties of nature, any landscape or seascape or starry night meets that requirement and therefore puts us in a mystical frame of mind. The same is true if we have an ear for music. Not only the works of the great musical masters, but even a simple melody that sings from the heart, evoke a mystic response.

What the Jewish people should mean to the individual Jew may be illustrated by the famous answer given by George Malory, one of the greatest mountain climbers, when asked why he wanted to climb Everest. He simply replied, "Because it is there." Likewise when we are asked, "Why remain Jews?" the only reason we should feel called upon to give is: "Because the Jewish people is here and we are part of it." Unless we feel that to belong to the Jewish people is a high spiritual adventure which has intrinsic value regardless of consequences and practical ends, our Jewishness is tantamount to the interest of casual tourists in foreign countries.

Since the Jewish people is indispensable to the Jew as a human person, and since it has always given him the feeling of being in *rapport* with God, identification with the Jewish people provides Jewish religion with the indispensable dimension of the mystical. On the face of it, nothing should seem more obvious, yet it is the very obviousness that seems to have led many a Jewish thinker and theologian to develop a blind spot for the mystic character of this self-identification with the Jewish people. They seem to see in it only the socio-psychological significance which the non-Jewish social scientist, as an outsider, can see in it. But if they would stop to consider for one moment the entire regimen of Jewish religious practice and ritual and note the extraordinary fact that the individual Jew never takes part in them without associating himself with the whole House of Israel, they would begin to sense the extent to which this association with the Jewish people is not merely a socio-psychological, but a definitely mystical, experience.

A New Zionism, pp. 114–16.

12. Observations

If we read with understanding the prayers we recite in a Jewish service, we would discover that they are meant to be a means of getting us to identify ourselves with the Jewish people, and of arousing in us a passionate yearning that our people rise to great spiritual heights.

"Everything ideal has its natural basis; everything natural has its ideal fulfillment," said Santayana.

That is why Judaism must have the Jewish people as its basis; and that is why the Jewish people must find its fulfillment in Judaism.

The character of a people derives, in large part, from the circumstances under which it is born.

The people of Israel, having been born in redemption from bondage, has the love of freedom and the sense of human dignity deeply engraved in its consciousness.

What the Crown is to England, that the Land of Israel is to the Jewish people—"an unsurpassed symbol both of continuity and unity."

Eretz Yisrael is to the Jewish people what the skin is to the human body.

As the skin joins the human body to its environment, so does Eretz Yisrael join the Jewish people to the rest of the world.

Nothing develops personality like success in a task.

Nothing, therefore, is so essential to Jewish personality as success in the task of establishing security in the State of Israel.

The establishment of Israel should not mean an addition of one more nation to the roster of the world's troublemakers, big or little.

It should serve as a retroactive rationale for all that the Jewish people has hoped for throughout the thirty-three centuries of its checkered career.

Part of the mystery of peoplehood is that we feel impelled to live for posterity, and that posterity will look to us for life's meaning.

Not So Random Thoughts, pp. 219–29.

III

The Quest for the Divine

2. Religion and Magic

Genuine religious symbolism is a late development in religion. It comes into being when rites and observances are practiced for what they do to stir the mind and the heart religiously. They are a means of enabling man to commune with himself, or with his fellow men, about things divine. On the other hand, if they are supposed to influence directly any supernatural being to extend help, or to withhold from doing harm, they are theurgic.

Theurgy* assumes the presence of mysterious forces in animate or inanimate objects, or in the environment generally. Those forces, it is assumed, can be summoned or exorcised by means of prescribed formulas or actions. Whether regarded as invisible or as residing in visible objects, they are of an impersonal or demonic character. They lack the kind of superhuman personality that is associated with divinity. A god is worshipped, but a demon is feared. Demons are supposed to act automatically, in response to theurgic rites or formulas, just as the electric lamp lights up or the bell rings when an electric button is pressed. The fact is that to most people God is not really God but a magnified demon. That is why they cannot dissociate religion from supernaturalism. . . .

Before the advent of modern science and technology, it was difficult even for the mentally gifted to abandon entirely the theurgic habit of mind. They noted that language, which articulates man's will, effects changes in the human and physical environment. Therefore words were to them not merely symbols that enabled the mind to think, remember, and imagine, but actual realities, or forces, that could put other realities or forces into motion. The tendency of the human mind to reify, that is, to treat as a thing whatever it has a name for, grew so strong that it gave rise in the Middle Ages to a type of thinking known as "realism," in contrast with the view held by those who refused to reify words or concepts, the view known as "nominalism." That philosophical quarrel had an important bearing on the idea of God.

Judaism Without Supernaturalism,
pp. 38–40.

---

*Theurgy is the performance of magical rites designed to coerce supernatural powers into fulfilling human desires.—eds.

3. Supernaturalism

The supernaturalist conception of salvation is based, in Jewish tradition, upon the following series of assumptions:

1. In the first place, divinity completely transcends humanity, of which it is the absolute antipode. God is not subject to any empirical law of nature. Having created the world and having fixed its laws, He can, at any time, destroy the one and suspend the other. Such is the logic inherent in all of Jewish supernaturalist tradition, down to our own day. From that standpoint, the miraculous events recorded in the Bible, including the theophanies, particularly the one on Mount Sinai, are extraordinary but by no means impossible phenomena. In fact, such phenomena are needed to demonstrate not only the power but the transcendence of God.

The existence of a transcendent God is not to be proved by abstract philosophical reasoning, but by the sensate experience afforded by miracles and theophanies. It therefore goes without saying that no attempt should be made to detract from the literal description of them, as historical events which are in contravention to the regular course of nature. All interpretations of them that try to render them comparable to ordinary experience must be ruled out. Thus, when the crossing of the Red Sea is said to have coincided with the ebbing of the waters at its most northern point and the death of the pursuing Egyptians to have been caused by the return of those waters, the sense and purpose of the miracle narratives are completely falsified.

2. Secondly, according to the tradition, God's intervention in the regular order of the world is not only a demonstration of His existence and power. It is also an evidence of His special love for the people of Israel. For no other people does God work miracles, and to no other people does He reveal Himself or declare His will. Prophecy is exclusively for Israel. Even when He vouchsafed the gift of prophecy to Balaam, it was for the sake of Israel.

How then are the other nations ever to know God, and how can they be expected to render Him allegiance? The answer is: Let it be Israel's task to proclaim those miracles and divine self-manifestations to all the world. When prophecy was still in vogue, the Prophets performed that role in behalf of their people. When prophecy was silenced and psalmody took its place, the Psalmist calls upon Israel to "make known His [God's] deeds among the nations" (Ps. 105:1). This is the theme, for the most part, of the *Hallel* psalms.

This exclusive privilege granted to the people of Israel, to have witnessed the many miracles which God performed in their behalf, is what renders Israel a chosen people. That should be sufficient to prove that the doctrine of Israel's chosenness is rooted in supernaturalism. Any interpretation which attempts to sidestep that fact and to give the impression that the chosenness of Israel is merely a way of stressing Israel's having chosen God to be *its* God, or Israel's having been the first to have come upon the profounder truths of religion, is as much a misinterpretation and falsification of the truth as is the "naturalization" of the miracles.

3. This brings us to a third aspect of supernaturalism: That all the great miracles and theophanies took place in the beginning of Israel's career and were not repeated in later years is no mere accident. The logic behind that fact is that there was something intrinsically sacrosanct about the past which rendered it worthy of having harbored all those eyewitness proofs of the reality and greatness of God. Not all who lived then were worthier than their descendants. Indeed, only two—Joshua and Caleb—out of the entire generation of the Wilderness did deserve to enter the Promised Land. But the mere fact that God chose to reveal Himself in the early past, and has remained "hidden" ever since, is sufficient to sanctify that past.

Judaism Without Supernaturalism, pp. 21–23.

4. God and the Nature of Man

The only alternative to the traditional and supernaturalist conception of God's self-manifestation that can make a difference in people's lives is not the metaphysical approach but the social-behavioral one. It may well be that the human mind is forever and intrinsically incapable of grappling *existentially* with ultimates and is permanently and inherently limited to theorizing about them *conceptually* or by means of ideas—which are abstractions from reality. That God, as ultimate reality, is unknowable is a commonplace of all thinking other than that which is entirely naive. Theologians constantly remind us that all our affirmations concerning God have to be translated into negatives, if they are to approximate the truth. Consequently, religion which aims to improve human nature and the conditions of human living cannot be based on the ultimate nature of God. Its field of operations must be the nature of man. It has to focus its attention on that aspect of man's nature which is in need of being fully humanized, on what the human being ought to become, if he is to reflect the image of God. It is the business of religion not to give a metaphysical conception of God but to make clear what we mean by the belief in God, from the standpoint of the difference that belief makes in human conduct and striving.

Judaism Without Supernaturalism, pp. 26–27.

5. How Believing in God Functions

Since the experience about the world and ourselves is determined by the society and civilization into which we are born, the conception of God should be related to them and they should be made more meaningful by it. This discussion being carried on by us, as Jews, what we have to know is: How did the conception of God function in the consciousness of the Jewish people and in the various stages of the Jewish civilization? In short, how did the conception of God function in Judaism? To this question, the following is the answer:

The conception of God in Judaism has not functioned either as a philosophical truth or as a theological dogma. It is not a philosophical truth, because it is not the product of reflection or reasoning. It is not a theological dogma, because it is not the product of any attempt to reconcile the traditional idea of God that came down from the past with any particular philosophy or world outlook. The conception of God in Judaism is historical and functional. It is historical and functional in the sense that (1) it has fostered the unity and individuality of the Jewish people, (2) it has made for the good life, and (3) it has held out hope for the future. Such is the God of Abraham, Isaac, and Jacob; the belief in Him is the product of the universal need of human nature for courage, hope, and self-improvement.

1. To foster the unity of the Jewish people, the conception of God in Judaism is given concreteness through the extraordinary events in the career of Israel, beginning with Abraham's migration from Ur of Chaldea. To foster the individuality of the Jewish people, the God of Israel has been conceived as demanding undivided loyalty and complete severance from the worship of any other deity.

2. To make for the good life, the God of Israel is assumed to have revealed to His people the Torah with its laws concerning what man is to do and what refrain from, and with its teachings concerning God's dealings with man.

3. To hold out hope for the future, God is conceived as certain to send the Messiah for Israel's redemption and to establish His Kingdom over mankind in the age to come.

All of the foregoing belongs to the thought-world of traditional Judaism. How far it can be retained and reinterpreted, and how much of it has to be rendered in the vocabulary of our thought-world, is subject to trial and error. This is part of the birthpains of a tradition in the making.

Questions Jews Ask, pp. 88–89.

6. God as Process

Without entering into a detailed and difficult analysis of the possibility of knowing what God is and how He acts, let the reader consider the case of Maimonides. No one in his senses can question Maimonides' genuine piety and belief in God or the greatness of his mind and character. To whichever of his writings we turn we find that he keeps on repeating that God and His attributes are one. He then goes on to explain that statement as follows:

When, for example, we are told that God is living, we should not take that to mean that God is a being who possesses the attributes of life, which He shares with other living beings, but that He is life itself. God and life are one and the same. Likewise, when we are told that God is good, we should realize that God and goodness are one and the same. Or when God is said to know all things, we should understand that to mean that God and knowledge are identical. For in the case of God, the knower, the act of knowing, and the object known are one and the same. Nor was Maimonides the first or the last to affirm that fact about God. Many other religious thinkers before him and after him affirmed the same about God.

The conception of God as cosmic Process has been subjected to considerable misunderstanding and misplaced resentment, as though it constituted a complete break with the traditional, or conventional, idea of God. Not only has its validity or truth been attacked but its very claim to being religious in character and compatible with prayer and worship has been challenged. Many an ill-informed critic has even charged that conception with being atheistic. What are life, knowledge, goodness, if not processes? They are certainly not beings or entities. Since God is life, knowledge, goodness, what else can He be but Process?

Modern scientific and philosophic thought regards all reality not as something static but as energy in action. When we say that God is Process, we select, out of the infinite processes in the universe, that complex of forces and relationships which makes for the highest fulfillment of man as a human being and identify it by the term "God." In exactly the same way, we select, among all the forces and relationships that enter into the life of the individual, those which make for his highest fulfillment and identify them by the term "person." God and person are thus correlative terms, the meaning of each being relative to and dependent on that of the other, like parent and child, teacher and pupil, citizen and state. God is the Process by which the universe produces persons, and persons are the processes by which God is manifest in the individual. Neither term has meaning without the other. So to conceive of God is to regard Him as personal, in the sense that He manifests Himself in our personality, in every effort of ours to live up to our responsibilities as human beings. At the same time He is not a person, since He cannot be compared with a human person, any more than the human person can be compared with one of his momentary acts.

Questions Jews Ask, pp. 102–103.

7. God and Spiritual Values

Much of the wisdom and aspiration of our ancestors is lost upon us because we no longer speak their language, though we may speak to the same purpose. The effort to recover the permanent values inherent in traditional religion is handicapped by the lack of imagination. An inflexible mentality takes every word in texts of ancient origin literally and ignores the *nisus* [effort, impulse] which created the word. If we disengage from the language of adoration the spiritual desiderata implied therein, we discover that the attributes ascribed to God represented the social and spiritual values formerly regarded as all-important. Those attributes are by no means limited in their meaning and application to the theurgic conception of God.

Just as the God-idea progressed from a perceptual image to a conception like the one which identifies God as the sum of all those factors and relationships in the universe that make for unity, creativity, and worthwhileness in human life, so can the attributes of God, which once were externalized and concrete, be translated into modern terms and made relevant to modern thinking and living. Men attributed to God their own highest desires and aspirations. They called Him creator, protector, helper, sovereign, and redeemer. These terms can now be identified with the highest and most significant aims of human existence and achieve a new force and vitality through this conscious process of identification. We can no longer believe that God is a mighty sovereign or that the universe is the work of His hands. In the light of the present development of the God-idea, however, we can see that God is manifest in all creativity and in all forms of sovereignty that make for the enhancement of human life.

Let us take, for example, the attribute of God as creator. Were we to approach it from the standpoint of medieval metaphysics, we would at once involve ourselves in the complicated problem of *creatio ex nihilo*, and land in a philosophic *cul-de-sac*. If we proceed by the functional method of interpretation, we can discern in the belief that God created the world an expression of the tendency to identify the creative principle in the world with the manifestation of God. This approach to the problem of creation is in keeping with the trend of modern religious metaphysics. In a sense, it is the very antithesis of the approach of traditional theology, yet, emotionally and volitionally, we can deduce the same practical and socially valuable results from the one approach as from the other—from the conception of God as the creative principle of the universe as was derived in the past from the conception of God as creator of the universe. For the creative principle is compatible in human life only with intelligence, courage, and goodwill and is hindered in its operation by arrogance, greed, and uncontrolled sexual desire.

God as helper and protector may be identified with the powers of nature which maintain life, and with the intelligence that transforms environment by subjugating and controlling the natural forces for the common good of humanity. In any act of social cooperation and goodwill, in the striving for finer human relations, in man's courage and moral resilience, in his conquest of fear and death, we can discern the operation of the divine principle—God made manifest. Likewise, whenever we experience a sense of stability and permanence in the midst of the universal flux, we experience the reality of God as helper.

The attributes of God as redeemer and sovereign can also be translated into terms of contemporary needs. According to tradition, when God revealed Himself to Israel at Sinai, He made Himself known not as the creator of heaven and earth nor as the sovereign of mankind but as the redeemer of Israel. In terms of the present world outlook, man's desire for freedom, his struggles to attain it, reveal the striving of the divine in man. The cosmic life urge is displayed in restiveness under restraint. When the life urge becomes self-aware in man's efforts to shake off intolerable restraint, God as redeemer is manifest.

The sovereignty of God denotes the primacy of spiritual values in human life. That God is sovereign means that those aims, standards, and interests which center about the belief in God are ends to which all other aims, standards, and interests are subordinate as means. Thus for the individual so to strive after wealth that it becomes to him the standard of all values, is a denial of the sovereignty of God. So are the attainment of power for its own sake and the subservience to power, regardless of the manner in which it was acquired or the purpose to which it is applied. In domestic life, the primacy of the spiritual values means placing love and the spirit of sacrifice above any selfish purpose. In economic life, the primacy of the spiritual means realizing that men count more than things, that production is not an end in itself. In national life, from the standpoint of internal relations, the primacy of the spiritual values implies aiming toward creation of opportunities for the many rather than maintaining privileges for the few; from the standpoint of external relations, it implies that international dealings be motivated by a desire for peace and cooperation rather than for war and domination.

Judaism as a Civilization, pp. 400–402.

8. Religious Humanism

This growth in the sense of interdependence of men and nations should be regarded as growth in the knowledge of God. This interdependence, however, cannot be achieved unless human beings organize themselves into organic societies. The only way to translate religious humanism into practice is to apply it to some particular society, be it family, tribe, nation, people, or church.

Thus I came to apply religious humanism to the Jewish people. Humanism represents a Copernican revolution in the conception of what should be central in an *authentic* perspective on human existence. In the mythological and metaphysical perspective, the belief in, or the idea of, God holds a position of centrality. According to religious humanism, however, centrality should be accorded to the belief in, or idea of, salvation or human fulfillment. Only authentic self-understanding can give us authentic ideas of fulfillment. Since the individual human being cannot possibly achieve fulfillment apart from some organic society, the organic society acts as an intermediary between the cosmos or nature and the individual, for those forces or processes in the latter which impel and help him to make the most of his life, of his potentialities and opportunities. Thus, it is normal for an organic society which functions as such an intermediary to evolve its own indigenous religion. Jewish religion is thus an indigenous religion, and Judaism is a religious civilization, particular in content and universal in form and reference.

What a Hallelujah would resound throughout the world if all peoples proclaimed that God was to be found in whatever there exists of man's urge to truth, honesty, empathy, loyalty, justice, freedom, and goodwill! Can one imagine Jews being bored by a Jewish religion that would dedicate itself to the purpose for which, according to the account in Genesis, God chose Abraham: "in order that he might instruct his children and his household after him to keep the way of the Eternal by doing righteousness and justice"? (Gen. 18:19)

Thus religious humanism, properly understood, does not negate religion as such. It negates only the mythological and metaphysical types of religion. What it does with the idea of God is to have us treat the term "God" not as a substantive noun like "gold" or "silver" but as a functional noun like "king" or "master." It is therefore a correlative noun, with salvation or human fulfillment as its correlate. This is the sense in which the term "God" is used in the Jewish scriptures. (Compare Numbers 15:41 and Zechariah 14:9.) Transposed into the key of functionalism, the term "God" denotes the power or process, both in the cosmos and in man, that makes for human fulfillment or salvation, both individual and collective, or for *normative* man.

"Between Two Worlds" in *Varieties of Jewish Belief,*
ed. Ira Eisenstein, pp. 140f.

9. God's Presence

Religious souls have never been satisfied with an awareness of God merely as an intellectual concept. They always craved a religious experience in which the reality of God would be brought home to them with an immediacy akin to our awareness of objects through the senses, and with an overpowering emotion that stirred every fiber of their being. In our various interpretations of God as the power that makes for certain desirable goals, there is one point that is not taken into account, and that is that we may accept these goals, without identifying the power that makes for them as God, as the spirit that so possesses us as to compel our adoration and worship. . . .

The purpose in the various attempts to reinterpret the God-idea is not to dissolve the God-idea into ethics. It is to identify those experiences which should represent for us the actual working of what we understand by the conception of God. Without the actual awareness of His presence, experienced as beatitude and inner illumination, we are likely to be content with the humanistic interpretation of life. But this interpretation is inadequate, because it fails to express and to foster the feeling that man's ethical aspirations are part of a cosmic urge, by obeying which man makes himself at home in the universe. Without the emotional intuition of an inner harmony between human nature and universal nature, without the conviction, born of the heart rather than of the mind, that the world contains all that is necessary for human salvation, the assumptions necessary for ethical living remain cold hypotheses lacking all dynamic power. They are like an engine with all the parts intact and assembled, but lacking the fuel which alone can set it in operation. The dynamic of ethical action is the spirit of worship, the feeling that we are in God and God in us, the yielding of our persons in voluntary surrender to those larger aims that express for us as much as has been revealed to us of the destiny of the human race. It is only this emotional reaction to life that can make humanity itself mean more to us than a "disease of the agglutinated dust."

The Meaning of God in Modern Jewish Religion, pp. 244–45.

10. Salvation in This World

The salvation that the modern man seeks in this world, like that which his fathers sought in the world to come, has both a personal and a social significance. In its personal aspect it represents the faith in the possibility of achieving an integrated personality. All those natural impulses, appetites, and desires which so often are in conflict with one another must be harmonized. They must never be permitted to issue in a stalemate, in such mutual inhibition as leaves life empty and meaningless, without zest and savor. Nor must they be permitted to issue in distraction, in a condition in which our personality is so pulled apart by conflicting desires that the man we are in certain moments or in certain relations looks with contempt and disgust at the man we are in others. When our mind functions in such a way that we feel that all our powers are actively employed in the achievement of desirable ends, we have achieved personal salvation.

This personal objective of human conduct cannot, however, be achieved without reference to a social objective as well. Selfish salvation is an impossibility, because no human being is psychologically self-sufficient. We are impelled by motives that relate themselves to the life of the race with as imperative an urge as by any that relate themselves to the preservation of our individual organism. "Love is strong as death" and frequently sacrifices life itself for the object of love. Although to every individual the achievement of personal salvation is his supreme quest and responsibility, it is unattainable without devotion to the task of social salvation. The thought "If I am not for myself, who will be for me?" in this striving for salvation always carries with it the implication, "If I am but for myself, what am I?" because we cannot even think of ourselves except in relation to something not ourselves.

In its social aspect, salvation means the ultimate achievement of a social order in which all men shall collaborate in the pursuit of common ends in a manner which shall afford to each the maximum opportunity for creative self-expression. There can be no personal salvation so long as injustice and strife exist in the social order; there can be no social salvation so long as the greed for gain and the lust for domination are permitted to inhibit the hunger for human fellowship and sympathy in the hearts of men. There is a sense in which it is still true that salvation is of the world to come, for its attainment is clearly not of today or of tomorrow. That it will ever be attained can never be demonstrated, but faith must assume it as the objective of human behavior, if we are not to succumb to the cynical acceptance of evil, which is the only other alternative.

The Meaning of God in Modern Jewish Religion,
pp. 53–54.

11. Salvation and the Divine

Man's yearning for salvation is the human form of the will to live, which is cosmic and characteristic of all living beings. In the case of man, the will to live is the will to abundant and harmonious living. It involves a conscious selection of goals of human behavior. These are equated by man with the will of God, but neither the quest for salvation nor the choice of goals is entirely man-determined. Human nature is a part of the larger world of nature, and man's salvation can only be conceived as a manifestation of a divine power both within and beyond man. That is why human salvation, or self-fulfillment, is inconceivable without God. God is that aspect of the cosmos that makes for man's salvation. . . .

Judaism Without Supernaturalism,
p. 119.

12. Human Needs

What is the best sort of life that men can live, what kind of life satisfies the maximum of human interests and releases the maximum of creative energy, what, in short, shall constitute the goal of human salvation can, of course, never be stated in a final formula. As life progresses we acquire new insights into possibilities of worthwhile experience. But at the present stage of human development, salvation would involve living according to the highest truth that experience has thus far revealed. Some of the most significant of these truths may be stated as follows:

1. For the individual, salvation should henceforth be regarded as consisting in the satisfaction of three primary needs. In the first place there are the physical needs the fulfillment of which constitutes what we

mean by health. Men seek food to sustain them, shelter to protect them from the elements, and the gratification of the mating instinct. In the second place, man needs love. He needs to feel that he is in close relationship to other human beings to whom he is important and who are important to him. Finally, man needs creativity. He needs the opportunity to express himself and to give effect to his purpose in work and play. If he lacks any of these conditions, if he suffers illness, loneliness, or enforced idleness and inactivity, he experiences frustration.

2. All human beings, regardless of race, nation, or creed, are equally entitled to be treated as ends in themselves and not merely as means to the satisfaction of other people's desires. Any form of slavery, exploitation, or oppression is an offense against human dignity and a bar to the attainment of salvation or life harmonious, abundant, and creative.

3. As ends in themselves men are entitled to realize their creative potentialities. This means that society must seek to provide men with the economic and cultural opportunities necessary for their maximum self-realization as persons. This is what is meant in the affirmation that men are created equal. They are created with an equal right to whatever opportunities exist in our society for making the most of their native capacities as human beings.

4. The purpose of society should be to enable each individual to achieve salvation. By organizing opportunities for social communion, intellectual intercourse, and collaboration in productive work, society can immeasurably add to the creative power of every individual member. Society must further insure that collaboration is effected by means that are consistent with, and tend to confirm, the principle of human dignity and equality.

The Future of the American Jew, pp. 206–207.

13. God and Creativity

Only the moral aspect of belief is nowadays of vital import. The moral implication of the traditional teaching that God created the world is that creativity, or the continuous emergence of aspects of life not prepared for or determined by the past, constitutes the most divine phase of reality. A modern equivalent of the notion of creativity, which tradition regarded as the very essence of Godhood, would be the concept of the latent and potential elements in the universe as making for the increase in the quantity and quality of life. Since a spiritual conception of life is consistent only with a world outlook which counts on the realization of much that is still in the womb of possibility, it implies the belief that both man and the universe are ever in a state of being created.

The Sabbath is regarded in Jewish tradition as celebrating the creation of the world. The modern equivalent of that interpretation of the day would be the use of it as a means of accentuating the fact that we must reckon with creation and self-renewal as a continuous process. The liturgy speaks of God as "renewing daily the works of creation." By becoming aware of that fact, we might gear our own lives to this creative urge in the universe and discover within ourselves unsuspected powers of the spirit.

The belief in God as creator, or its modern equivalent, the conception of the creative urge as the element of Godhood in the world, is needed to fortify the yearning for spiritual self-regeneration. That yearning dies down unless it is backed by the conviction that there is something which answers to it in the very character of life as a whole. There can hardly be any more important function for religion than to keep alive this yearning for self-renewal and to press it into the service of human progress. In doing that, religion will combat the recurrent pessimism to which we yield whenever we misjudge the character of the evil in the world. It will teach us to live without illusion and without despair about the future, with clear recognition of the reality of evil and creative faith in the possibility of the good.

The Meaning of God in Modern Jewish Religion, pp. 62–63.

14. Wisdom and the Belief in God

The biblical philosophy of history assumes man's relevance or importance to God. Modern man must experience God's relevance to man. An authentic conception of God is relevant to the facts of human nature and to the contemporary world. God as the power in nature and in the human species that makes for the salvation of men and nations gives purpose and meaning to their existence.

In the biblical account, the God of Israel created and ordered the world according to the laws of nature and created the people of Israel to live according to the laws of the Torah (cf. Ps. 19). Since both the laws of the Torah and those of physical nature are treated in the Bible as manifestations of *divine wisdom*, explicit homogeneity is implied between nature and nature's God (cf. Prov. 9 and Job 28). This conception negates the notion that belief in God is purely subjective, that it does not affirm the existence of a cosmic process. The cosmic process of universal reciprocity outside the human mind comes to be God only when it is experienced as cosmic interdependence, and, in the human world, as moral responsibility. God's relevance to man consists in impelling him so to control and direct his strivings as to satisfy all his life needs without reversion to strife and war.

The term "God" does not belong to the category of objective facts which are the subject matter of *reason* and *intelligence*. It belongs to the category of *values* which, as spiritual *factors*, are the subject matter of *wisdom*. Particularly in the Bible, wisdom refers to the experience and scale of values which answer man's vital needs.

How shall modern man reconstruct the traditional conception of God? Neither through mysticism nor reason but through the emotional experience of responsibility can we become aware of His existence as the power that assures man's fulfillment and survival. The mounting peril of human extinction through war can be averted only if the nations conduct their political and economic activities in the spirit of ethical nationhood. In the ancient mythological world Israel was expected to learn that lesson and to exemplify it among the other nations.

The Bible supports the reinterpretation of the belief in God in terms of human conduct that is Godlike, creative, and founded on justice through law. Thus, in mythological idiom, the Bible relates: "YHWH saw how great was man's wickedness on earth, and how every plan devised by his mind was nothing but evil all the time. And YHWH regretted that He had made man on earth and His heart was saddened" (Gen. 6:5–6). Demythologized, man's sin of irresponsibility culminating in violence, if unpunished, would not only disprove God's omnipotence, it would deny His very existence. The rabbinic tradition confirms this version of the belief in God as dependent on the behavior of man. The rabbinic comment on "You are my witnesses, says YHWH" (Isa. 43:10) reads: "If you are my witnesses, I am God; if you are not my witnesses, I am not, so to speak, God" (*Yalkut Shimeoni* quoting *Sifré* and commenting in the same spirit upon three additional texts). Mature wisdom or authentic religion depends upon faith in man. The reality of God can be experienced only when mankind acts in a way that makes for its creative survival.

Civilization is in greater danger than ever before because both the nuclear powers and the smaller nations conduct international relations on a level of moral irresponsibility. The very survival of mankind demands the modification of absolute sovereignty in the direction of ethical nationhood. From the very beginning that has been the purpose and meaning of Jewish existence.

The Religion of Ethical Nationhood, pp. 47–49.

15. God the Life of Nature

Our fathers acclaimed the God
Whose handiwork they read
In the mysterious heavens above
And in the varied scene of earth below,
In the orderly march of days and nights,
Of seasons and years,
And in the checkered fate of man.

Meantime have the vaulting skies dissolved;
Night reveals the limitless caverns of space
Hidden in the light of day,
And unfolds horizonless vistas
Far beyond imagination's ken.
The mind is staggered,
Yet soon regains its poise,
And peering through the boundless dark,
Orients itself anew
By the light of distant suns
Shrunk to glittering sparks.
The soul is faint,
Yet soon revives,
And learns to spell once more the name of God
Across the newly visioned firmament.

Lift your eyes, look up;
Who made these stars?
He who marshals them in order,
Summoning each one by name.

God is the oneness
That spans the fathomless deeps of space
And the measureless eons of time,
Binding them together in act,
As we do in thought.

He is the sameness
In the elemental substance of stars and planets,
Of this our earthly abode
And of all that it holds.
He is the unity
Of all that is,

The uniformity of all that moves,
The rhythm of all things
And the nature of their interaction.

He binds up the Pleiades in a cluster
And loosens the chains of Orion;
He directs the signs of the Zodiac
And guides the constellations of the Bear.

God is the mystery of life,
Enkindling inert matter
With inner drive and purpose,

He is the creative flame
That transfigures lifeless substance,
Leaping into ever higher realms of being,
Brightening into the radiant glow of feeling,
Till it turn into the white fire of thought.

And though no sign of living thing
Break the eternal silence of the spheres,
We cannot deem this earth,
This tiny speck in the infinitude,
Alone instinct with God.

By that token
Which unites the worlds in bonds of matter
Are all the worlds bound
In the bond of Life.

It is He who forms the mountains
And creates the wind,
And reveals His inner mind to man;
He who makes the dawn and darkness,
Who marches over the heights of earth;
The Lord, the God of hosts, is His name.

God is in the faith
By which we overcome
The fear of loneliness, of helplessness,
Of failure, and of death.

God is in the hope
Which, like a shaft of light,
Cleaves the dark abysms
Of sin, of suffering, and of despair.

God is in the love
Which creates, protects, forgives.

His is the spirit
Which broods upon the chaos men have wrought,
Disturbing its static wrongs,
And stirring into life the formless beginnings
Of the new and better world.

Thou art my portion,
O Eternal;
Thou art my share.
Thou wilt show me the path of life;
Fullness of joy is in Thy presence;
Everlasting happiness dost Thou provide.

Questions Jews Ask, pp.99–101.

16. Observations

Religion should be a series of self-corrective attempts on the part of man to become fully human.

The millennium will come when mankind learns to be half as afraid of the scientific hell of its own invention as it was for centuries of the theological hell of its own imagination.

The difference between philosophy and religion is like the difference between the dentist's knowledge of a toothache and the patient's knowledge of it. The former is essential knowledge; the latter existential knowledge.

Therefore philosophy without religion is like a dentist without a patient, and religion without philosophy is like a patient who has no dentist to cure his pain.

Religion is not intended to answer the ultimate questions of existence. It can only provide an effective protection against their shattering impact.

God will have established His Kingdom when religion and nationalism are made safe for the world.

To be a complete person one has to be part of something super-personal.

The God-impulse in us is not fear but hope, not helplessness but self-help, not despondency but courage, not the obfuscation of the mind but the light of reason, not the belittlement of what man is but the exaltation of what he might be.

Not So Random Thoughts, pp. 133–59.

IV

Torah in Our Day

1. The Torah's Fundamental Purpose

Before the Torah was promulgated, the need to integrate human life and give it meaning was felt only sporadically by a few individual saints or thinkers. The Torah represents the first conscious attempt on a large scale to read and understand the destiny of human life in order to learn the direction which man's efforts should take. The Torah is the first product of the awareness that the purpose of religion should be the salvation of the entire man and of human life as a whole.

The origin and nature of things interested the authors of the Torah primarily from the standpoint of the relation of those things to man's destiny. Likewise with the origin and nature of the world. The main purpose of the opening chapter of the Torah is not to give an account of creation but to teach that the world, as God created it, is a fit place for man to achieve his Godlikeness, or salvation.

All ancient peoples except Israel looked to various deities as the source of whatever kind of power they needed. One deity gave power over nature, another over enemies, etc. But to our ancestors, the God of Israel was the only source of all kinds of power, because their spiritual leaders taught them to use power as a means to the achievement of human destiny and to look to the God of Israel alone as the ordainer of human destiny. That is the real meaning of Jewish monotheism. Its classic formulation is: "God created the world." In the Torah, creation is not a metaphysical but a soterical truth, or a truth which has to do with man's salvation.

Hence it is not what the Torah text itself teaches that should constitute for us Torah but what it impels us to affirm as a means of salvation. What we so affirm may be the very antithesis of what the Torah teaches, yet since we are impelled to do so by the very aim of the Torah as a whole, we are merely extending its scope as did the *Tannaim* and *Amoraim**

---

*Tannaim and *Amoraim:* the earlier and later rabbis, respectively, who established the foundations of rabbinic or talmudic Judaism during the first seven centuries of the Common Era.—eds.

of old. This is simply another case of the principle that the law is sometimes fulfilled through the very suspension of it (*Bittulah shel torah zehu
yissudah*). The text may state laws and beliefs which we have long outgrown. In recognizing that fact, we necessarily stress the ideas and
standards to which we have grown up and which, assumedly, reflect
progress in the understanding of salvation.

Even if the standard we choose to live by deviates from the one prescribed in the Torah, so long as that standard is in keeping with the
fundamental purpose of the Torah, it is as much entitled to be considered Torah as the rabbinic and philosophic interpretations which
read into the Torah a great deal that was not there. The only alternatives
to that procedure are either no Torah or some new Torah. The first
alternative is unthinkable because it would put an end to the Jewish
people. The second alternative is unthinkable because it would destroy
the spiritual continuity of the Jewish people. We must therefore resort to
the evolutionary conception of the Torah as an ongoing process.

That conception, however, is bound to appear labored and artificial,
unless we take into account one of the fundamental principles on which
the Torah is based—namely, that God is to be sought in the history of
man's effort to learn the meaning of salvation and in the striving to
attain it. In the light of that principle, the very distance we have travelled away from those beginnings which are recorded in the Torah
should be treated as history of that kind. The slightest moral or spiritual
advance which any law, institution, or event recorded in the Torah
reflects should be noted as constituting the initial leap into a new dimension of human evolution. But the advance since the one recorded in the
Torah should figure equally as Torah, for it marks the growth which the
Jewish people has achieved in its efforts to apprehend the meaning of
salvation and salvation's God. This is what we mean by saying in our
prayers: the Torah is "our life and the length of our days."

The Greater Judaism in the Making, pp. 509–11.

2. The Torah: Righteousness into Law

The term "Torah" is so frequently translated "Law" that we are apt to
lose sight of the fact that the Torah is much more than a code of laws.
But the fact that Torah is so commonly translated as "Law" is significant. The Torah does emphasize the importance of law, and discussion
of the legal aspects of Jewish civilization, known as the *halakah*, looms

large in the literature of Torah. The Torah seeks to translate righteousness into law. All modern efforts at social reconstruction prove Paul to have been wrong in maintaining the primacy of faith-righteousness and are a vindication of the Jewish religion which insists on the primacy of law-righteousness.

The progress of mankind is a movement from the notion that the world is governed by arbitrary whim to the realization that this is a law-governed world. Law-mindedness is that attitude of mind which seeks out the inherent nature of the realities it copes with in order to discover their potentialities for the achievement of truth, beauty, or goodness. The attitude of law-mindedness toward physical realities has given us science. The change from the notion that the elements of nature are controlled by an arbitrary will to the discovery that those elements act in accordance with predictable and uniform laws has increased a thousandfold the possibilities of health and life, has made the world infinitely more habitable, and has immeasurably increased our capacity for growth and development. Law-mindedness in matters of human creativity has given us the arts. It was due to the discovery of the great uniformities in the physical form of man, and the unsparing self-discipline which the Greeks cultivated in the arts, that they became the world's exemplars in human creativity. The long years of apprenticeship and training to which the musician, painter, and sculptor must submit in order to achieve success proves that those laws which its devotees conform to have not been arbitrarily devised by a few master artists but are inherent in the very nature of the beauty which man seeks to create.

Jews may be said to have contributed to human values the intuition that social life is not the plaything of arbitrary human wills, but is subject to intrinsic laws which cannot be violated with impunity. This law-mindedness, applied to human relations, gives rise to law-righteousness. Law-righteousness has little, if anything, in common with that efficiency in social organization which multiplies laws on the statute books. It is rather the recognition that social give and take must conform to certain fundamental laws that are as intrinsic to human nature as the law of gravitation is to matter and that by reckoning with those laws the human being can achieve a fullness of life from which he is otherwise precluded. The Jews were not expert either in the discovery of the laws of physical nature or of those governing the fine arts, but they possessed a deep insight into the inherence of law in the art of living together.

The Meaning of God in Modern Jewish Religion, pp. 315–17.

3. Torah as Self-Government and Self-Education

How could that "law and order" which is to be the conscience of the Jewish people and its impetus to self-transcendence operate? The answer the Torah gives is the following: self-government, self-education, with a view to self-perpetuation. Each of these forms of functioning is stressed in the Torah so conspicuously and so emphatically as to leave no room for misunderstanding. The revelation of the Kingdom of God as "law and order" is limned in the story of the three wayfarers who were entertained by Abraham as he was sitting in the heat of the day outside his tent. One of those wayfarers was none other than YHWH, and the other two were angels who were to function as witnesses of the crimes for which the cities of Sodom and Gomorrah were to be destroyed. However, YHWH did not allow Himself to destroy them, although He had noted their criminality, without the testimony of two witnesses who visited the cities and reported what they had found there. YHWH is represented in that story as teaching Abraham a lesson in the way justice was to operate. He had chosen Abraham for the purpose of having Abraham instruct his descendants to conduct themselves in keeping with the principle described in Genesis as "righteousness spelled out into law," the way of YHWH, or as we would now say, the function of His being a God, namely, responsibility as "law and order." The fact that *tzedakah* means responsibility is evident from the use of that term in modern Hebrew for charity rather than for legal justice, which it meant in ancient usage. Common to legal justice and to charity is the sense of responsibility.

The duty of communal self-education is stressed in the command to the parent to impress upon his children the importance of loving YHWH, who represents the conscience of the people of Israel, with all of one's heart, one's soul, and one's strength, and that the parent should talk to the children about it at home, on the road, when lying down, and when rising up. What civilization other than that of the Jews has stressed the sacred duty of transmitting its spiritual heritage from generation to generation as a means of self-perpetuation? This is further underscored by the covenant relation between YHWH and Israel, committing both of them to everlasting union. The covenant relationship plays a very emphatic and significant role in the whole of Jewish tradition. The fact that it is actually translated into a religious rite accounts in large part for the survival of the Jewish people.

If Not Now, When?, pp. 120–21.

4. Viewing the Torah Dynamically

The existential reality of the Jewish people and certainly the religious significance of its peoplehood are inconceivable apart from the Bible. A Jew's relation to the Bible is not to be merely that of one interested in an ancient literature or in a collection of extraordinary writings. To begin with, an American Jew, for example, should as a Jew feel toward the Bible as he feels as an American toward the Declaration of Independence and the Federal Constitution. As these give being, name, and status to the American nation, so the Bible gives them to the Jewish people. That attitude should be cultivated in the Jewish child toward the Pentateuchal Torah. This constitutes the seriousness with which it should be approached. To take the Torah seriously requires, in the first place, to learn to view it dynamically, that is, as subject to change and development. The Bill of Rights, or the Amendments to the Federal Constitution, are what give the latter its dynamism. That fact has its analogy in the growth of Jewish law and interpretation since the canonization of the Pentateuchal Torah. Seen in this light, whatever new developments take place in Jewish life, in democratic response to new and unprecedented challenges and emergencies, should be regarded as Torah and as equally binding. Although Jews seem at present very far from adopting such an attitude toward the Torah, it represents an inevitable goal, if the Jewish people is to survive, and if Jews are to realize their peoplehood for their own spiritual enhancement and for that of the world.

As to the rest of the Bible, the historic act of its canonization in itself marks that expansion of Torah which constitutes its dynamic character. In the Talmud, everything outside the Pentateuchal Torah is called *divré kabbala*. Although the rabbis treated *divré kabbala* as *less* authoritative than the Pentateuchal Torah, they stressed the divinely inspired and edifying function of the rest of the Bible. The edification which the modern Jew should derive from the Histories, the Books of the Prophets, the Psalms, and the Books of Wisdom should consist not only in a heightened spiritual mood, but also in a deepened Jewish consciousness.

Judaism Without Supernaturalism, pp. 35–36.

5. The Torah: Creation of
the Jewish People

The historical approach implies that the Jewish tradition is a human phenomenon subject to the natural laws of human behavior and to the normal action and reaction between human life and the environment. Those who accept that approach are not at all impressed by that tradition's claim to supernatural origin. They recognize that claim itself as entirely natural and normal, and as being, under the conditions of cultural development which obtained in pre-modern times, a way of expressing awareness of supreme worth and binding authority.

If then the Jewish tradition is a natural phenomenon, the Jewish people, instead of appearing in the light of a passive recipient, has to be reckoned with as its creator, and the tradition itself has to be viewed as both the stimulus and the product of that people's will to live and to render its life worthwhile. As a natural phenomenon, a tradition represents the past stage of that collective life process which we identify as a civilization. It is also a civilization as matter for transmission to the coming generation or as matter for education. In accepting the Jewish tradition, we are not accepting the ideas, habits, attitudes, and institutions as the petrified sediment of a lived past but as pent-up energy which, when released, generates new life. Thus the alternative to regarding Judaism as a specific tradition which consists of supernaturally revealed laws and teachings is to regard Judaism as a civilization which is both the product and the incentive of the will to live as a people.

The Future of the American Jew, p. 377.

6. The Torah Testifies to the
Reality of God

Today we are in a position to perceive that the experience of our people was not unlike that of other peoples, and we are able to explain, with the aid of the human sciences, the origin of legal institutions and to trace most of the features, which are unique in any civilization, to specific conditioning circumstances. It becomes, therefore, too pretentious for us to assume that our Torah is the *only* way of life for *all* peoples. We may recognize its value as the organized effort of our people to realize its highest ideals, and this may make it truly a way of salvation for the Jewish people. No other doctrine and discipline can serve them as well because, as a matter of historic fact, no other doctrine and discipline developed out of the exigencies of their own collective life in response to their own special needs and as an expression of their own collective purpose.

Evaluated in this light, the Torah may still be considered as a divine revelation in the sense that it testifies to the reality of God as the spirit that promotes righteousness in the world. To assert this is not, however, to affirm what our fathers meant when they spoke of *Torah min hashamayim*. It affirms that the Torah reveals God, not that God revealed the Torah. It assumes that the process by which the Torah actually came into being is divine, in the sense that it is a manifestation of the will to salvation or life abundant and that the doctrines and laws of other civilizations, being part of the same process, also are divine. To be sure, they are divine only to the extent that they actually do express principles which help men to live well; a limitation that applies also to Jewish law.

The modern Jew cannot, therefore, look to the Torah as a source of authority, in the sense that whatever it permits is right and whatever it forbids is wrong. He reverses the process and says: Whatever is right should be incorporated in our Torah, and whatever is wrong should be eliminated from our Torah. Inasmuch as no man can know, merely on the basis of personal experience, what is right and wrong in every situation, the traditional standards of right and wrong cherished by our people, and the institutions sanctioned by the Torah as aids to spiritual discipline, can and should be regarded with reverence, and should be observed, wherever experience has not challenged their validity. But we must not cling to the standards of the past, if they work mischief in the present. This is what happens often even to legal institutions which were beneficent in their day, but which have become detrimental to the realization of our highest ideals in the circumstances under which we live.

The Future of the American Jew, pp. 381–82.

7. A New Method of Interpreting the Torah

The purpose of reinterpretation should be to set forth the intrinsic merit of the Torah. . . .

For the regulation of conduct, for the formulation of duties that shall act as a restraint upon our evil inclinations, for a cultivation of a historic consciousness through which we may behold the divine guidance of our people, for a philosophy of life which would establish the proper spiritual relations of the Jew to his people, and of his people to the world, for all these we must go to the Torah, where they are elucidated with an amount of definiteness and detail that leave no room for uncertainty. . . . The Pentateuch is an institution, while the other parts of Scriptures are only great literary masterpieces of divinely inspired writers. . . . The method of interpretation, which will reckon with the Torah as an institution, . . . is tantamount to reading the Torah in the light of the entire body of teachings to which it has given rise. To interpret the Torah from the viewpoint of its institutional character is to recognize that ideas may be held in a potential form, in the same way as the oak is held potentially in the acorn. . . .

Furthermore, the Torah consists of both narratives and laws. This itself should supply us with a very important principle of interpretation. The term "Torah" has, through a mistranslation, become synonymous with Law, while, as a matter of fact, the term "teaching" would have been more correct though less graceful. But the mistranslation has been responsible for the neglect of the true significance to be derived from the relation between the narrative and the legislative parts of the Torah. They are not simply put together at random, but are so interwoven as to be essentially connected with each other. The laws of the Torah are not merely given in the background of the history of Israel. They are developed as a sort of corollary of that history. . . .

An interpretation of the legislation in the Torah should enable us to see in it the practical application of what might be termed the religious philosophy, which is unfolded in the narrative portions. . . .

Finally, the method of interpretation here urged will have to view the Torah *sub specie unitatis*. It must assume that, however diverse the age, authorship, and circumstances of the different fragments that constitute the Torah—if the theory of the critics as to its documentary character be the correct one—they became tributary to some dominating ideal in the mind of Israel the moment they were woven into the context of the Torah. In this new position, each fragment is to be regarded as having parted with most of its own local color and associations, and as having become instinct with the predominating aim that was responsible for bringing them together into one Torah. In being made part of a canon, the different component elements of the Torah lost part of their temporal associations and assumed an eternal significance. From that time on, the Jewish interpretative imagination began to weld the Torah into a consistent unity.

"The Supremacy of the Torah," in *Reconstructionist* 30:7 (May 15, 1965) [originally written in 1914], pp. 14–16.

8. Torah as Lifelong Moral Education

A Torah-less Judaism may hang on to life for a generation or two, but its end is inevitable. Hence, our problem is what to do to reinstate the Torah in the life of the Jew. To be sure, we cannot any longer expect the Torah to be utilized by the Jew as the sole humanizing and civilizing agency. We may, however, so interpret its scope and function as to give it first place among the ethical and cultural influences that shape his life. Why limit Torah to the study of texts, all-important as those texts are, when in reality Torah represents a living and continuing process rather than a final attainment? Torah should remind us of the truth that Judaism can function as a way of life only so long as the Jew is engaged in a lifelong process of moral education. The duty of Torah should signify the duty of treating life as an art which it is our business to keep on perfecting. Like all arts, the art of life can be perfected only by taking thought. When our people will accept this larger significance of Torah, they will inevitably go back to the classic literature of the Jewish people; for, you cannot touch upon any phase of the problem of life without reckoning with the wisdom and experience of Israel as embodied in our sacred writings.

This truth that lifelong moral education is the paramount religious duty of the human being is far-reaching enough to constitute a world mission, if we are looking for one. No one takes us seriously when we boast that we are entrusted with the mission to teach righteousness. But if we were to adopt as our mission the learning of righteousness, we would, no doubt, render a much-needed service to the cause of civilization.

A New Approach to Jewish Life, pp. 62–64.

9. The Torah and the Moral Law

The unique element in the Jewish religion consisted in the conscious recognition that the chief function of the belief in God was to affirm and fortify the moral law. It is one thing to obey an inherent principle of the human mind, but it is another to be conscious of that principle and to apply it to a critical situation. The outstanding characteristic of the Jewish religion is its conscious emphasis upon the teaching that the moral law is the principal manifestation of God in the world. This teaching is summed up in what is perhaps the most significant statement in the entire literature of religion: "The Lord of Hosts is exalted through justice, and God the Holy One is sanctified through righteousness" (Isa. 5:16).

As a result of historic vicissitudes, that prophetic teaching found concrete embodiment in the adoption of the Torah as the guiding instrument of national and individual life. The identification of God as the author of righteousness or the moral law was thus translated into the identification of God as the author of the Torah. We should therefore recognize in the doctrine of Torah *min hashamayim*, of the Torah as divinely revealed, the original prophetic discovery of the moral law as the principal self-revelation of God.

The Meaning of God in Modern Jewish Religion, pp. 302–303.

10. Torah as a Source of Spiritual Values Today

When we reflect that the Torah tradition is the embodiment of Israel's quest through the ages for the moral law that expresses the will of God, it appears absurd to entertain even for a moment the thought that tradition may be valueless to us in our continuation of this quest which our nature as human beings imposes on us. The Torah is not infallible; but even its errors, when submitted to study and analysis, may prove instructive and enlightening. We learn the moral law as we learn natural law, by trial and error. If we study the Torah in this candid yet reverential spirit, it will continue to be a means of revelation to us, disclosing to us those spiritual values which, since they constitute the value of life, are the only possible evidence of God.

The Meaning of God in Modern Jewish Religion, p. 312.

11. Torah as Affirmative and Creative Adjustment

It is not . . . the traditional Torah, or the Jewish civilization as it has come down from the past, that can any longer elicit the attitude that it is of supreme worth to the Jew and his people. The traditional Torah must be reinterpreted and reconstructed so that it becomes synonymous with the whole of a civilization necessary to civilize or humanize the individual. Individual self-fulfillment is possible only through affirmative and creative adjustments to a series of concentric and overlapping relationships within the human world, supplemented by a similar adjustment to the world as a whole. All relationships of the individual to his family, to the opposite sex, to friends, to community, to nation, to mankind, and to the world as a whole are potentially capable of evoking affirmative and creative adjustments. This process in every relationship that applies to a Jew is the career of Torah, or the career of the Jewish civilization.

Torah should mean to the Jew nothing less than a civilization which enables the individual to effect affirmative and creative adjustments in his living relationships with reality. Any partial conception of Torah is false to the forces that have made for Judaism's development and survival. Torah means a complete Jewish civilization. But to the Jew in the Diaspora it must, in addition, spell the duty of beholding in the non-Jewish civilization by which he lives a potential instrument of salvation. He must help to render that civilization capable of enhancing human life as the Torah enhanced the life of Israel. If, like the Torah, it is to be worthy of fervent devotion, those whose lives it fashions must be convinced of its intrinsic righteousness.

Judaism as a Civilization, p. 414.

12. Torah Must Advance with Human Progress

Traditionally, Torah has been understood as the supernaturally revealed way of life, and its scope was limited to whatever could come within the frame of that meaning. Henceforth, however, Torah will have to encompass every phase of Jewish life and thought, from the standpoint of its bearing on what has always been the main function of Torah—namely, the salvation of man. By relating the satisfaction of life's basic drives, the physiological and the social, to the supreme need of achieving the maximum human potential, life comes to be lived in a religious spirit. The purpose of Torah can never become outdated. To be successful as a means, however, Torah must advance with the progress of human life. Modern Judaism demands freedom to search more deeply and to understand more realistically than was possible in the past what constitutes salvation.

If we are to enlarge the scope of Torah, in the spirit of the verse "He magnifieth Torah and enhanceth it," (Isa. 42:21) we have to widen its traditional perspective. Torah should henceforth embrace that aspect of Jewish life which is traditionally designated as *derekh eretz*. The two principal connotations of *derekh eretz* are: "secular interests" and "ethical interests." These have to be made to figure in Torah to the same degree that they figure in actual life, and thus to become part of religion as a way of life.

Our first task is to identify the pragmatic implications of Torah, or the specific ways in which it has functioned hitherto in the Jewish consciousness. The next step is to ignore those implications which have become obsolete and to elaborate and implement the rest. There are, in fact, only two implications which have become obsolete: (1) that the Pentateuch, or the Torah of Moses, is a supernaturally dictated text, and (2) that it alone is the final source of whatever is authoritative in Jewish life, whether in terms of law or of social control. On the other hand, there are far more relevant implications than obsolete ones.

The very existence of an "oral Torah" alongside the "written Torah" implies the need for conceiving Torah not as a static code but as an expression of the dynamic process of spiritual growth, through adjustment to new realms of thought and action. That adjustment was regarded in the past as sanctioned by the tradition itself. It was, however, to a larger extent actually dictated by the urgent need to arrive at some modus vivendi which submitted to the irresistible demand for change while maintaining the illusion of keeping the tradition unchanged.

A New Zionism, pp. 153–54.

13. The Modern Expansion of Torah

In formulating a program for the modern expansion of Torah, based on a conception of salvation as achievable on this earth, we have to take into account the following facts or factors:

In the first place, a philosophy of salvation cannot function in a vacuum. It not only reflects but is integral to some generally accepted universe of thought, some specific pattern of ideas, hopes, and values which happens to figure in men's minds at the time. . . . It is inevitable, therefore, that in our day whatever philosophy of salvation we adopt will reflect what we consider the most authoritative thinking of our time.

Secondly, in contrast with the tendency in the past to assume that there can be but one acceptable idea of salvation, we have to realize that the day of unanimity and uniformity in men's thinking on that subject is over. We must learn to live with the fact that there are varying types of temperament and mentality, and that each such type builds a different universe of thought, and correspondingly forms a different idea of salvation. [Henry Nelson] Wieman and [Bernard E.] Meland, in *American Philosophies of Religion* (1936), describe four different types of "thought-traditions" current in our day, namely, supernaturalism, idealism, romanticism, and naturalism.

Insofar as we American Jews are necessarily influenced by the currents of American life and thought, whatever Torah tradition we are to foster is bound to reflect one or the other of these four types of religious consciousness with their corresponding conceptions of salvation. Although a bridge of mutual understanding can be built connecting these four types of religious consciousness, there is no reason why we should minimize their differences. There is need, however, to emphasize their equal legitimacy. That is tantamount to saying that religious pluralism is as inevitable in Judaism, or Jewish civilization, as it is in our non-Jewish environment.

Thirdly, a philosophy of salvation which is to be developed in the spirit of the Torah tradition cannot afford to confine itself to general ideas about human nature and destiny. It will have to be coextensive with all that we understand by a way of life. It will, therefore, have to deal, from a normative standpoint, with all those higher needs of the human spirit which have come to be better understood by reason of the general advances in the knowledge of human nature. All those needs are being studied at present in the human sciences only in a descriptive, or objective, fashion. They will henceforth have to be studied also from the standpoint of ethics and religion, in order that we may know specifically what is wrong with our present-day world, and what will have to be done to set it right.

A tradition is great, not so much by virtue of its actual pronouncements as by the incentive it affords to human growth and self-improvement. The greater the fund of knowledge and experience with which we come to it, the richer and the more significant are the lessons we can derive from it.

Questions Jews Ask, pp. 387–89.

14. Lessons from Others and Self-Criticism

We may well equate the study of Torah with Plato's conception of education. "Those who are rightly educated generally become good men," says Plato, ". . . It is the first and fairest thing that the best of men can

1. Religious Naturalism

The history of religion may be said to be the history of the different interpretations which men have given to their experience of the environment or the cosmos as dependable, from the standpoint of what they regard as salvation. The modern-minded person wants particularly to know which interpretation of this experience is compatible with a naturalistic philosophy of life.

There is a naturalistic philosophy of life with which religion or spirituality of any kind is incompatible. That is the philosophy which reduces all manifestations of life, including thought, to mere operations of matter and physico-chemical causes. In such a philosophy, there is no room for belief in spiritual values as having any inherent reality.

But there is a type of naturalism which recognizes qualitative distinctions between lower and higher orders of being. That type of naturalism allows for creative or emergent evolution, and for the autonomous functioning of mind and spirit. For that kind of philosophy, the data of rational and spiritual experience are not merely by-products of sense experience. Truth, justice, love are conceived as operating in their own right and helping to bring order out of chaos. Hence there is no reason for dismissing the experience of selfhood or personality as illusion. By the same token, we must accept as genuine the experience of Godhood, which is to the environment or cosmos what selfhood or personality is to the body. To these two spiritual qualities, selfhood and Godhood, we must add "society," which occupies a position intermediate between them and shares something of the nature of each. Though all these three are data of natural experience, they transcend the brief life of the individual human being, and redeem it of its merely temporary character, in that they enable him to lay up resources and create potentialities that outlast him.

Questions Jews Ask, p. 95.

ever have, and which, though liable to take a wrong direction, is capable of reformation. And this work of reformation is the great business of every man while he lives" (*Laws*, 644).

We deliberately introduce this passage from Plato's *Laws* for two reasons. First, we wish to suggest that broadening the concept of Torah implies among other things realizing that we Jews have no monopoly on the wisdom of life. On the contrary, the wisdom which we should display as synonymous with Torah should consist in our learning from the wisdom of all peoples, both ancient and modern, acquired by them in the course of their striving for the fulfillment of human destiny. Plato, for example, in the same context from which the above passage is quoted, identifies human fulfillment with "the ideal perfection of citizenship." The traditional Torah, on the other hand, addresses itself to Israel with the precept "Thou shalt be perfect with the Lord thy God." (Deut. 18:13)

Secondly, we wish to give Torah a connotation of directed growth and development. That is an idea or value which is lacking in our tradition. The capacity to be self-critical, to recognize that Torah or education may have taken "a wrong direction," and that "this work of reformation is the business of every man while he lives," is essential not only as a means of regenerating the tradition but also of perpetuating it. As a tradition succeeds in reforming or reconstructing itself to meet new needs of man, it acquires a new lease on life.

A New Zionism, pp. 155–56.

15. Achieving Existence as a Torah People

The radical change which took place under Pharisaic influence in the traditional conception of reward and punishment and which completely revolutionized the purpose and the meaning of Jewish existence then came about so slowly as to be imperceptible. Nowadays, a change in Jewish ideology has to take place forthwith and with full awareness that it is, from the standpoint of world outlook, a break with the kind of religious rationale that was accepted by our ancestors or forebears. Moreover, in the past, all that was needed to meet the challenge was to reinterpret the traditional ideas about God, the world, and man. Nowadays the Jewish situation is such that reinterpretation is far from enough. What is urgently needed is a social structure, or polity, that would enable the Jews throughout the world to function as an organic people. They cannot function as a nation in the modern sense of the term nor as a church in the modern sense of the term. They have to find a way of functioning as a civilizational people, united by a bond of voluntary allegiance to a civilization or Torah, the purpose of which is to achieve fulfillment, both individual and collective, along lines which permit continuity in change and unity in diversity. In other words, the Jews have to achieve existence as a Torah people, with Torah understood as coming forth from a modern Zion. The establishment of the State of Israel is only a spearhead of a movement to create that new kind of social structure or polity. So far, no thought has been given to the forging of the spear itself.

The Purpose and Meaning of Jewish Existence, p. 10.

16. The Contemporary Study of Torah

We cannot afford to defer any longer the need of recovering for the study of Torah a position of primacy in the life of our people. To achieve that purpose, we have, first, to become fully aware of the specific needs which the study of Torah fulfilled in the past, and, secondly, to give the *status* of Torah to whatever content, or material of study, is necessary to fulfill those needs in our day.

The following are the needs which the study of Torah fulfilled in the past:

It provided the Jews with an awareness of themselves as a people, united by a corporate self-awareness, or we-feeling.

It taught Jews what they were to regard as salvation, or the highest good, both as individuals and as a people, and by the same token it taught them what to believe about God as the power that makes for salvation.

It taught our ancestors what they had to know and do in order to achieve salvation, or the highest good.

Accordingly, for the modern Jew, the study of Torah, or its equivalent—Jewish culture and education—has to embrace whatever knowledge would enable us Jews to retain our individuality as a people, discern our true destiny, and know the means and methods of achieving it.

The attainment of such normative knowledge involves not only taking into account all that is now generally accepted as factual and helpful in the art of living. It also involves utilizing the entire Jewish tradition to check, illustrate, and implement whatever inference we may derive

from the modern approach to our problem as Jews. Our tradition would
then be utilized functionally in the same spirit, though not in the same
way, as when Rabbi Akiba drew upon the written Torah to give authority to what was accepted as normative in his day. That is the only way
our tradition can keep on growing and renewing itself and keep abreast
of the general progress in human experience and the wisdom of life.
That is the only way we Jews can solve the problem of living in two
civilizations, our traditional one and the civilization of the country of
which we are citizens.

Questions Jews Ask, pp. 383–84.

17. Observations

Only a modern orientation can sustain our devotion to tradition.

The ideas and ideals which a tradition transmits constitute spiritual
capital.

Belonging to the past, they are like currency of a country from which
we have migrated.

If they are to be put into circulation, they have to be converted into the
currency of the present-day world.

The process of conversion is known as interpretation or reinterpretation.

That process enables the spiritual energy stored in a tradition to continue operating in worlds far different from those in which it arose and
grew.

Directing and acting are said to "make" the play.

Similarly, effective and relevant interpretation "makes" tradition.

The foremost problem in Jewish religion is how to get Jews to take the
Bible seriously without taking it literally.

It is a sign of childishness to accept the great religious myths as literal
truths, a sign of adolescence to regard them as delusion, and a sign of
maturity to appreciate their spiritual implications.

An excellent clue to the understanding of the Bible is to realize that it is
the product of the endeavor by Israel's Sages, priests, and Prophets to
reeducate their people. They sought to eradicate misconceptions about
life, God, man, and the world, and to put in their place new conceptions.

The Bible is the first, and so far the only, evidence that a people can reeducate itself. Maybe that fact should constitute its main claim to being divine.

To interpret the Torah properly, we must remember that the whole of it is more than the sum of its parts.

The difference between our Torah and other ancient and modern law codes is that the chief aim of those law codes is to establish law and order in society, whereas the chief aim of the Torah is to enable man to become fully human.

The account of the fall of man, in the opening story of Genesis, is the ancient way of reminding us that man is only on the way to becoming human.

The future of man as a free spiritual being cannot be divorced from his past endeavors to become one.

It is necessary to be rooted in a tradition in order to have not only something to live by, but also something to rebel against.

The ancient authorities are entitled to a vote—but not to a veto.

If tradition is to be a means to our growing up, it has to be partly outgrown.

We should feel toward our tradition as we should feel toward our country:
   My tradition right or wrong: if right, to be kept right; if wrong, to be set right.

Those to whom every inherited folly is holy are mainly to blame for there being so many to whom everything holy is folly.

The cure for anxiety about the future is not nostalgia for the past.

At first men struggle to be free from nature; that gives rise to tradition. Then men struggle to be free from tradition, to get back to nature.

Only a progressive is entitled to recite the benediction of "Sheheheyanu."
   For the conclusion of the benediction reads, "Vehiggianu lazeman hazeh" (He has caused us to reach this time), i.e., "He has brought us up to date"!

Jewish tradition consists of the written Torah, together with the interpretation given it by the Jewish folk spirit. That interpretation constitutes the oral Torah.
   In what way does the interpretation given by the Jewish folk spirit differ from that given by an individual commentator who does not embody that spirit?

The difference can be explained by what a music critic once said about the playing of Rachmaninoff.

"When an average performer," he said, "sits down before the piano, he becomes smaller and smaller and the instrument becomes larger and larger.

"When a performer of the class of Rachmaninoff sits down to play, suddenly the piano begins to diminish and fades into a miniature, until finally it seems to disappear altogether—and you are left alone with the man and the music."

The written Torah is the piano; the Jewish folk spirit is the performer.

When those who incarnate the Jewish folk spirit interpret the written Torah, the latter fades into a miniature, and you are left alone with the Jewish folk spirit and the divine music.

Tradition puts Judaism in fetters. It is not enough to remove the fetters; what Judaism needs is wings.

Not So Random Thoughts,
pp. 255–88.

V

Interpreting the Torah, the Prophets, and the Rabbis

1. Introductory Myths
   of the Torah

It has become urgent to analyze the mythological elements of the Jewish religious tradition and to identify those aspirations or spiritual values in it which are relevant for individual fulfillment and universal peace. The functional, rather than allegorical, method of demythologizing the Torah should reveal the purpose and meaning of Jewish existence. . . .

The myth of Creation in the entire first chapter of Genesis is a figment of the primitive imagination. The story about the Flood depicts a heaven with windows through which the waters poured down to swell the waters below the earth.

The myth that God made man in His own image implies that God and man share the transcendent element of Godhood. Thus man only attains humanity when his life reflects the reality of God. Though man and beast have much in common, the divine in man sets him radically apart. Unlike other great civilizations of the Near East which worshipped animals as gods, the world of the Bible distinguished between the human and the subhuman. This humanistic and moral idea defines the function of the mythical Creation story.

Ostensibly, the Garden of Eden myth conveys God's expectations of man; God did not want man to eat the fruit of the tree of knowledge of good and evil. But what is meant by "the knowledge of good and evil"? When that phrase occurs in Deuteronomy (1:39), it reads: "your children that this day have no knowledge of good or evil." And young King Solomon asked God to give him "an understanding heart to judge Thy people, that I may discern between good and evil"(1 Kings 3:9). These passages declare that the knowledge of good and evil relates to the difference between right and wrong and that God, not man, is the sole source of such knowledge. (The Hebrew Bible did not propound moral relativism or situational ethics.)

Transposed into humanist terms, the Garden of Eden legend emphasizes that man's self-interest is no gauge of right and wrong. Only a transcendent awareness of reciprocal responsibility in accord with the dictates of nature's God can determine moral and spiritual values. When Cain killed Abel and subsequently disavowed all responsibility for his brother, he took the law unto himself and set into motion the degeneration of the human species. Violence resulted from Adam's transgression in substituting self-will for the law and order which are the will of God.

As man's transgressions multiplied, the contagion corrupted all creation. Therefore, the myth relates, God regretted that He had created man and brought on the Flood. But in the exceptional character of Noah—who is portrayed as reflecting the divine purpose—God discerned the creativity that overcomes the entropy in nature and in man. After the Flood, which virtually returned creation to chaos, God dictated to Noah the law and order which, if observed, would assure the survival of mankind. The myth represents God as promising no more floods or cataclysms. Ironically, it is man who now has the power to turn the earth back to original chaos. A functional interpretation of the Flood myth and of God's covenant should warn mankind to bring its morality into the same century as its weaponry.

In a naive attempt to explain the origin of nations, the author of the City and Tower of Babel myth portrayed God as confounding the language of mankind. Through division men would be prevented from contravening the divine purpose of creation: "And the Lord said: 'Behold they are one people, and they all have one language; and this is only what they begin to do; and now nothing will be withholden from them, which they propose to do' " (Gen. 11:6). But the evils of nationhood are not inherent in the division of mankind into ethnic groups and national entities. It is the ethical character of nationhood which decides whether division and diversity bode good or ill for creative survival. Without ethical motivation in this age of megaton missiles and "acceptable" ninety (as opposed to one hundred and twenty) million casualties, the menacing reality forecast in the myth may come to pass: "Behold [the nations] have one language [that is, the capability of annihilation]; and now nothing will be withholden from them, which they propose to do."

When Abraham welcomed God and His two angels, disguised as strangers, their colloquy sounds the keynote of the religion of Israel. Mythically, the episode relates how YHWH instructed Abraham in what was to be the distinctive moral trait of the nation to be founded by him. That nation was to set an example to the other nations of the way to administer justice through law. Hence the display of the legal process as later set forth in the Torah, including the testimony of at least two witnesses (Deut. 17:6). Without such testimony even the flagrant violence of Sodom and Gomorrah against strangers could not be punished. Discounting the element of myth in this legend, we have here unmistakable evidence of ancient Israel's aspiration to function as a paradigm of ethical nationhood.

When Abraham received a last-minute reprieve from the divine command to sacrifice his only son, Isaac, the angel of the Lord said: "Do not lay hands on the lad . . . for I know now that you revere God." Why does this myth stress reverence for God? Because Abraham, by his unquestioning obedience to God's will, made possible the rise of an eternal people. He renounced the cycle of violence and lawlessness which Adam and Eve, through their disobedience, had precipitated.

However, the fact that so bizarre a myth could find a place in the Torah does call for an explanation. That story undoubtedly arose at a time when human sacrifice was practiced in some of the pagan nations with which ancient Israel came in contact. Those who first learned to worship the God YHWH no doubt refused to be outdone by the pagans in their devotion to YHWH, to whom human sacrifice was an abomination. Thus out of the tension between those two conflicting attitudes toward YHWH there was bound to arise the kind of a myth in which that conflict was resolved. Abraham was tested and he withstood the test.

The Bible defines the goal of Jewish existence in terms of the glorification of God. In Deutero-Isaiah God refers to ancient Israel as "My people, Mine elect, the people which I formed for Myself that they might tell of My praise" (Isa. 43:20–21). How seriously Israel regarded the glorifying of God is manifest in its unique genius for psalmody. To be sure, polytheistic religions have psalmody. But praising the gods singly or in concert—in the hope of winning their favor or deflecting their wrath—has nothing in common with the Hebraic conception. The frequent reference in the Bible to the special significance of knowing God's name seems almost certainly to prove that the term "name" in Hebrew either denotes or at least connotes the idea of function. Thus we read: "I will set him on high because he knows My name; when he calls upon Me I will answer him" (Ps. 91:14–15).

Even in this mythical form the notion that God created man to honor Him presupposes a radical and qualitative difference between the human and subhuman. Ancient Israel refused to deify animals because of their superior physical powers. So profound was its abhorrence of such blasphemy that the Israelites were enjoined from representing the Deity in any form.

The biblical conception of God is unique. Great thinkers such as Kepler and Spinoza conceived of God as synonymous with nature. To the biblical scholar Ezekiel Kaufman, the God of Israel represented purposiveness in antithesis to blind fate. Insofar as nature is creative and functions according to the will of God, predictable law may be identified with that creative aspect of nature which impels and helps man to achieve creative survival. Despite its mythical aspects, the traditional belief that God created man to glorify Him had all the force of objective fact. That concept impelled ancient Israel to accept the praise of God as its mission in life and the *raison d'être* for its nationhood. It became the chief motivation for Jewish survival in the midst of hatred and persecution. Its authentic elements of individual and collective commitment still define the goal and purpose of Jewish survival.

The Religion of Ethical Nationhood, pp. 35–39.

2. Revelation

Undoubtedly the assertion that the Ten Commandments were spoken by God at Sinai, taken literally, conveys a fact which is in conflict with the modern man's outlook. But a knowledge of the workings of the ancient mind and of the way it was wont to report its profoundest experience has taught us to penetrate beneath the surface of a tradition and to get the functional significance of that tradition, from the standpoint of the attitudes and behavior it was intended to call forth. There is a large area of feeling and experience for which even the most articulate lack the right expression. Suppose an ancient people, untutored in philosophic speculation, had the irresistible intuition that the ethical values stemmed from a source other than that of individual expediency—by no means incredible—how could they put that intuition into words other than those recorded in the Jewish tradition? As what else than a revelation from God could they possibly describe this experience of compelling certainty? The sense of inner compulsion which a highly important truth always carried with it led the ancients to ascribe that truth to a source which belonged to a different dimension of being from that of normal experience. Such a source could only be divine revelation.

"A Philosophy of Jewish Ethics," in *The Jews*, ed. Louis Finkelstein, p. 1017.

3. The Biblical Philosophy of History

So persistent are the problems of human life dealt with in the Bible, so comprehensive and consistent is the scope of its philosophy of history, that despite the naiveté of some of its concepts the Bible is vitally relevant today for the renewal not only of the Jewish people but of all mankind.

The biblical philosophy of history is cast in the form of a drama, with God and Israel in the foreground as the principal protagonists. Against the backdrop of other nations Israel is presented as their paradigm. As the drama unfolds, it emphasizes that human beings can learn to control and direct the satisfaction of their vital needs only when they are divided into nations, each of which conducts its affairs in a spirit of justice and law. Ultimately such individual and collective responsibility will establish the Kingdom of God on earth through the abolition of national rivalries and war.

God is the central character of the drama. He is represented as having created the world with all that is in it for the sake of man, and as having created man to glorify Him. That assumption, which underlies traditional religion, clarifies what the biblical writings meant to their authors and contemporaries. . . .

The Bible asserts that God governs mankind and directs the panorama of creation for the sake of His own name and glory. Furthermore, the entire course of nature and human history manifests His infinite power and inexorable justice—tempered by forgiving mercy. Since according to this premise every event in history reflects the power and justice of God, the biblical record of the people of Israel reveals a definite plan which gives purpose and meaning to those events. . . .

Thus from the beginning of mankind's history to its culmination with the establishment of God's Kingdom on earth, the Bible conceived history as a revelation of God's purpose with mankind. History was not regarded as a progressive evolution of the human species through its own conscious efforts to rise above what it has in common with the subhuman. When man's knowledge of the universe was geocentric and his conception of God was anthropomorphic, primitive wisdom was theocentric. Its theology spoke in terms of man's relevance to God as a means to God's prestige.

The Religion of Ethical Nationhood, pp. 44–47.

4. The Religion of the Prophets

It may be said without exaggeration that no single belief contributed so much to the unique development of the Jewish religion as the belief that the God of Israel was someday bound to reveal Himself in His full glory and power to all the world. This belief proved to be the main driving force for the prophetic movement. The primary task of the Prophets was not merely to announce this belief—since it was universally assumed to be true—but to interpret in its light whatever disaster seemed imminent. The upshot of their interpretation was that the Day of the Lord was a day of doom for all who rebelled against YHWH, and that only those who would repent and return to YHWH would be spared. Had not their contemporaries taken for granted the advent of the Day of the Lord, the Prophets would have had nothing to which to address themselves. As it was, that postulate proved the most potent vehicle for communicating the moral and spiritual urge by which they were obsessed. What the modern person experiences as a relentless inner urge the ancients experienced as a compulsion coming from some outside mysterious being— usually the god they worshipped. The Prophets, therefore, could do no other than identify as the command of YHWH the urge that drove them to make known what the Day of the Lord had in store for their people.

The religion of the canonical Prophets is not quite identical with what is commonly understood by the term "monotheism." That term usually designates the outcome of an intellectual development which could not possibly have been carried on in early Israel. God, as monotheism conceives Him, is a metaphysical being whose traits and attributes have nothing in common with anything in human experience. When we say that God is all-knowing, or all-good, it is with the qualification that we are using a terminology which in strictness is totally inapplicable to God. Why then do we use it? Simply because we have none better. No such sophistication could ever form part of the Prophets' idea of the God of Israel. YHWH still retains His proper name. He is not merely God, but the god *par excellence,* the one being who has more right to be called a god than the deities of the other nations. YHWH, in the estimate of the Prophets, comes up to the standard of what a god should be. The other beings for whom godhood is claimed are not unreal or imaginary, but they have not the qualities essential to being a god. They may be considered evil spirits, or good spirits, but they are not gods because they lack the power and the holiness of YHWH.

There was something paradoxical about the God of Israel. On the one hand, He was conceived as possessing all those traits that made Him the God of the whole world, and, on the other, as content to put up with one little rebellious people for His nation. None felt the paradox more keenly than the Prophets. They were at great pains to find some degree of commensurateness in the relationship between God and Israel. They tried, as it were, by a *tour de force* to change Israel from an average people dominated by the blind impulses of superstition and greed into a holy people that might deserve, by virtue of its purity and righteousness, to be the people of YHWH. This is the reason for their unremitting opposition to any entangling alliances with other nations. Israel must remain unique and solitary.

The inevitable conclusion concerning the solity of the God of Israel to which the Prophets felt themselves driven did not comport in the least with the kind of religion they saw their people live by. In the sanctuaries of Israel were to be found all the paraphernalia of altars, pillars, and images, all the feasting and abandon that one could behold at any of the sanctuaries of the false gods. The people's adoption of a syncretic religion, which bore all the earmarks of Canaanitish custom and ritual, indicated no awareness that the God of Israel was totally incomparable with the so-called gods of the nations. Along with their failure to mark the supreme Godhood and holiness of the God of Israel in the worship at the sanctuaries, the Israelites actually flouted His supremacy in their daily life, and in their political affairs. They disregarded the laws of justice which had been promulgated in His name in former days when they still retained the simple nomadic customs. Their rulers were continually engaged in political intrigues with the rulers of the neighboring nations. This always led to the aping of foreign customs. Since YHWH was all-powerful, Israel did not need the protection of the great empires, nor did it need to enter into conspiracies with neighboring peoples for the overthrow of those empires. Those who resorted to such measures evidently had not much faith that the God of Israel was able to defend His own people. It was but one step from lack of confidence in the God of Israel to the adoption of other gods with whose peoples Israel sought to form alliances.

The Prophets were not merely social reformers or preachers of morality voicing their protests against the social wrongs of their day in the language of the religion familiar to their hearers. They were primarily believers in and ardent devotees of YHWH. What rendered them so devoted was that they saw in Him the only supernatural being who was truly a god, because, in addition to being all-powerful, He was the patron and defender of the oppressed. They were sensitive to the injustice committed by the strong against the weak. Godhood, therefore, could mean but one thing to them—the will and the power to vindicate the right. They were certain that YHWH had the will to vindicate the right because of the many ordinances and precedents ascribed to Him in the interests of justice and purity. None of the deities of the neighbors was known to be so insistent upon righteous dealing. Accordingly, YHWH alone possessed all the attributes of Godhood; He alone was truly a god. They were certain that, before long, He alone would be acknowledged as God, and to Him only would divine honors be rendered.

The crises which betokened oncoming upheavals and which the Prophets interpreted as heralding the Day of the Lord had their beginning in Assyria's resumption of a career of conquest, after having been held to her own borders for almost half a millennium. She sought once more an outlet to the Mediterranean. The peoples of the many small kingdoms that stood in the path of her ambition were thrown into panic. Alliances and counteralliances against Assyria were the order of the day. The cooperation of Judah and Israel was sought by their neighbors. It was evident that some great catastrophe was impending.

To the devotees of YHWH, it was unthinkable that the gods either of Assyria or of the little peoples which were seething with fear and unrest could have anything to do with the oncoming calamities. Many in Israel, no doubt, concluded that the gods of the conquering Assyrians were apparently more powerful than the deities of the other peoples, more powerful even than YHWH. Resistance was, therefore, futile; the best policy was either to make alliance with Egypt, or court the favor of Assyria and her gods. The Prophets could not possibly permit such a conclusion to go unchallenged. They would not brook the thought that YHWH was inferior to any other deity. Since YHWH was the only supernal being who by reason of His power and righteousness could be deemed God, they believed that He alone was the prime mover of the destinies of nations. It was YHWH and no other god, they concluded, who let loose the devastating hordes which were about to sweep over countries and carry away populations. Whether He sends the Assyrian, the Scythian, or the Babylonian hordes, it is because the peoples of the invaded countries had aroused His indignation through cruelty or immorality. How will Israel fare in the oncoming doom of the nations? No better than the rest. The Israelites, to be sure, were at one time the object of YHWH's special love and interest. Their history was replete with accounts of the marvelous deeds their God had wrought in their behalf from the time He redeemed them from Egypt. Gratitude should have impelled them to repose implicit faith in YHWH and obey His laws; yet they proved recreant. Nothing, therefore, could save them from the universal disaster.

As much as the Prophets had to contend against those who in their hearts believed that YHWH would have to succumb to alien gods, they had an even more difficult task in combating the patriotic optimism of the "false prophets" and their adherents, who argued, "Is not YHWH among us? No evil will come upon us." One of the popular beliefs which fortified this optimism was that YHWH would someday manifest His power over the nations by granting Israel a spectacular victory over its foes. Such was their interpretation of the long-awaited Day of YHWH. It was at this juncture that the Prophets appeared and warned the Israelites that their God was about to display His glory but with consequences to them other than those that had been expected. The great cataclysm that would ensue would destroy all enemies of YHWH, those within Israel as well as those without. All who disobeyed the law of YHWH, who oppressed the poor, who grew rich through exploitation, or who worshipped strange gods were His enemies, and would feel the impact of His wrath. "Woe unto you that desire the Day of YHWH," cried the Prophet. "Wherefore would ye have the Day of the Lord? It is darkness, and not light . . . even very dark and no brightness in it" (Amos 5:18, 20).

This preoccupation with the belief concerning the Day of YHWH placed the Prophets in the forefront of those who have done most to influence the course of mankind's religious development. They prodded their people into realizing that the attribute of Godhood ought not to be bandied about freely and bestowed upon every candidate and claimant, from crawling reptiles to kings and emperors. For the first time in the history of religion, the man of average intellectual and spiritual grasp was called upon to appreciate some of the implications of his idea of God. This was not the product of abstract thought; it was the result of the continual "speaking betimes and often" of the Prophets who proclaimed the belief in the Day of the Lord, and interpreted it in its relation to current events.

Subsequent events proved the truth of the frenzied warnings uttered by the great Prophets. The fall of Samaria was a complete vindication of YHWH's power and character. But it took more than one Prophet, and more than one manifestation of YHWH's wrath, to raise Him in the minds of His worshippers to the position which He finally attained. Not even the Prophets, aided though they were by the course of events, could have brought about such a result. The work of the Prophets would have remained futile if there had not arisen a band of anonymous zealots, including priests of the Temple at Jerusalem, who not only consolidated the results of the Prophets' preaching but also laid the foundation of a theocratic commonwealth. These anonymous zealots labored more or less in secrecy during the reign of Manasseh, when the voice of prophecy was silenced and a new influx of foreign religious practices, chiefly from Babylon, presented a new danger to the worship of YHWH. During that period the traditions concerning YHWH were gathered and revised, and the laws attributed to Him were reformulated so as to be in accord with His character as a God of righteousness. All of these efforts finally bore fruit. Upon the death of Manasseh, the prophetic party, consisting of Temple priests and disciples of the Prophets, became active again. In the year 621 B.C.E., when the scroll of the Torah was found, a new covenant was made with YHWH. Henceforth there was to be a definitive instrument which was to serve as the criterion of obedience to the will of YHWH, a written Torah.

Although that covenant marks the beginning of the Jewish religion as based upon a written Torah, a long time elapsed before the Torah came to occupy the place of primacy in the life of the Jews. Outside the limited group of priests and Prophets, the deeper and more spiritual conception of the God of Israel was still unknown or unpopular. It was only after the stupendous efforts of Prophets like Jeremiah and Ezekiel, and of others who have left no writing behind or whose writings have remained anonymous, and after Jerusalem and the Temple were destroyed and the people had experienced all the horrors of war and exile, that the prophetic conception of the God of Israel and of His dealings with His people came to be generally accepted. It was only then that Jews were animated with a sincere desire to know and obey His Torah. During the century and a half following the destruction of the First Temple, Jewish life was in the process of reorganizing itself as a theocratic civilization. It was as such that Judaism functioned virtually until the destruction of the Second Temple.

Judaism as a Civilization, pp. 357–62.

5. The Afterlife and the Individual

Until the fourth century B.C.E., the Jewish religion, in common with the less-developed religions, assumed that man maintained relationship with God only during his lifetime. Theories of what happened to the human being after death, though they provided a rich source for magic, did not become part of the body of religious ideas or practices. Such magic known as necromancy was drastically forbidden and condemned. Israel's ideas about the condition of the dead originally resembled those generally entertained by the peoples of the Near East during the first stages of urban culture. People then thought that death came after the principle or spirit of life left the body, although they had no definite ideas of what happened to the spirit after its departure. The prevalent notion that the shades, or shadowy doubles, of those who died spent the rest of their existence in a subterranean pit known as Sheol, seemed to have no practical implications for the human being while alive.

Though ancient man could not believe that death meant complete extinction, he formulated no definite belief in the immortality of the soul as part of religious doctrine. All customs and institutions that in the ancient world attended the burial of royal personages, as, for example, in Egypt, and that seem to have been interwoven with the religious life of the people, only prepared the way for the later emphasis upon religion as a means of redeeming the human soul from the power of death. For it must be remembered that royal personages were regarded as gods whose life was necessarily immortal. It was only in its later stages, especially in the traditional form handed down to us, that religion came to look upon the continuance of the ordinary man's relationship with God, even after death, as a matter of course. But the ancient Israelite took for granted that this relationship was severed at death. The prospect of such severance, rather than that of personal annihilation, was what he dreaded about death. "In death there is no remembrance of Thee; in Sheol who shall give Thee thanks?" (Ps. 6:6). "For Sheol cannot praise Thee; they that go down into the pit cannot hope for Thy truth" (Isa. 38:18). Thus the fact of death, far from entering the circle of beliefs, emotions, and practices centering around the conception of God, constituted the cessation of religion as it did of life itself.

Whatever outward influence may have contributed to the adoption of the belief in resurrection during the fourth century B.C.E., it was undoubtedly concurrent with an important psychological development which took place in Jewish life—the emergence of the individual. Many adumbrations of this development may be found in the Deuteronomic law, in Jeremiah and Ezekiel, but only when the belief in resurrection became a part of the Jewish religion were the claims of the individual recognized, not only in the religion of the few who were spiritually eminent but also in popular religion. Before then it was assumed that the individual suffered the fate of his people, no matter what his own deserts were. But from now on, man was regarded as a being who was judged as an individual, not as an indistinguishable unit in the mass. When God would create the new heaven and new earth, all the dead would rise again, all would be judged, and according to their deeds they would gain the world of the blessed or be destroyed forever.

Apparently the belief in resurrection was accepted when people clearly perceived that, despite all assertions to the contrary, man did not receive his just deserts in this world. The Bible produces sufficient evidence to show that the claims of the individual are asserted with increasing emphasis not long after the reforms introduced by Ezra and Nehemiah. Some of the Psalms, the books of Job and Koheleth, attest the persistent questioning of the then-traditional conception of retribution. As a result, some became skeptical and broke with Jewish religion entirely. Others, after an extreme effort of the will to find a solution, acquired serenity. This solution, reflected in Psalms 73 and 92, amounted to a categorical reaffirmation of the belief that the prosperity of the wicked does not endure, and that their end is all the more disastrous because of the unmerited prosperity which they enjoyed. Yet experience belied these brave affirmations. In times of conflict with foreign and Jewish rule, in the tyranny of the powerful over the humbler and more pious members of the population, men saw the triumph of those who were manifestly evil. All too often the wicked ended their days in peace and left behind them numerous progeny who showed not the least tendency to come to terms with those whom their fathers had persecuted. At that critical juncture, the belief in resurrection saved the Jewish religion. For it was possible now to affirm that the time of judgment and retribution was not in the here and now, but at the end of days, when God would become the king of the world, who would judge the quick and the dead. Thus did the faith in the power and justice of God take on new life.

Judaism as a Civilization,
pp. 366–68.

6. After the Temple's Destruction

When the Second Commonwealth was destroyed, the Jewish religion underwent vast changes in emphasis, due to the fact that instead of being the principal means of national self-expression, it became the one and only means. Such a role has not been played by any other religion in the world. Because of this unique function served by the Jewish religion, it is by no means an easy task, if not an altogether impossible one, to describe Jewish traditional religion correctly in terms used to describe other religions. Terms like "national" and "universal" do not apply to it. If already in the days of the Second Commonwealth the Jewish religion became *sui generis* by becoming the *principal* national preoccupation, it became infinitely more so when, through the loss of the last vestige of political independence, it became the *only* medium through which the national consciousness and will of the Jewish people found an outlet. All the religious ideas, emotions, and habits were very much intensified in order to further the survival of the nation. Not that the conservation of national existence was deliberately professed as an end in itself, but subconsciously the will to live as a people henceforth colored every element of the religion, its ideas, attitudes, and practices.

The most important result of the fact that religion became the sole outlet of national self-expression was the conservation of the revelational basis of the belief in God. It is evident that no reasoned conception of the existence and nature of God could possibly have formed the basis of Jewish unity. It is impossible for any reasoned conception to gain uniform acceptance unless it is backed by some authoritative body which can arrogate for its decrees the validity of supernatural revelation. This was what the Christian synods did. But even they would have been ineffective if the emperors, in order to conserve the unity of the Roman empire, had not added the weight of their authority to the synods' decrees.

With the lack of an external force to sanction any reasoned theology, the Jewish religion was compelled to retain as its sole basis the purely revelational conception of God, a conception that remained free of any admixture of philosophical investigation into the problem of God's existence or His nature. The traditional Jewish religion as interpreted by the *Tannaim* and *Amoraim*, and as conceived and lived by the sixty generations of the Jewish people preceding the present era, contributed nothing to the conception of God that had not been known in the era of the Second Commonwealth. On the contrary, that conception was somewhat narrowed because of the national motif interwoven with it. That does not mean that the scope of the God-idea in Judaism was reduced to the needs of Jewish national survival. The danger that God would be conceived once again as a sort of tribal or national deity was long past. But the conception of the universe as a whole shrank to smaller proportions by very reason of the central place which Judaism accorded in it to Israel.

Judaism as a Civilization, pp. 369–370.

7. The Different Modes of Rabbinic Interpretation

How has it been possible for all of the various writings in the Bible to arouse and keep alive the awareness of God, to fortify the national consciousness, and to serve as a guide to conduct over so many generations, amid all possible climes, and under so wide a range of varying circumstances? The answer is that the Bible is not merely a text or collection of texts; it is what the interpreter derives from, or reads into, those texts. The meaning of any passage in the Bible is not what the surface reading of it seems to convey, but what the interpreter reads out of, or into, it. The interpreter himself is not a scientific scholar interested in objective fact. What the scholar finds may at best be the raw material out of which the Bible was formed, but not the Bible itself. The interpreter, on the other hand, is a Jew who has, in common with the rest of his people, the threefold interest of having the Bible give him a keen awareness of God, a deepened consciousness of his people, and a passionate devotion to the right way of life. This is what the Jewish interpreters have always tried to find in the Bible. As a result of their efforts, we Jews are by this time in possession not of one version, but of four different versions of the Bible, and we are on the eve of evolving a fifth version.

The four versions of the Bible are the products, respectively, of the four different kinds of interpretation: *Peshat, Remez, Derush,* and *Sod.* A brief characterization of each type of interpretation will make clear wherein it gave rise to a different version of the Bible.

Peshat means literal interpretation; yet it would be incorrect to say that the ancients were always true to the literal meaning of the text, when they thought they were giving its *Peshat.* It is doubtful whether most of the statements which speak of God in human terms retained their literal significance after they were incorporated into the Bible. The verse in Genesis which speaks of God as having smelled the sweet savor of Noah's sacrifice, or the oft-repeated phrase "a sweet-smelling offering to the Lord," may be the desiccated remains of an ancient way of speaking. A safe description of *Peshat* might, therefore, be the following: That which constituted the functional meaning of the text, or that meaning of it which formed the basis of action or belief, at the time it came to be part of the Bible.

Derush is not just any kind of interpretation that departs from the original or literal meaning of the text. As one of the four types of biblical interpretation, *Derush* refers only to those meanings which the *Tannaim* and *Amoraim* have read into the Bible, and which constitute the content of the *Midrashim* and the groundwork of the *Gemara* in the Talmud. The five years which, according to the *Mishnah* in *Avot,* should be devoted to the study of the Scriptures, were to be spent in learning the *Derush* of the Bible. The term *"debé rav"* appended to one of those collections of rabbinic interpretations betrays the early school environment in which the Bible was taught, in the light of *Derush.*

It is important to mention some of the main rabbinic doctrines and interests that changed radically the original or literal meaning of the Bible text. The belief in the world to come, as the world in which alone man achieves salvation, transformed such simple statements as those which refer to life, or to long life, as a reward for obedience to God, into promises of reward in the world to come. The dominant rabbinic interest at that time was to give biblical sanction to accepted norms, in civil and ritual law. We have, accordingly, the well-known reinterpretation of "eye for eye" as a money fine, and of the threefold repetition of the ordinance forbidding the seething of the kid in its mother's milk as the basis of all those practices which forbid the mixing of milk and meat diets. When in the former years the child would be taught "Humesh with Rashi," he was introduced at once into the version of the Bible, which is the product of the rabbinic method of interpretation, known as *Derush.* This was the version of the Bible which bulked largest in the Jewish consciousness during the eighteen centuries of premodern times. The only exception to this was the Song of Songs, which will be dealt with in the next category.

A third version of the Bible, which is the least popular, is the product of *Remez*. *Remez* refers to metaphorical or figurative rendering of a text. As a method of interpretation, it is found even in those rabbinic writings which are generally characterized as *Derush*. The interpretation of the Song of Songs, for example, as symbolic of the love that unites God and Israel, though part of Amoraic literature, properly belongs to *Remez*.

Remez refers to that perspective in Judaism which resulted from the impact of philosophic thought, whether Platonic or Aristotelian, on the Jewish tradition. The whole of Philo's exegesis has the effect of giving us an entirely different version of the Bible from that which either *Peshat* or *Derush* yields us. According to this version, the Bible presents, in symbolic form, teachings and values derived from Plato and the Stoics. Ibn Ezra's commentary on the Song of Songs and Isaac Arama's commentary *Akedat Yitzhak* on the Pentateuch belong to the same genre of exposition as that of Philo. Maimonides and Albo read many philosophical ideas into the Bible, thereby transforming the character of whole sections of it.

The version of the Bible which was the product of the method of interpretation known as *Remez* reads like a treatise on subjects like the following: the good and evil inclination, the relation of philosophy to revelation, of human reason to human passion, of the spirit to the body, and of the intellect to the feelings. That version includes, also, the discussion of such ethical themes as prudence, courage, humility, and temperance. Under its influence biblical characters, places, and events become embodiments of philosophic problems which are dealt with by Plato and Aristotle. One can understand why this interpretation of the Bible should have antagonized the strict traditionalists. They saw in it a danger to the authoritative or rabbinic rendering. Abba Mari Don Astruc, the famous leader, in the beginning of the fourteenth century, of the opposition to the rationalism of the Maimonists, in his *Minhat Kenaot*, a letter addressed to the talmudic scholars of France and Spain, accused the rationalists of reducing the entire section of the Torah from Genesis to Exodus to nothing but allegory.

Finally, we have the Bible of the mystics, which is the product of the method of interpretation known as *Sod*. What the Torah is, according to Jewish mysticism, is summed up in a well-known passage in the *Zohar* which reads as follows: "Woe to the man who says that the Torah intends to relate to ordinary stories and everyday affairs. If that were the case, it would be possible even nowadays to compose a Torah dealing with everyday affairs, a Torah that could be of greater excellence than the one we have. Even the worldly princes would then seem to possess books of greater worth than the Torah. We could use those books as a model and compose a worldly Torah. The truth is that all the matters dealt with in the Torah are of a supernal character and contain sublime mysteries."

To the Jewish mystics, the Torah was in all literalness the very instrument wherewith God had created the universe. Hence the author of the *Zohar* reasons that, since the angels in descending to the earth put on earthly garments, as otherwise they could neither stay in the world nor could the world endure them, "the Torah which created all the worlds and which sustains them" must certainly have had to put on earthly garments. "The stories of the Torah are only her outer garments, and whoever looks upon that garment as being the Torah itself, woe to that man—such a man will have no portion in the next world . . . . Stupid people see only the garment, the mere narratives. Those who are wise envisage the body. But the really wise can penetrate to the soul, the root principle of all, namely the real Torah."

We can perhaps best appreciate the perspective on life which the Bible opened up to the Jewish mystics if we recall that they were, with only few exceptions, not given merely to passive contemplation. They were, inherently, men of action. They believed that a knowledge of the various combinations and permutations of the words of sacred Scriptures would enable them to gain power over the forces of life. Moreover, as *Jewish* mystics, their main purpose in striving to attain such power was to be able to redeem Israel from exile. To be worthy of wielding such power, they assumed that they had to discipline themselves in all of the *mitzvot*, both ethical and ritualistic. With purposes such as these to be achieved through the study of sacred writings, the thought-world which those writings opened up could not but be radically different from the thought-world which emerged from any of the other three methods of interpretation described above.

The diversity among the thought-worlds of the four different versions of the Bible is only half the story. The other half of the story is that there was something to these four versions of the Bible which made them one, besides the mere fact that the same text and language underlay them all. After all, these versions of the Bible cannot but be the product of human nature, as it functioned in the Jewish people. Each version represents the moral and spiritual values which the Jewish people evolved, in response to the particular environment in which it found itself.

The Jewish people, however, had lived for a long time in a world which is not reflected in any one of these four versions. Before any of them arose, the Jewish people had already been in existence for nearly a thousand years. That period may be roughly placed between 1600 and 600 B.C.E. It was then that the Jews produced the greater part of the writings contained in the Bible. Those writings had not yet been canonized. At that time those writings were only a kind of proto-Bible. That is the Bible which is being reconstituted by means of modern biblical scholarship. Reflecting as it does the first thousand years of Israel's career, this proto-Bible must be included at some point in the educational curriculum. Unfortunately, in a good many instances, biblical scholarship, especially as it was fostered in Germany,* was motivated by anti-Jewish prejudice and the desire to defame the Jewish people. That fact justifies the late Solomon Schechter's quip that Higher Criticism was a form of Higher Anti-Semitism. It would be a fatal mistake, however, to allow this quip to obscure the new vistas that biblical scholarship has opened up in our understanding of the first period of Israel's history.

The proto-Bible reflects the period of spiritual gestation, when the tendencies, attitudes, and habits which later became part of the Jewish consciousness were taking shape. During that period the empires of the Nile and Euphrates were at the zenith of their power, and Israel found itself, together with numerous other peoples, competing for a place on the bridge between those empires. Tribal and natural deities, surrounded by hosts of all manner of spirits and angels and demons, then jostled one another in the imaginations of men. From a study of the proto-Bible, we begin to realize how Israel finally emerged from that medley of peoples and religions as a highly self-conscious nation, with a clear perspective and well-knit life pattern that took into account the whole of the then-known world. In a sense, that outcome was a far greater miracle than any recorded in the Bible itself.

The Future of the American Jew, pp. 452–56.

8. The Study of Torah**

What the study of Torah meant to the Jew may be inferred from the following saying of Rabbi Berekiah and Rabbi Hagiga of Kephar T'humin: "The whole world is not equal in value to one word of the Torah. All the *mitzvot* are not equal to one word of the Torah." The verse in Proverbs (8:11) "Wisdom is better than jewels" is interpreted as implying that neither *mitzvot* nor good deeds can compare in value with the study of Torah. The Torah was to the Jew not a mere series of narratives and ordinances which had come down from the past, nor was its divine authorship assumed in the ancient conventional manner of ascribing to the god of the nation whatever code was authoritative. In the words of the rabbis, "The Torah was not to them like an ancient edict with which no one reckons, but like a recent one which everyone is eager to read."

Despite the frequent reiteration of the contrast between the God of

*In the nineteenth century.—eds.
**The traditional sources upon which this and the following two sections are based are to be found in the footnotes of the original texts.—eds.

Israel, the sole creator and maintainer of the universe, and the false gods of the other nations, it never lost its edge. Fully conscious as the Jew was of belonging to the only people that worshipped the true God, he could not but thrill to the possibility of communing with Him in the course of learning what God would have him do. When a man reads a letter from his beloved, he does not only read what it says, but, pondering over every word, imagines her communing with him. Likewise when the ancient rabbis studied Torah, they relived the experience of divine revelation.

The Greater Judaism in the Making, p. 100.

9. The Observance of *Mitzvot*

With all the emphasis that was placed on the study of Torah, and with the opportunity that it afforded the keener minds to display their mental power in hair-splitting arguments, the danger that it might become an end in itself was all too imminent. Hence the numerous warnings sounded against forgetting that "not learning but doing is the chief thing." Rabbi Hanina ben Dosa said, "He whose works exceed his learning, his wisdom will endure, but he whose learning exceeds his works, his learning will not endure." That learning and works are to each other respectively as branches and roots is carried out in a lengthy analogy by Rabbi Elazar ben Azaria.

A most striking paradox in the rabbinic literature is the one which was formulated at the end of the protracted discussions on the part of Rabbi Tarfon, Rabbi Yose, and Rabbi Akiba as to which was more important, study or works. They finally came to the conclusion that study was more important, because it led to works. The rabbis state distinctly that the reward for study and the punishment for neglecting it are greater than the reward for performing works of piety and punishment for neglecting them. The consensus, however, is that study is a means to works. Even Rabbi Meir, who is the greatest advocate of study, advises, "Let thy works exceed thy learning."

Rabbi Simeon ben Halafta said, "Whoever studies and does not practice is liable to suffer greater punishment than he who has not studied at all." This he illustrated by a parable. A king who had an orchard brought to it two caretakers. One was in the habit of planting trees and hewing them down, and the other neither planted nor hewed. Certainly the former is more deserving of punishment. Elsewhere we are told: "He who only studies Torah but does not engage in pious works is as though he had no God."

Obedience to God's will is regarded as leading to individual and collective bliss, both in this world and in the next, but that is neither the purpose for which the *mitzvot* are intended primarily nor the main reason why they should be obeyed. That is the idea underlying the oft-quoted teaching of Antigonos of Soko, "Be ye like servants who minister to their master without thought of reward." Those who observe the *mitzvot* for the sake of material advantage or personal aggrandizement are denounced. Said Rabbi, "A man who observes the *mitzvot* for an ulterior purpose had better not been born."

We are so accustomed to think of human welfare as the purpose of ethical and spiritual conduct that we find it difficult to enter sympathetically into the state of mind of the ancients. To them human welfare, though undoubtedly important as a criterion of value, never figured consciously as such, when the question of God's will was involved. The welfare of others was a motive for doing good to them, not because of any altruistic considerations, but because putting at the service of others whatever one possesses, be it wealth, learning, or energy, was itself deemed a great blessing. To do good was a blessing, because it expressed compliance with the will of God. In Scripture, conformity to God's will is assumed to be a sufficient sanction for all the laws, statutes, and ordinances associated with His name.

Nevertheless, neither in the Pentateuch nor in the Prophetic writings do we note any tendency to minimize expectation of reward or fear of punishment. Material advantages are frankly promised as a consequence of doing God's will. There is not slightest intimation in Scripture that obeying God for the sake of reward is unworthy of man's highest loyalty to Him. On the other hand, though the Sages of the Talmud stress no less emphatically the principle of reward and punishment, they frequently deprecate making the expectation of reward or fear of punishment the main motive of conduct.

We are told that the resistance which we often experience when we try to live in accordance with the precepts of the Torah is to be welcomed, because it affords us the opportunity to subordinate our own will to the will of God. Hence the feeling of being weighed down by the will of God as by a yoke is not deplored; it is treated as the normal state of mind in man's relation to God. If the performance of the *mitzvot* were easy, or if they did not run counter to man's will—in other words, if they were not felt to be a yoke—how would one know that they really represented the will of God? Being sure that the *mitzvot* express God's will and obeying them because of that fact are of the very essence of rabbinic Judaism. Not that God is arbitrary in His precepts, or that there is no intrinsic purpose to them. Even a law like that of the red heifer has a reason. God simply did not want that reason to be generally known; He revealed it only to Moses.

Rabbi Nahman ben Isaac attached such importance to obeying the will of God as the all-controlling motive of the practice of the *mitzvot* that he put the matter paradoxically by saying: "A transgression performed with the intention of serving God is better than a *mitzvah* performed with no such intention." This urge to perform the will of God has given rise in rabbinic literature to the metaphor "to afford delight to the Holy One, blessed be He." The true saint is he who so loves God that his one purpose in life is "to afford God delight." Every Jew felt it incumbent upon him to give heed to the teaching of Judah ben Temma, who said: "Be bold as a leopard, swift as an eagle, fleet as a gazelle, and strong as a lion to do the will of thy Father in heaven."

The conception of the *mitzvot* as affording man the opportunity of deliberately obeying the will of God enables us to understand the attitude of the rabbis toward what we ordinarily call the ethical laws. The rabbis evaluated human conduct differently from the way we do. They regarded the opportunity to do the will of God as the highest privilege granted to man, to which all else was secondary. They were religionists first and foremost, and nationalists and moralists only secondarily. They were in all literalness God-intoxicated. Hence, we must not at all be surprised that they considered the *mitzvot* "between God and man" as ends in themselves, and the *mitzvot* "between man and his neighbor" as indispensable means to those ends.

Ahad Ha'am was mistaken in assigning to the Jewish people an inherent tendency to treat ethics as occupying a position of primacy in Jewish religion. The entire rabbinic and philosophical tradition is opposed to that assumption. The primacy of ethics in man's relation to God is compatible only with man-centered religion, the kind of religion that was unthinkable in premodern times. The shift in Jewish religion of the center of gravity from ritual observances to ethics is at the very heart of the metamorphosis which Judaism is undergoing.

There can be no question that the *mitzvot* "*par excellence*," or those which, according to Rabbi Simeon ben Yohai, may be termed "messengers of the Holy One, blessed be He," are the commandments pertaining not to human relations but to ritual observances. When the Sages interpret the verse "Thou art beautiful, my beloved" (Song of Songs 4:1) as referring to the *mitzvot* insofar as they confer beauty on Israel, the *mitzvot* which are singled out are the following: the heave-offerings to the priest, the tithes, the gleanings, the corners of the field for the poor, the fringes on the corners of the garments, the phylacteries, circumcision, *mezuzah, sukkah, lulav, ethrog,* prayer, the reading of the *sh'ma*. In addition to these, also the following are enumerated elsewhere: the prohibition against an ox and ass plowing together and the one against sowing mixed seeds, the commandment to offer certain portions of the animals to the priest, the prohibition against shaving the hair of the head and of the beard, the commandment to build a parapet to the roof. All those *mitzvot* God bestowed upon Israel in order to afford them the opportunity to earn their share in the world to come.

Moral actions assume a new significance insofar as they confer glory upon the name of God for having commanded them. They are regarded as means of sanctifying God's name—*kiddush ha-shem*—because they lead even the ignorant and the non-Jew to acknowledge the greatness and goodness of the God of Israel. On the other hand, immoral conduct that leads to the profanation of God's name—*hillul ha-shem*—subjects one who is guilty of it to far greater punishment than if he were judged merely on the basis of the harm he does to his fellow man.

Rabbinic literature abounds in moral teachings which inculcate honesty, humility, peace, forgiveness, loving-kindness, and similar traits. The Sages declare the sin of pride as tantamount to displacing, as it were, God from the world; the penalty is that the sinner will have no share in the resurrection. The reason probably is that one who is proud plays the god and thus sets himself up as the rival of God. Breaking a promise is equivalent to the sin of idol worship. Sycophancy and flattery consign one to *Gehinnom*. *Derek eretz*, in the twofold sense of morals and manners, is declared to have preceded the Torah by two thousand years. An entire treatise by that name is devoted to a detailed enumeration of moral laws. Yet it cannot be said that Rabbinism considers the most scrupulous fulfillment of these moral laws the acme of human attainment: though, to be sure, they are an indispensable prerequisite to communion with God, which can be achieved only through the study of Torah and the observance of the ritual *mitzvot*. In this regard the rabbis merely reflect the Psalmist's idea that to be "clean of hands and pure of heart" makes one worthy of ascending the mount of the Lord (Ps. 15:1–2, 24:3–4).

As a rule, we are more likely to appreciate a good which we alone happen to possess than one which we share in common with others. The moral laws of the Torah were known to be common to civilized mankind, and their possession did not distinguish the Jews from other peoples. Only in rare instances, as with the feeling of shame or pity, is there a suggestion of a specifically Jewish trait. The ritual laws, on the other hand, were confined to Israel. Believing as the Sages did that Israel was God's chosen people, they could not but see in the ritual *mitzvot* an irrefutable proof of that belief. "Beloved are the Israelites, whom the Holy One, blessed be He, has surrounded with *mitzvot* by bidding them to place phylacteries on their heads and arms, a *mezuzah* on their doorposts, fringes on the four corners of their garments. . . . The matter may be compared to a king who said to his wife, 'Adorn yourself in all thy jewels in order that you may please me.' So did God say to Israel, 'Be distinguished by means of the *mitzvot* in order that ye may please Me.' "

The Greater Judaism in the Making, pp. 106–11.

10. The World to Come

Few rabbinic sayings have so impressed themselves on the Jewish consciousness as the well-known saying of Rabbi Jacob ben Korshai which describes this world as a vestibule before the world to come, and which urges that we should spend our days on earth with a view to meriting a share in that world. When Rabbi Eliezer took sick and his disciples came to visit him, they said to him: "O our master, teach us the ways of life, so that we may attain through them the life of the world to come."

The belief in the world to come is, in rabbinic Judaism, seldom, if ever, confused with the belief in the coming of the Messiah. That is because in the minds of the talmudic Sages, the two aspects of Judaism—the national and the individual—were accorded distinct, though equal, significance. Rabbi Eleazer of Modiin is quoted as saying: "If you will succeed in keeping the Sabbath, the Holy One, blessed be He, will give you six good portions: the Land of Israel, the world to come, the new world, the Kingdom of the House of David, the priesthood, and the Levitical offices." "The world to come" or *ha-olam ha-ba* is the one in which the individual is granted his due reward; "the new world" refers to the Messianic age, when the Jewish people is destined to experience redemption from exile.

The belief in the world to come was another one of the main issues on which the two ancient sects, the Sadducees and the Pharisees, were divided. To the Sadducees, the Torah was fundamentally an instrument of national life and not of individual salvation. They could, therefore, have but little sympathy with the Pharisaic interpretation of the Torah which regarded it as being also an instrument of individual salvation. This function of the Torah figures prominently in the Mishnaic treatise known as *Pirkey Avot*.

That treatise is not intended, as is generally assumed, to be merely a random collection of ethical teachings; it is a collection of statements by the greatest of the *Tannaim* on the primacy of the study of the Torah. Nothing can be more important than a share in the world to come; the best means to achieve it is through the study of Torah. That is the main motif of *Avot*. The custom of reciting a passage from the Mishnah Sanhedrin before reading on Sabbath afternoons a chapter of *Avot* emphasizes this motif. That passage states: "All who are of the people of Israel have a share in the world to come." The reason for granting them this special privilege is that they accepted the Torah, which is a means to the attainment of life eternal.

The spirit of Tannaitic sayings collected in *Avot* is one of exhortation to the individual to make the best use of the means at his command to achieve salvation. Hillel urges the learned man to love peace and strive for peace, and to love his fellow men. The most concrete way such a man can show his love for them is by bringing them nigh to the Torah, for "he who has acquired words of Torah has acquired for himself the life of the world to come." "A share in the the world to come" is the term used for the reward which awaits the individual after death. Thus when we read, "Rabbi Eleazer said: 'Be thou alert to study Torah . . . and know before whom thou laborest and who is the master of thy work to give thee the wages of thy toil,' " "wages" refers to salvation in the world to come for the individual who has labored in the study of Torah.

How great their share is depends upon how much of the study of Torah and the practice of the *mitzvot* they engage in while they are still in this world. "If thou hast learned much Torah," says Rabbi Tarfon, "they give thee much wages, and faithful is the Master of thy work who will pay the wages of thy toil. And know that the giving of the reward to the righteous is in the time to come." Rabbi Akiba is no less emphatic as to the bliss which awaits those who have lived up to the duty of engaging in the study of Torah and the performance of *mitzvot*. "They have whereon to rely," he says, "and the judgment is a judgment of truth, and all is made ready for the banquet."

The analogy of the world to come to a banquet is a favorite one in rabbinic literature. It is the basis of the above-quoted statement by Rabbi Jacob: "This world is like a vestibule before the world to come: prepare thyself in the vestibule, that thou mayest enter into the banquet hall." The underlying assumption is that this world is a place where men should strive to do the will of God and that the world to come is for enjoying the reward of that striving. This distinction between the two worlds gave rise to the comparison of the world to come to the Sabbath. "The enjoyment of the Sabbath is but a minute fraction (a sixtieth) of the enjoyment in the world to come." On the principle that only he who has prepared enough for the Sabbath has enough to eat when the Sabbath arrives, we are told that he who has laid up deeds of piety in this world may expect the bliss they will yield in the world to come. Even in the statement of Abba Arika (Rav) which says that in the world to come there will be no eating nor drinking, the simile of the banquet recurs again. Thus we are told that "The righteous sit with their laurels on their heads and enjoy the splendor of the *Shekinah*." This refers to the custom in vogue among the ancients of having the guests wear laurels at banquets.

The Sages themselves were doubtful as to what would happen to the world and to man after the advent of the Messiah. Neither Samuel's statement concerning the Messianic age nor Rav's statement concerning the world to come helped to remove that doubt. Maimonides tried to square the views of both Rav and Samuel with his own philosophic assumptions. He assumed that the present world order was not likely to be changed. For that reason he welcomed Samuel's statement that there was to be no distinction between the present world order and the one which would obtain during the Messianic era, the only difference being that during the Messianic era the Jews would be freed from foreign rule.

Maimonides assumed that no physical body could possibly be immortal, since, as a compound, it must in time disintegrate. That led Maimonides to conclude that those who would be resurrected would die again; only their souls were immortal. There is, of course, an evident contradiction in his reasoning. By the same token that bodies could be resurrected, they could be kept alive eternally. We must remember, however, that Maimonides sought to reconcile tradition with reason. By this compromise he managed to pay deference to both reason and tradition.

According to the view predominant in rabbinic Judaism, the "Messianic age" is that era of *this* world which will begin with the advent of the Messiah. That advent marks an end to "this world" or the present age. On the other hand, the term "world to come," or as some render it, "the age to come," denotes the eternal life of those who have been resurrected. Thus a familiar prayer reads: "There is no one to be compared to Thee, O Lord, in this world, neither is there any beside Thee, O our King, in the world to come. There is none but Thee, O our Redeemer, for the days of the Messiah; neither is there any like unto Thee, O our Savior, for the resurrection of the dead." In that prayer, each appellation for God denotes a different manifestation of His divinity.

Those who will have died before the advent of the Messiah, and had lived a fully worthy life, will be resurrected when his advent takes place. They are destined to enter forthwith *ha-olam ha-ba* (the world to come). All others, however, on being resurrected, will be judged on the Day of Judgment. Those found incorrigible will be utterly destroyed. The rest, known as "the one-third," mentioned in Zechariah (13:8), will pass through the ordeal of purgation by fire, and thereafter live forever. This is, in simplified form, the tradition concerning the resurrection. That tradition did not attain as definitive a form as have most of the theological concepts in rabbinic lore.

Ha-olam ha-ba, the world to come, is the present world re-created. This is unmistakably evident from the following saying: "The division in the world to come will not be like the division in this world. . . . In the world to come everyone will own land that is situated on mountainous ground as well as on a plain and in a valley. The imperfections of this world, which are the consequence of Adam's sin, will be eliminated. In that re-created world, Eretz Yisrael will abound in those extraordinary blessings which were foretold by the Prophets Isaiah and Ezekiel."

The *Amora* Rav's conception of the world to come is radically different and does not seem to have been shared by the other Sages. "In the world to come," he said, "there will be neither eating nor drinking, no begetting of children, no business transactions, no envy, no hatred, and no rivalry; but the righteous will sit with laurels on their heads and enjoy the brightness of *Shekinah*." The general opinion, however, seems to have been that even in the world to come the human being will retain his physical nature with its needs, though he will be free from the domination of the evil *Yetzer* (the inclination to evil). It was assumed that mankind would then achieve the perfection which Adam originally possessed before he committed the sin that corrupted the human race.

Thus, to have a share in the world to come meant being eligible for the life of eternal bliss. That is the ultimate destiny of the individual human being, as a person in his own right. On the other hand, the conception of "the Messianic age" refers to the future of the nation. Traditional Judaism in all its teachings and precepts aims simultaneously at the twofold goal of national redemption and individual salvation. Corresponding to those two goals are the two aspects of its life pattern, the national and the individual, according to which the Jew is expected to order his own life.

At the basis of the other-worldly conception of salvation, or human destiny, is the belief that this world is intrinsically marred by sin and suffering. It therefore is altogether unfit to be the scene of man's self-fulfillment. In this vale of tears, life at best is merely like a fleeting shadow. The words "which I command thee this day to do them" (Deut 7:11) are interpreted by Rabbi Joshua ben Levi as follows: This day refers to man's life in this world, as the time for obeying God's commandments. As for the reward, that will come on "the morrow," when man enters the next world. That world is not the spiritual heaven which, according to the medieval philosophers and theologians, is the abode of divinity, the ministering angels, and the souls of the righteous. It is none other than the world we live in, re-created and restored to the condition it was in when it first came from the hand of God, and when "He saw everything that He had made, and behold it was very good." In that re-created world, "The light of the moon will be as the light of the sun, and the light of the sun will be sevenfold, as the light of seven days."

To effect the transition from this world to the next, man has to pass through the ordeal of death. Nothing perhaps so characterizes the ancient mind as its bizarre notion of death. It seemed unable to regard death as a normal part of the world order. In rabbinic writings, for example, it was assumed that man was not meant to die, but to live forever. "The whole effort of philosophical thought," writes Ernst Cassirer, "is to give clear and irrefutable proof of the immortality of the human soul. In mythical thought the case is quite different. Here the burden of proof lies on the other side. If anything is in need of proof, it is not the fact of immortality, but the fact of death."

According to Rabbi Judah bar Ilai, it was Adam who brought death on mankind. Elsewhere he mentions the fact that Elijah did not suffer death. This should prove that if Adam had not sinned, he would not have died. The *Amora* Rav Ami states that every death is caused by sin, and that sickness is a punishment for transgression. This statement gives rise to a discussion in which various Tannaitic passages are introduced to prove that it was Adam's sin that had brought death on mankind. There is no dissent from this assumption. We are told that, when the Israelites stood at Mount Sinai, God wanted to exempt them from death, but was prevented by His irrevocable decree which had imposed death on Adam and his descendants.

According to Rabbi Yose, exemption from death was the condition on which Israel was willing to accept the Torah. Rabbi Hama bar Hanina said, "Adam would not have experienced the taste of death, if not for the fact that some of his descendants were bound to consider themselves gods." Rabbi Jonathan said to him, "If that were true, only the wicked should suffer death and not the righteous." To which Rabbi Hama replied: "That would lead the wicked to practice insincere repentance and to perform *mitzvot* for ulterior motives." According to Rabbi Jonathan, "The reason the wicked die is that they might cease provoking God. The reason the righteous die is that they might rest from their continual struggle with the evil *Yetzer*." According to Rabbi Simeon ben Lakish, "The wicked die because of their sins. The righteous, on the other hand, accept death willingly so as not to appear to be motivated in their righteousness by the fear of death; for that they will be rewarded doubly in the world to come."

Not a single one of the foregoing *Amoraim* seemed to have conceived death as a normal phenomenon. Those who take that view of death cannot possibly regard the troubles of human life as purely accidental, or the destructive forces of nature as part of the original creation. They invariably look to a future in which the present condition of the world will be replaced by one in which there will be no suffering or death.

The Jews, moreover, developed an elaborate eschatology with regard to the soul. It dealt with the state of the soul during the interim between death in this world and life in the world to come. It also included accounts of *Gan Eden*, *Gehinnom*, and the Day of Judgment. In rabbinic times the Garden of Eden, or Paradise, was conceived as the region on earth where God had placed Adam. Though the rest of the earth had deteriorated since the days of the Flood, the Garden of Eden was believed to have remained in its original state of perfection somewhere on earth. The waves of the great Flood stopped at its gates. In *Gan Eden* the souls of the dead are said to abide after having undergone their purgation in *Gehinnom*, which was supposed to be situated somewhere beneath the earth's surface. The Sages assumed that one of the three entrances to it was near the Hill of Zion, in the historical Valley of Hinnom. Whatever sins man commits during his life have to be expiated during the interim existence in *Gehinnom*.

In *Shevet Mussar*, an ethical treatise which appeared in 1712, the author gives the following detailed description of *Gehinnom*: "The lower [i.e., earthly] *Gehinnom* is a vast space extending over myriads of acres. The more the wicked increase in numbers, the larger it grows. It is divided into many regions where suffering is meted out in varying degrees of severity, so that every sinner may have meted out to him the punishment he deserves. The fire which exists there is sixty times as hot as the fire in this world. There are coals as large as entire mountains. In the midst of *Gehinnom* there are rivers of pitch and sulphur, which well up from the deeps. Moreover, all kinds of evil demons and devils are begotten by the evil deeds of the wicked. Our Sages say: 'Every transgression one commits becomes an accusing angel.' These accusing angels are added to the evil spirits which have been in *Gehinnom* since its creation. All of them inflict different kinds of wounds on the body of the wicked. Some hang and choke the wicked, others gouge out their eyes. The torture depends upon the gravity of the sins committed."

The fact that, in talmudic Judaism, other-worldliness does not take the form of asceticism, or that it does not imply that the present world is hopelessly beset by sin, has led many modern Jewish and non-Jewish theologians to maintain that Judaism, in contrast to Christianity, is mainly concerned with this world. That contrast is entirely unwarranted. A small treatise on conduct which dates probably from the Geonic period prescribes the way of life which a scholar should pursue. Among other things it says: "A scholar should act on the thought: 'I take no pleasure in the good things of this world, since life here below is not my portion.' "

Christianity has added to the other-worldliness which it emphasizes in common with traditional Judaism, the disparagement of the bodily functions. Indeed, traditional Judaism itself was not entirely averse to asceticism. On the contrary, there were times in Jewish life when asceticism was the vogue. Rabbi Simeon ben Yohai and his son lived for twelve years in a cave to avoid the Roman terror. They spent those years in mystic contemplation. When they finally emerged, they saw with astonishment and dismay a farmer tilling the soil. " 'The people neglect eternal life,' cried the rabbi, 'and busy themselves with temporal life.' So great was his anger that wherever he turned his gaze, the crops withered. But a voice from heaven protested: 'Have you come to destroy My world? Go back to your cave!' " This talmudic passage reflects an ambivalent attitude toward asceticism.

The Greater Judaism in the Making, pp. 75–82.

11. Continuity with Our Past

We are now in a position to understand what actual historical fact is conveyed in the statement that the Jewish religion maintained its continuity for three thousand years. When we speak of the continuity of a religion, we do not mean that its teachings and prescribed modes of conduct have remained unchanged. This is the continuity of a stone, but not of a living organism. The living organism possesses a dynamic identity because of the life principle that animates its constantly changing elements. To comprehend the continuity of a religion, it is necessary to think of the religion not as an abstract entity existing by itself, but as a function of a living people and as an aspect of the civilization of that people. The common denominator in the different stages of the Jewish civilization is not to be sought in the tenets and practices, but in the continuous life of the Jewish people. Without the continuity of social life, without the countless generations of men, women, and children who lived and cultivated their social and spiritual heritage and transmitted it to the generations following, the religion of the Jews of the Second Commonwealth could not have been continuous with the religion of the Israelites who entered Palestine.

But while the transmission of the spiritual heritage from generation to generation is sufficient to account for its *actual* continuity, it is necessary to point to some factor which operates to prevent the changed outlook and mode of life from destroying the *feeling* of continuity. That factor has been the tendency to reinterpret religious values which have come down from the past so that they can serve as a vehicle for the expression of teachings and ideals which have relevance to contemporaneous ideas and needs. The articulate or symbolic form of those values remains the same; it is the significance that is new. Reinterpretation of religious values is spiritual metabolism. It is a form of that law of growth which, by an uninterrupted transfer of life from the old to the new, renders vital change a very means to vital sameness and continuity.

We have seen how the Prophets prepared the way for the transformation of the Jewish religion from a henotheistic religion into a theocratic one, and how eschatological speculation transformed it from a theocratic into an other-worldly religion. Likewise, during the other-worldly stage of the Jewish religion there developed a theology which prepared the way for the next and fourth stage of the Jewish religion. The principal function of Jewish theology was to fit the biblical and rabbinic conception of God into the framework of the philosophic concepts which had come to be regarded as setting forth the truth about reality. Although medieval Jewish theology believed it was merely reaffirming the Jew's allegiance to traditional beliefs, it indirectly paid sufficient homage to reason to prepare the way for a type of religion in which reason—in a sense sufficiently large to include our deeper insights and intuitions—is the only guide and authority.

Judaism as a Civilization,
pp. 381–82.

VI

Interpreting Medieval and Modern Judaism

1. The Philosophers Reconstruct Rabbinic Judaism

To what extent rabbinic Judaism underwent metamorphosis when synthesized with Greek philosophy may be seen from the following teachings of medieval Jewish theology:

1. According to rabbinic Judaism, salvation (or the fulfillment of human life) can be achieved only through the study of Torah and the practice of the *mitzvot*. According to medieval Jewish theology, it can be achieved only through contemplation of the truth concerning the nature of reality or of the divine government of the world; this is what the Jewish theologians understood by study of Torah in its esoteric sense. They accepted Aristotle's view of the moral virtues as being, in the words of Matthew Arnold, only "the porch and access to the intellectual, and with these last is blessedness." At the hands of the Jewish theologians, also the conception of prophetism underwent a radical change. In rabbinic writings, the Prophet is conceived merely as the "messenger of God," or *malak*, whose intellectual powers had nothing to do with his being selected by God to exhort and instruct. In philosophic writings, however, the Prophet is viewed as a great thinker whose intellectual powers were so extraordinary as to render him qualified for his prophetic mission.

2. Rabbinic Judaism is not troubled by the anthropomorphic conception of God. But medieval Jewish theology's principal task is the vigorous deprecation of anthropomorphism. It explains away the anthropomorphisms in the Bible as purely metaphorical, on the rabbinic principle of "the Torah speaks in human idiom." That principle was intended originally to apply only to the legalistic rendering of the Torah text. As such, its purpose was to offset the tendency to derive legal conclusions from what appeared to some *Tannaim* to be verbal redundancies; it had nothing to do with questions of theology.

3. Rabbinic Judaism was not in the least disturbed by the problem which miracles presented from a philosophic point of view. Now, philosophically, miracles imply changes in God's will in accordance with

circumstances occasioned by man. That conception of miracles is incompatible with the assumption that God's will is immutable. Those statements in rabbinic writings which have a bearing on the miracles of the Bible are not motivated, as is wrongly assumed, by the foregoing consideration. To the rabbis, the miracles are part of their Israel-centered view of the world, and their comments on miracles have to be understood in that light. For the theologians, however, the philosophic considerations are primary. Maimonides,* therefore, treats the miracles as having been built into the structure of the world when God created it. Gersonides,** who tries to steer a middle course between tradition and reason, arrives at a highly sophisticated explanation of miracles which seems to satisfy the demands of neither.

4. Rabbinic Judaism sees no contradiction between the conception of God's infinite power and the many attributes ascribed to Him such as those in Exodus 34:6–7, which imply that He is influenced by factors outside Himself. On the other hand, Jewish theology, finding it necessary to describe God in negative terms, gives a negative meaning to the attributes ascribed to God in the foregoing verses in Exodus, since their affirmative meanings imply limitations on God's being and power.

5. Rabbinic Judaism is unaware of any contradiction between God's foreknowledge and man's free will. The usual interpretation given to Rabbi Akiba's statement in *Avot* 3:19 as implying an awareness of such contradiction is incorrect. The phrase *hakol tzafui* in that statement does not mean "everything is foreseen," but "everything is beheld." Hence what Rabbi Akiba says is not "Everything is foreseen, yet freedom of choice is given," but "Everything is beheld *and* freedom of choice is given." What he wishes to emphasize is not God's foreknowledge but God's *knowledge* of whatever man does or thinks. Jewish theology, on the other hand, never wearied of seeking a solution for the apparent contradiction between God's foreknowledge and man's freedom to choose between obeying and disobeying the will of God.

6. Rabbinic Judaism sees no need for attaching any meaning other than a literal one to biblical stories in which human traits are ascribed to God. Jewish theology either interprets those stories allegorically, or it considers them as visions or dreams. It does not regard them as accounts of objective events. This applies especially to stories like those of Creation, the Garden of Eden, the Tower of Babel, the three divine visitors to Abraham, and Jacob's struggle with the angel. In the case of the theophanies recorded in the Bible, medieval Jewish theology resorts to the novel concept of *kavod nivra,* a kind of visible being created for the occasion, or an existing light too dazzling for human eye to behold,

*Rabbi Moses ben Maimon, popularly known as RAMBAM (1135–1204), author of *The Guide of the Perplexed*.—eds.
**Rabbi Levi ben Gershom or RALBAG (1288–1344), author of *The Wars of the Lord*.—eds.

except after it has passed. The basis for this novel view is the biblical term "the glory of the Lord" and the rabbinic term "*Shekinah.*"

7. Rabbinic Judaism recognized only one kind of authoritative law, namely, the supernaturally revealed law contained in the Torah. It regarded that law as intended to help the Jew attain his well-being in this world and bliss in the hereafter. Jewish theology, on the other hand, as represented by Joseph Albo in his *Ikkarim,* which is a kind of abbreviated Jewish *Summa Theologica,* accepts the classification formulated by Thomas Aquinas of three kinds of law—namely, natural law (the medieval equivalent for our term "moral"), positive law (formulated in some human code), and divine, or supernaturally revealed, law. According to this classification, the Torah as supernaturally revealed law is contrasted with moral and humanly formulated law. This classification has given rise to the modern distinction between religious and secular, a distinction which has only helped to confuse thinking and darken counsel.

8. Rabbinic Judaism deprecates the interpretation of the *mitzvot* as having a purpose other than that of affording the opportunity to serve God. It insists on their being observed as divine decrees, or as means of teaching man to obey God's will without any ulterior purpose. Jewish theology, on the other hand, takes it for granted that ritual practices have the additional purpose of improving man's character. Ritual practices which seem devoid of such purpose are regarded as inferior in sanctity or importance.

Rabbinic Judaism has a special category for duties pertaining to interpersonal relations. It assumes, however, that the Torah lays down in each case what is right and what is wrong. Jewish theology introduces an additional ethical norm which emanates from reason. That norm is usually the one suggested by Aristotle's "Golden Mean." According to Maimonides, who makes a point of stressing the "Golden Mean," it is identical with whatever conduct the Torah prescribes. He considers it the principle underlying the Mishnaic treatise of *Avot.*

9. Rabbinic Judaism sees no difficulty in conceiving God as exercising individual providence over the life of every human being. Jewish theology regards such providence as being exercised in accordance with the intellectual development of the individual. If the individual has failed to develop his intellect, divine providence knows him only as a member of the general species "man." To be an object of God's special care, a human being must develop his intellectual powers.

10. Rabbinic Judaism accepts the principle of reward and punishment. Jewish theology finds it necessary to retain the belief in divine retribution, but, in doing so, it draws a sharp distinction between the body and the soul, insofar as they are objects of reward or punishment. The soul is conceived in philosophical terms suggested by Aristotle. According to him, man possesses three souls—the vegetative, the ani-

mal, and the human. Of these, the human soul, which is synonymous with the intellect, is the only one that survives the body. But its survival consists in being united with what is termed the Active Intellect of the world, third in the order of spiritual beings, of which the first two are God and the Separate Intelligences. Maimonides; Hillel ben Samuel (1220–95) of Verona, Italy, in his *Tagmule ha-Nefesh*, and Hasdai Crescas (1340–1410) of Barcelona, Spain, in his *Or Adonai*, explain allegorically the statements in rabbinic writings concerning *Gan Eden* and *Gehinnom*.

11. Rabbinic Judaism assumes that in the world to come the human body will be so perfected as not to be subject to the hunger, ailments, and deterioration which mark its present life. We seldom meet in rabbinic writings any attempt to describe in detail the process of bodily resurrection. Otherwise, that belief is accepted as a matter of course. The theologians, on the other hand, find resurrection a troublesome belief. Admitting that it has to be accepted on faith, they recognize that it calls for stretching that faith. Maimonides, however, is the only one who refuses to accept unqualifiedly the traditional idea concerning the resurrection. Though he accepts that part which affirms the reunion of the soul with the original body, or with a new body, at some time after death, he cannot accept the traditional assumption that this reunion is to be eternal. The body, being a compound substance, must ultimately disintegrate and fall away from the soul.

All of the foregoing deviations from rabbinic Judaism show that medieval Jewish theology evolved a radically different universe of thought from that of the rabbinic tradition. Medieval Jewish theology was based on an attempt to reconcile authoritative tradition with the conclusions of reasoned thought. The Jewish theologians themselves were unaware how radically different their own point of view was from that of tradition. This unawareness was due to their lack of historical perspective. One has only to read Maimonides' Introduction to his Commentary on the *Mishnah* and the one to his Code, for his account of the transmission of the Torah from Moses to his successors, to realize how uncritical of tradition Maimonides was, from the standpoint of objective history.

The Greater Judaism in the Making, pp. 116–20.

2. Jewish Mysticism and the Jews

What especially contributed to the hearty welcome which Judaism extended to mystic lore, in contrast with the antagonism toward philosophy, was the central place assigned in that lore to the people of Israel. The very opening chapter of the *Zohar* dwells at length upon the supernatural powers wherewith the people of Israel is endowed. The centrality of Israel did not remain merely an exalted abstraction. It was made the basis of the very practical hope which kept the Jewish people alive, the hope that the promised Messiah would appear and redeem it from exile and subjection. Jewish mysticism interpreted this redemption of the Jewish people as synonymous with the redemption of the *Shekinah*, thus giving to that redemption a cosmic dimension. It taught, furthermore, that the advent of the Messiah depended upon the conduct and inner life of every Jew. When a Jew kept his inner life free from sin and obeyed the *mitzvot* of the Torah, he brought about those changes in the very nature of the universe which speeded the redemption of his people.

According to the *Zohar*, the *mitzvot* are a part of the very process whereby the world came into being. To be sure, all rational philosophies likewise stress self-discipline as indispensable to the attainment of that clarity of mind which is necessary for the perception of the truth and for the unclouded judgment that can distinguish clearly between good and evil. On the other hand, the observance of ritual precepts lies outside the domain of rational philosophy. Indeed, they even have to be apologized for, and their value defended on grounds which often seem far-fetched. Quite often, these very grounds serve as a reason for their nonobservance, because once their purpose is recognized, it seems attainable without all the effort expended in their observance.

With mystic lore, however, the case is entirely different. In the first place, both ritual practice and self-discipline come to be indispensable means to the cultivation of that lore and to the attainment of the mystic state of mind or of soul. The sense of power, of being an efficient cause, is one of the most vital urges in human nature, and that urge is satisfied by the self-discipline which is a prerequisite to mystical speculation. Likewise, the ritual observances, upon which Jewish mysticism lays great emphasis, are not merely a means of securing reward in the hereafter. On the contrary, their reward is assumed to be near at hand, in the form of added power which the one who observes them acquires.

Jewish mysticism did not merely emphasize the importance of the ritual precepts; it assigned to them a theurgic function by ascribing to them meanings (*kavanot*) which were expected to endow one with the power to control, or manipulate at will, the forces of the cosmos. The Jewish mystics seemed to share with all other medieval mystics the ambition to compete with alchemists and other dabblers in primitive science in their attempt to wrest from nature those secrets which place it at the command of the human will. "That the doctrine of *kavanah* in prayer," writes G. G. Scholem, "was capable of being interpreted as a certain kind of magic seems clear to me; that it involves the problem of magical practices is beyond any doubt."

Together with the observance of the *mitzvot*, the study of Torah and engaging in prayer are repeatedly stressed in Jewish mysticism. Whatever contributed to man's salvation or *tikkun ha-nefesh* (setting the soul in order) was regarded as contributing also to *tikkun ha-olam* (setting the world in order). *Tikkun ha-olam* was tantamount to the restoration of the original harmony of the universe, of the lower with the upper worlds, and of Israel with God.

In contrast with the theurgic potency associated in Jewish mysticism with the traditional way of life, Jewish philosophy or theology saw the highest good in the realization of the Hellenic ideal of intellectual contemplation. The entire regimen of Torah, *mitzvot*, and prayer had for the Jewish philosopher only the instrumental value of providing the environmental conditions necessary to enable the intellectual elite to achieve their self-fulfillment or salvation. It is no wonder, therefore, that philosophy did not have the slightest chance of appealing to the heart or mind of the average Jew.

The reason mysticism always exercises an attraction for the human mind is that it seems to hold out the promise of coping either theoretically or practically with the problem of evil. Apart from mysticism, all that traditional religion has to offer is the regimen of moral and religious duties, accompanied by the promise that those who lay up sufficient merit in this world will be amply compensated in the hereafter for the evils suffered in this world. Jewish theologians tried to argue evil out of existence. They took the position that existence was intrinsically and necessarily good. Hence evil was merely nonexistence.

Jewish mysticism, on the other hand, not only recognized the reality of evil but was preoccupied with the problem of combatting it in *this* world. It viewed the evils that troubled man as rooted in the very constitution of the universe. To combat them, man had to measure himself against a foe of cosmic proportions. Having no conception of the possibility of resorting to the control of natural forces through scientific knowledge of their operation, the Jewish mystics concluded that for man to be equal to the combat, he had to be clothed with more than human power.

The Greater Judaism in the Making, pp. 126–28.

3. The Philosophy of Moses Mendelssohn*

The basic assumption which underlies Mendelssohn's position with regard to the mutual relations of state, religion, and Judaism is that the human being can reach a high point of spiritual development only when he is entirely free to choose his course of action. The state, which is inherently a coercive agency, fulfills a necessary function, but should have nothing to do with the spiritual life of its citizens. Religion, on the other hand, which is a means of rendering man spiritual, should not have to resort to coercion. Neither should Judaism, which is both a religion and a system of divine legislation, have to resort to coercive sanctions. Mendelssohn's failure to take into account the fact that religion functions as a social process, and not merely as a system of beliefs acquired through tradition or arrived at by the individual on the basis of his own experience, renders his notions of church-state relations unworkable. However, he is not always consistent. Though he would not have the state meddle with the religious beliefs of its citizens, he would nevertheless grant it the right to compel its citizens to believe in God, providence, and immortality, on the ground that those beliefs are indispensable to the moral life.

No less paradoxical than his rationalist view of the relations between church and state is his attempt to interpret Judaism from the standpoint of his philosophic conception of religion, and to vindicate his adherence to Jewish tradition. He maintains that Judaism cannot be regarded as a religion in the usual sense of the term. "I believe that Judaism," he writes, "knows nothing of a revealed religion, in the sense in which it is taken by Christians. The Israelites have a divine legislation: laws, judgments, statutes, rules of life, information of the will of God, and lessons on how to conduct themselves in order to attain both temporal and spiritual happiness. Those laws, commandments, etc., were revealed to them through Moses in a miraculous and supernatural manner, but no dogmas, no saving truths, no general self-evident assumptions. Those the Lord always reveals to us, in the same way as to the rest of mankind, by nature and by events, but never in words or written characters."

The assumption implied in the foregoing passage is that reason, rather than revelation, is the source of those truths which are essential to

*Moses Mendelssohn (1729–86): distinguished writer and philosopher; leading figure of the movement for Jewish enlightenment (Haskalah) in Germany; author of *Jerusalem or On Religious Power and Judaism* (1783).—eds.

salvation. Mendelssohn identifies salvation with bodiless immortality of the soul and its bliss in the hereafter. Such salvation is not the monopoly of any church or religious communion. It is accessible to all human beings who cultivate their reason adequately.

To Mendelssohn, religion meant only that which reason revealed concerning God. The notion of a supernaturally revealed religion, therefore, appeared to him to be self-contradictory. Judaism, on the other hand, was to him "revealed legislation," and not a religion. He may have derived that conception of Judaism from Joseph Albo's *Ikkarim*; to Albo, as well as to Thomas Aquinas in his *Summa Theologica*, conformity to revealed, or divine, legislation was a prerequisite to salvation, and only that religion's communion, or church, which was in possession of such legislation was qualified to be an instrument of salvation. To Mendelssohn, however, all legislation, whether divine or human, was intended to enable man merely to make the best use of what this world had to offer. On the other hand, salvation, or life eternal, was attainable only through the activity of reason. In that opinion one may discern the influence of Maimonides.

The Greater Judaism in the Making,
pp. 187–88.

4. Abraham Geiger* and Reform Judaism

The history of Judaism is, to Geiger, the story of the Jews as the people of revelation. As such, it is not only history, but also religion. The Jews were the only people among whom arose a long line of Prophets. To them was vouchsafed this unaccountable inner illumination and revelation. The Prophets had to labor hard and long before they could get their people to grasp their message. The way in which the people of Israel interpreted the God-idea was necessarily conditioned by their cultural development during the different periods of their history. The progress which the Jews achieved in their ethical and spiritual comprehension of God is their spiritual odyssey. The awareness of that odyssey, according to Geiger, must henceforth constitute the Jewish historical-religious orientation, on the basis of which the Jews should plan their future. This, he maintained, was the only conception of Jewish history which furnished the Reform movement with a philosophy and a program.

*Abraham Geiger (1810–74): scholar and rabbi; a leading figure in the Reform movement in Germany.—eds.

With this purpose in mind, he applied himself to the task of reconstructing the traditional orientation into one based on the assumption that God revealed Himself through the entire history of the Jewish people. In order, however, to interpret Judaism properly, he deemed it necessary to treat the biblical period as of cardinal importance, for it was then that prophecy flourished. It was, therefore, the period of divine revelation *par excellence*. The first and most difficult step in the evolution of Judaism was to wean away early Israel from the heathen forms of divine worship, which included sacred prostitution and human sacrifice. To Geiger, the struggle that went on during the early centuries in the career of the people of Israel between the Prophets and their contemporaries, the former urging spiritual worship and the latter clinging to the barbarous practices of their neighbors, was a manifestation of the divine spirit striving to take possession of the collective Jewish consciousness.

The Greater Judaism in the Making,
p. 236.

5. The Essence of Isaac Mayer Wise*

To Wise, Judaism was Mosaism, a universal religion that had been divinely revealed to Moses. In the course of years, it assimilated numerous extraneous beliefs and practices. All those acquisitions had helped the Jews to create for themselves the shell of nationhood within which they had sought safety against the physical and spiritual onslaughts of the hostile world around them. With the advent, however, of the new era of enlightenment and freedom, particularly in the United States, with its Constitution to guarantee the permanence of that era, Judaism had the opportunity of becoming at long last what it was originally intended to be. It could become "Mosaism in action." All that it needed was to rid itself of all those oriental elements in it that were narrowly national and intrinsically alien to its spirit. It should concentrate on the ethics and theology of the Ten Commandments which are the very basis of all civilization. "The religion of the future," he said, "will be Judaism in its pure and denationalized form."

His optimism was unbounded. He had not the least doubt "that his system will and must triumph all over this country, and is THE Judaism

*Isaac Mayer Wise (1819–1900): Reform rabbi in America; the central figure of early Reform Judaism.—eds.

of the coming generations . . . *that before this century will close,* the essence of Judaism will be THE religion of the great majority of all intelligent men of this country."*

All that optimism sprang from a faith in America and love for its institutions which only one who had come from the oppressive and suffocating atmosphere of reactionary Europe of the thirties and forties of the nineteenth century into the freedom-loving sections of the United States could possibly experience. America spelled for Isaac M. Wise the advent of the millennium and of the Kingdom of God on earth. "The dominion of popes and nobles," he wrote in 1852, "found its grave in the progress of civilization, being opposed to liberty; so the dominion of monarchs equally odious will also find its grave in the rushing wave of time." The main basis for his extravagant expectations for America was its Federal Constitution which separated church from state. That fact, combined with the unity of language, the rapid growth in the means of transportation and communications, the freedom of press, and the prevalence of common sense, he was sure, would make of the heterogeneous elements of this country, by the beginning of the twentieth century, "not only the most numerous and wealthiest nation, but also ONE nation."**

Two great obstacles stood in the way of the realization of his great hopes for America and Israel: Orthodox Christianity and Orthodox Judaism. . . .

Wise assailed Orthodox Judaism not for its creed but for its religious regimen. He deprecated the emphasis which Orthodox Jews placed on the meticulous observance of dietary laws. He maintained that the prescribed rules of ritual practices often served as a means of salving consciences. Wise, nevertheless, recognized the role those observances had played in unifying the Jews and giving them a sense of solidarity, which he valued highly. But even that could not atone, in his opinion, for the moral and spiritual complacency and the cultural stagnation which were generally the concomitants of strict adherence to ritual observance. He attributed the failure of Judaism to become a universal religion to its fixation on ritualism.

> *The Greater Judaism in the Making,*
> pp. 278–81.

---

*Dena Wilansky, *Sinai to Cincinnati* (New York, 1937), p. 33.
**Ibid.

6. Lessons of the Reform Movement

Judaism cannot possibly release the highest potencies in the Jew unless its teachings be made compatible with fearless freedom of thought, and unless its institutions and practices are revised with a view to their utmost ethical effectiveness.

We are aware that the Reform movement has tried to remold Judaism in accordance with those purposes. The leaders at least may be credited with a sincere desire to save Judaism from destruction. Have they succeeded? The criterion of a successful Jewish reformation would naturally be, Does it tend to make the Jew more Jewish? Who will venture to claim that result for the Reform movement? It should not be difficult by this time to diagnose the failure of the Reform movement. Two factors have contributed to that failure, one negative and the other positive. The negative factor was the omission to prepare the laity for changes in Judaism. To be capable of adapting any social or spiritual institution to new conditions of life and thought, we must evince new moral energy, an energy that expresses itself in a readiness for self-denial. Otherwise, convenience is liable to be given priority over principle. This has been the experience of the Reform movement. It has allowed considerations of political and social status to dictate what shall or shall not be Judaism. It should have reformed the Jew before it attempted to reform Judaism. It should have inspired him with a new self-respect. It should have disciplined him into a sterner regimen of Jewish duty, at the same time that it modified the content of Judaism.

The positive factor that has contributed to the failure of the Reform movement has been its complete misconception of the nature and function of Judaism. It claims that Judaism is a religious system of life, a system which God has enabled the Jew to evolve for the good of mankind. To communicate that system of life is the Jew's destiny and mission. That conception of Judaism involved changing the status of the Jews from that of a people yearning for its lost homeland into an international organization at home everywhere. The function of that organization is to preach the unity of God, and to further the brotherhood of man. Such a mission would pledge us to active propaganda against trinitarian Christianity and against all forms of privilege and militarism. If that were taken seriously, it would be more dangerous to be a Reform Jew than to be the most violent radical. Only a few daring spirits would venture to belong to an international organization of that kind. By setting up an impossible goal for the Jewish people, the Reform movement has reduced Judaism to an absurdity.

The failure of the Reform movement should not daunt us from trying again. Since most adjustments in human life proceed by the trial-and-error method, we should not be discouraged because the first trial happens to be an error. By avoiding the two fundamental mistakes of the movement, we might hit upon a workable and satisfactory solution of the problem of Judaism.

A New Approach to Jewish Life,
pp. 22–25.

7. Modern Orthodoxy

The outstanding trait of Orthodoxy is the clarity and forthrightness with which it affirms its theological doctrine. It bases Judaism upon implicit faith in the written and the oral Torah as the supernatural revelation of God's will. "The Torah," says Samson Raphael Hirsch (1808–88), "is an eternal code set up for all ages by the God of eternity." Orthodoxy is at no point vague or half-hearted in its affirmation that the Torah does not belong to the category of human writing. It insists that the Jew must believe that Moses was merely a passive amanuensis, recording at divine dictation each word of the Pentateuch, and simultaneously learning those interpretations and laws which constitute the authoritative rabbinic tradition. In that respect it reaffirms in unqualified fashion the teaching of Jewish tradition, both rabbinic and medieval.

"Let us not delude ourselves," says Hirsch. "The entire matter reduces itself to this question: Is the statement, 'And the Lord spoke to Moses,' which introduces all the laws of the Torah, true or not? Do we not believe that God, the Almighty and All-Holy God, spoke thus to Moses? Do we mean what we say when, in the circle of fellow-worshippers, we point to the written word of the Torah and declare that God gave us these teachings, and that these teachings are the teachings of truth, and that He thereby implanted in us everlasting life? Is all this a mere mouthing of high-sounding phrases? If not, then we must keep those commandments, fulfil them in their original and unabbreviated form. We must observe them under all circumstances and at all times. This word of God must be accepted by us as an eternal standard, transcending all human judgment, as the standard according to which we must fashion all our doings. Instead of complaining that it is no longer in conformity with the times, we should rather complain that the times are no longer in conformity with it."

In keeping with this literal understanding of the supernaturally revealed character of both the written and the oral Law, the spokesmen of Orthodoxy combated the new approach to the study of Judaism, which is known as *Die Wissenschaft des Judentums* (The Scientific Study of Judaism), and which is based on the attempt to explain the content of a teaching or tradition in the light of its historic context. Beside Samson Raphael Hirsch, the most outstanding among those spokesmen were Israel Hildesheimer (1820–99), founder of the Orthodox Rabbinical Seminary at Berlin, and Marcus Lehmann (1831–90), editor of the *Israelit* of Mainz, Germany. They rightly sensed that any attempt to explain a religious practice or teaching in relation to its historical context detracted from its eternally binding character. As divinely enunciated teaching or established practice, the contents of the Torah had to be regarded as absolutely true, infallible, and immutable.

The Greater Judaism in the Making,
pp. 320–21.

8. Conservative Judaism and the Historical School

The Conservative movement was at first identified with the Historical School in Judaism, the members of which were among the principal founders of the scientific study of Judaism. The historical approach to Judaism is basically a secularization of Jewish learning. It applies to Jewish learning the objective historic-critical approach. Before the nineteenth century, that type of Jewish scholarship was unknown. The one outstanding exception was Azariah di Rossi, who flourished in Italy during the latter half of the sixteenth century. The spirit of the Renaissance had then penetrated the inner life of Italian Jewry. Di Rossi, however, was the only outstanding Jew in whom that Renaissance spirit awakened a sense of historical and critical method in the study of the Jewish past. That approach constitutes a break with tradition, despite the attempt of most of those who have employed it to make it appear as in reality a continuation of the ideal of learning which prevailed in the past. Di Rossi's classic work *Meor Enayim* was anathemized and ordered burned by Rabbi Joseph Karo, the author of the *Shulhan Arukh*. . . .

The aim of the historical study of Judaism, as set forth by Immanuel Wolf in the first issue of the *Zeitschrift für Wissenschaft des Judentums* (Berlin, 1823), was to evolve a knowledge of past Jewish achievement in the field of intellectual, ethical, and spiritual values, and to relate those values to the historical background and the specific environmental conditions under which they arose. It was expected that such knowledge would open the eyes of non-Jews to the fact that the Jews, throughout their historical career, had been creators of significant cultural values, and that they did not have to justify their continued existence as a people on the ground of their belonging to a supernatural order of reality.

It was assumed that non-Jews would change their attitude toward Jews as a result of this new knowledge concerning them. Thus not only would Jews gain the goodwill of their gentile neighbors, but they themselves would also arrive at a better understanding of their own people and its past. They would be cured of the sense of inferiority to which they had become subject, as soon as they ceased to believe in the literal account of the events recorded in the Torah. The claim of the Reformists that the Jews were entrusted with the mission of keeping alive the cause of true religion somehow failed to strike a responsive chord. There was need for something that was in keeping with reality, with the way Jewish life had actually functioned, to revive in the Jew his waning self-respect. The Jew had to be made to feel that the people he belonged to had a significant history which reached down to his own day. By becoming aware of that history, his people would cease to have for him a kind of ghostlike character, and would acquire all the traits of a living, normal people.

The Greater Judaism in the Making,
pp. 355–57.

9. Conservative Judaism and Romanticism

Concern with the preservation of one's national tradition and conservation of the traditional institutions of one's nation, which are the two factors of nineteenth-century nationalist German romanticism, went into the making of Conservative Judaism. . . .

The fact is that the underlying principle of Conservative Judaism, which would have the salvation of the individual Jew depend upon his fostering an intensive Jewish consciousness by identifying himself with the people of Israel, promises more than it fulfills. That principle sounds as though it really affords both inspiration and guidance to the modern Jew, as though it provides the way to his self-fulfillment, in that it enables him to achieve the synthesis of what is best in his tradition with what is best in the modern world. Upon careful scrutiny, however, that principle turns out to be a method of salvation by evasion. It evades outward difficulties and inner conflicts, instead of coming to close grips with them.

Conservative Judaism possesses that trait in common with romanticism by which its beginnings were largely influenced. Romanticism is known to seek an anchorage in some calm water rather than ride the rough seas. It is especially fond of retiring into memories of the past, and it usually manages to select such memories as are pleasant and capable of affording a sheltered retreat. When the high hopes we place on man's reason and initiative to redeem himself from the evils that beset him are frustrated, and we find that the main result of the exercise of reason and initiative has been to despoil society of faith and idealism, and to give added stimulus to selfishness and aggression, we naturally yearn for the good old days of simple faith and unsophisticated morals.

No amount of wishing on our part, however, can actually bring back the conditions which obtained in the past. Not even the most vigorous efforts to create them artificially are of much avail. The result is that we spend our days mostly in nostalgic yearning for the past. Since we fail to achieve the object of that yearning, we conclude that the nostalgia is a spiritual experience, worthwhile in and for itself. We nurse our inner malaise and actually come to enjoy it. Needless to say, it renders us impotent to deal effectively with present realities. The old fable about the mountain's shaking and trembling only to produce a mouse is enacted time and again, particularly in the area of *halakah*, or Jewish law. During Prohibition days in the United States, halakic interpretation was resorted to in order to permit the use of grape juice when reciting the *kiddush* benediction over the Sabbath. Currently it is being resorted to in order to permit the inclusion of an unenforceable clause in the outdated type of marriage contract (*ketubah*), in the vain hope of overcoming serious divorce complications which are the result of the inferior status assigned to the woman in traditional law.

The Greater Judaism in the Making,
pp. 354, 369–70.

VII

Judaism and Community in America

1. Separation of Church and State

It is incumbent upon American Jews to demonstrate how they expect to solve the problem of living in two civilizations simultaneously. That is a problem which they share with their fellow Americans who are adherents of other faiths. Each of those faiths has to be lived in its historic civilizational context, if it is not to be reduced to a series of abstract platitudes. Insofar, however, as their adherents wish to integrate their own lives into the general American civilization, they have the task of enriching it by bringing to it some special contribution from their own historic civilizations. That raises the question: What would Jews have to do to excel in the field of religion in such a way as to enrich American life?

To answer that question we must take into consideration the anomalous condition in which the American people finds itself religiously. To prevent the historical religions, which lay claim to being supernaturally revealed and to being the sole means to salvation, from engaging in mutual conflict for political and cultural domination, the American Constitution has adopted the principle of separation of church and state. So far as domination is concerned, the Constitution has been effective. But that has not prevented the main religious bodies, like the Roman Catholic Church and the outstanding Protestant churches, from seeking to influence legislation and education in favor of their respective ways of life. It has fallen to the lot of the Jews to urge legislation and education in keeping with the principle of separation of church and state. On the face of it, every such attempt of Jews is made to appear as a move in the direction of secularism and irreligion. In being staunch supporters of the American Constitution, Jews ought to be regarded as good Americans trying to have other Americans live up to their commitment, but life does not work that way.

The fact is that the constitutional amendment pertaining to the separation of church and state has far-reaching implications which those who enacted it probably never contemplated. That is where all the trouble comes from. Sooner or later, all Americans will have to face up to those implications. American Jews have to do so now, if they wish to do their share as a group in extricating American civilization from the predicament in which it finds itself in relation to religion.

The Greater Judaism in the Making,
pp. 474–75.

2. Democracy and Religious Freedom

The American conception of democracy, which is pertinent to the future of Jews outside Israel, is unmistakably implied in the Federal Constitution. That Constitution, in prohibiting the adoption of any law which would deprive anyone of religious freedom, precludes the totalitarian form of state or church which would declare, for example, Roman Catholics to be un-American because they insist upon identifying themselves with the Vatican and papacy. Indeed, Jews would never think of asserting their prerogatives to the same extent that the Roman Catholics do. It could never occur to Jews to ask the state to exempt them from school taxes, even if they undertook to provide for the complete education of their children. Since Jews frankly accord primacy to American civilization, there is no basis whatever for charging them with trying to set up a ghetto, or with halting the process of cultural interpenetration, when they seek to foster their own Jewish heritage.

Religious freedom is meaningless unless it include the recognition of cultural-religious autonomy. Cultural-religious autonomy, on the other hand, does not mean segregation or separation from the rest of the population. Western society is so constituted that, if it is to retain the values of individual personality and freedom, it must do nothing to undermine the two associations which have hitherto been the most potent means of social control—namely, the institution of the family and the religious fellowship. The stability of the former depends upon the stability of the latter. Non-Jews need those two social agencies to counteract the totalitarian tendencies of the modern state. By the same token, Jews need to retain the integrity of their family institution and of Jewish peoplehood.

The Greater Judaism in the Making,
pp. 453–54.

3. Democracy in Judaism

As a consequence of historical experience, man's intelligence has come to regard democracy as the most authentic method of human creative survival, since both the maturity of the individual and international peace call for a conception of human life in which the individual and society have to be conceived as means to and ends for each other. Consequently, the next stage in Judaism has to incorporate democracy into its set of values.

"Answer," in *The Condition of Jewish Belief*,
ed. Editors of *Commentary*, p. 119.

4. Democracy and Jewish Law

Jewish law cannot function except in a society whose collective will it expresses. That collective will must make itself felt not only through prescriptions, but also through sanctions. The renunciation of Jewish legal autonomy has destroyed the organic character of Jewish society and has rendered Jewish law inoperative. To reinstate Jewish law, it is necessary to reestablish Jewish society. The problem takes on one form in Eretz Yisrael, another in the Diaspora. In Eretz Yisrael, the great need is for a code of civil law to govern all human relationships. In the Diaspora, Jewry must organize voluntary constitutional communities that would regulate Jewish interests, and formulate such laws as would be binding on all Jews. Though ritual regulations cannot be included as part of Jewish constitutional law, they need not be left to individual caprice. Ritual regulations would be observed by members of voluntary associations that would undertake to abide by them.

By such democratic processes Jewish law could again be made to function in Jewish life.

The Future of the American Jew, pp. 400–401.

5. Organic Jewish Community

The only way to overcome that fragmentation of Jewish life is to have Jews form themselves into organic communities that would function as the instruments of Jewish life as a whole and that would meet all its needs, in the order of their urgency and importance. Such a community would have to be democratically organized and represent all Jews who wish to be identified with it. Those who at present serve the various organizations and federations would then serve the entire community. Such reorganized communal life would not only coordinate Jewish activities efficiently, it would also integrate the Jew into the living body of the Jewish people, and give him that inner security which comes from belonging and from being wanted and welcomed.

The Greater Judaism in the Making, p. 456.

6. Reorganizing the Jewish Community

It is neither necessary nor possible to do more than indicate certain principles which have to be followed in the formation of an organic community. The first principle is that all who definitely desire to see Jewish life fostered, regardless of how they conceive the form or content of that life, should be eligible for membership. The first step in the self-discipline which the pronounced survivalists among us must take is to cooperate with all who prefer to remain Jews, on any terms whatsoever. No one but a fanatical believer in his own particular brand of Jewish survivalism would withhold membership in the Jewish community from those who conceive of Jewish survival differently from the way he does. One has to be blind to the complexity of our inner problem to claim to have found the only true solution, and to refuse to cooperate with anyone who disagrees.

We must have faith in the capacity of the Jewish people to determine for themselves the character of Jewish life. Indeed, not only must no Jew be excluded from the Jewish community for his opinions and beliefs, but the community must provide in its administration for a proper and proportionate representation of every Jewish trend. Each such trend should be given a chance to organize its own adherents and to pursue its own program, so long as it recognizes the right of Jews of other schools of thought to do likewise.

Secondly, if the Jewish community is to be a means of having the individual Jew experience the reality and vitality of the Jewish people, it follows that those institutions and agencies whose main function is to foster Jewish consciousness should occupy a position of primacy. Accordingly, the synagogues, the communal centers, and the institutions of elementary education and higher learning should constitute the nucleus in the organizational pattern. How to get the various Jewish denominations to operate harmoniously within the communal frame is by no means as insuperable a problem as we have been wont to think. In many large cities, Jewish educational bureaus manage to serve diverse types of Jewish educational institutions, from the most secular to the most Orthodox. This proves that it is possible for widely differing groups to find a common ground. By the same token, it should be possible to establish in each community a synagogue and center bureau that would perform a similar function for the spiritual and cultural needs of the adults.

Thirdly, the multiplicity of organizations and their tendency to perpetuate themselves and to retain their independence might seem to preclude their integration into a united community. The experience, however, with the existing federations and welfare funds throughout this country, which have succeeded in bringing together for common action the most diverse institutions and agencies, shows that the difficulties in the way of their committing themselves to a positive program for Jewish life are not insuperable. Moreover, if we follow the principle that it is always best to avail ourselves of existing forces and agencies instead of liquidating them and beginning *de novo*, there would be no occasion for any of them to feel aggrieved. Being the spontaneous expression of the will to organized effort, they are the medium through which the conservation and growth of Jewish life could best be furthered. All organizations and agencies at present engaged in specific tasks should, therefore, continue what they are doing, but they should be required, in addition, to be represented in local community councils. All organizations and agencies that are national in scope should have representation in, and give an accounting to, all the local community councils of those localities where they have branches. The community council should in each case be a reviewing, coordinating, and initiating body, from the standpoint of the all-dominant purpose of giving the Jew the courage, and providing him with the resources, to live as a Jew.

In a number of cities, Jewish community councils have already been formed; in others they are in the process of formation. At present, they virtually have no definite purpose, except that of exploring, or perhaps even generating, the sentiment for Jewish unity. Given the affirmative purpose of strengthening the morale of the Jew, we would have in the community councils the groundwork of an overall national Jewish community. An overall council, which would constitute the executive committee of that community, would be representative of all areas of opinion and have first-hand acquaintance with local problems. It could, therefore, well be trusted not to treat perfunctorily its task of reviewing and coordinating the activities of the different sections of our people, and initiating needed lines of action.

Many technical problems are bound to arise. How shall we deal, for example, with large Jewish populations in metropolitan centers, or with sparse Jewish populations in rural areas? Such problems are by no means insoluble. In metropolitan centers, a maximum, like twenty or twenty-five thousand, might be entitled to a local community council. In the case of rural areas, on the other hand, a population minimum and a geographic maximum might be combined to form a unit that would be entitled to a community council. These and similar details could be worked out by those who are expert in matters of this kind.

In a word, Jewish communal life should be organized on the following principles:

1. The inclusion of all who desire to continue as Jews.

2. The primacy of the religious and educational institutions in the communal structure.

3. Democratic representation of all legitimate Jewish organizations in the administration of the community.

The Future of the American Jew, pp.118–20.

7. Criteria of Jewish Loyalty

In view of the changed conditions in Jewish life, the criterion of loyalty to Judaism can no longer be the acceptance of a creed, but the experience of the need to have one's life enriched by the Jewish heritage. That experience should be formulated not in terms of dogmas but in terms of wants.

The following wants supply the measure by which we may in our day test our loyalty to Judaism.

1. We want Judaism to help us overcome temptation, doubt, and discouragement.

2. We want Judaism to imbue us with a sense of responsibility for the righteous use of the blessings wherewith God endows us.

3. We want the Jew so to be trusted that his yea will be taken as yea, and his nay as nay.

4. We want to learn how to utilize our leisure to best advantage physically, intellectually, and spiritually.

5. We want the Jewish home to live up to its traditional standards of virtue and piety.

6. We want the Jewish upbringing of our children to further their

moral and spiritual growth, and to enable them to accept with joy their heritage as Jews.

7. We want the synagogue to enable us to worship God in sincerity and in truth.

8. We want our religious traditions to be interpreted in terms of understandable experience and to be made relevant to our present-day needs.

9. We want to participate in the upbuilding of Eretz Yisrael as a means to the renaissance of the Jewish spirit.

10. We want Judaism to find rich, manifold, and ever new expression in philosophy, in letters, and in the arts.

11. We want all forms of Jewish organization to make for spiritual purpose and ethical endeavor.

12. We want the unity of Israel throughout the world to be fostered through mutual help in time of need, and through cooperation in the furtherance of Judaism at all times.

13. We want Judaism to function as a potent influence for justice, freedom, and peace in the life of men and nations.

Sabbath Prayer Book, pp. 563f.

8. Congregations and Community

The type of organization which American Jews must evolve for their spiritual salvation is a radically different instrument from that upon which they have been taught to depend of late; namely, the congregation. The congregation as constituted at present is likely to prove the most serious obstacle to the creation of a normally functioning Jewish community. To understand how the congregation, which is usually regarded as the mainstay of Jewish life, can stand in the way of its healthy development, it is necessary to become better informed about the true nature of the congregation. We might then be able to determine its proper place in Jewish life.

The delusion under which most Jews labor, whether they be Neo-Orthodox, Reformists, or radicals, is that the congregation is the same as the synagogue—that social institution through which the Jewish spirit has made itself articulate during the last twenty centuries. Hence the sacrosanct attitude with which the congregation is regarded by those who are identified with it, and the violent opposition to it on the part of those who have broken with the traditional expression of the Jewish spirit. What both groups should learn is that the congregation is only a recently evolved form of social organization. Jews have come upon it absentmindedly, as it were, in the course of their efforts to work their way from medievalism to modernism. It is a sort of hit-or-miss experiment which the Jews have been trying out in their attempt to adjust themselves to the new social and political conditions resulting from the Emancipation.

Two factors have contributed to the rise of the congregation. One has been the political emancipation which was usually accompanied with the understanding, either tacit or expressed, that the Jews would reduce the scope of their communal activity to a minimum. The other factor has been the loss of homogeneity in ideas and practices. Contact with a variety of cultures and with people in different stages of cultural development has changed the Jews into an almost hopelessly heterogeneous human mass. This has narrowed the basis of communal cooperation among them. In their desire, therefore, to conserve their collective life and traditions, Jews have done the next-best thing, by organizing themselves into congregations which are homogeneous groups united for the purpose of fostering Jewish life.

The congregation, as the Hebrew equivalent of that term indicates, aims to be a miniature *kehillah*, to fulfill for the Jew all those functions which the *kehillah* fulfilled in the past. This, however, it cannot possibly do, because the principle of homogeneity extends to economic status as well as to background and perspective. That means that the whole nexus of communal interests which constitute Jewish life could never arise within the congregation as such. Accordingly, if a Jew wants to express himself fully as a Jew, he must look elsewhere than to the congregation. Then why not accept the need for extracongregational organization as inherent in the very nature of Jewish life? Why not proceed to make the principal unit of Jewish interaction not the congregation, but the community which includes all Jews living in a town or in a district of one of the larger cities?

The congregation as a self-contained unit is a detriment to the religious, no less than to the communal welfare. By making the element of religion the main bond of unity among the members, religion becomes highly subject to misunderstanding. It is set up as something apart from other Jewish interests. This is neither wholesome nor in keeping with tradition. In the end, both religion and the other interests suffer. Religion is rendered abstract and contentless, confined in the main to worship and ceremonies, while the other interests are secularized and dejudaized.

It cannot be denied that the congregation has served a useful purpose as a temporary means of warding off the complete disintegration of Jewish life, which was bound to set in with the breakup of the pre-Emancipation type of Jewish community. This explains how the congregation has come to eclipse all other types of organized effort as a means to Jewish life. But, when temporary remedies or stopgaps are relied upon as permanent sources of strength or support, they usually lead to great danger. In a normally organized Jewish community, provision will have to be made for worship and the conduct of religious observances and rites. There will have to be synagogues and rabbis as there were in the *kehillah* of old. But the synagogue must not be the exclusive clubhouse of a homogeneous group, nor must the rabbi be monopolized by those who can pay his salary. Rabbis, as well as social workers, center executives, and other functionaries should be appointees of the community as a whole.

Moreover, organization on congregational lines as the social framework of Jewish life in America contains an intrinsic weakness insofar as it lacks the element of socialized authority. Whether a people expresses its will through the state, which is government by a lay body, or through the church, which is government by an ecclesiastical body, the collective will takes the form of law. The normal individual does not want to be a law unto himself. In his actions and in his impulses, he requires the sanctions and restraints imposed by a will which is supraindividual. Human nature demands that some pressure be brought to bear from without, and does itself create the source of that pressure—community life. Social life has as much need of a measure of involuntarism as physical life.

A person is a member of a nation not by choice, but by virtue of the pressure of the cultural group into which he is born. That pressure is exerted in the first instance through the family. If nationhood has played a useful part in the evolution of the race, it has been due, in no small degree, to this involuntarism which characterizes it. If, then, Jewish nationhood is to function in the Diaspora, its principal manifestation must be this very element of involuntarism characteristic of national life. The congregation cannot supply it because it is too small, intimate, and transient to be authoritative. There is a growing tendency to treat synagogue affiliation as a luxury to be enjoyed when times are good and money plentiful. But as soon as the financial status of the members slumps, the affiliation is one of the first luxuries to be surrendered, and once dispensed with, it is seldom resumed even with the return of prosperity.

Judaism as a Civilization, pp. 290–93.

9. Religion and the State

The traditional policy of the separation of church and state is inadequate, because it overlooks the fact that, among modern nations, nationalism is itself a religious program of salvation, and that government utilizes this program for the organization of power. Democracy is virtually a doctrine of national salvation, and the public schools are, to all intents, religious institutions which attempt to utilize this doctrine of national salvation, as a means of promulgating social solidarity and effective collaboration among the citizens of the nation. The problem of church and state should, therefore, for the purpose of this discussion, be restated as the problem of the relation of the traditional historic religions to the various emergent national religions of the modern world.

When medievalism gave way to modernism, the effect on religion was twofold: (1) religion began to be secularized, and (2) nationhood began to be religionized.

Religion has become secularized in that it has come to regard the promotion of social welfare as within its scope. Though it may still cling to the doctrine that true salvation is reserved for the experience of the soul after death, nevertheless, unlike medieval religion it regards the participation of men in movements designed to promote human welfare in this world as conditioning their salvation in the next. It does not classify the world and the flesh, along with the devil, as inherently anti-God. It does not commend an ascetic withdrawal from the responsibilities of political and economic life as virtuous conduct. On the contrary, it organizes social action, exercises political pressure on legislatures, and makes the promotion of social justice and world peace definite objectives of its program of salvation.

On the other hand, nationhood has become religionized. The function of the state is no longer limited to defending its citizens against foreign aggression and policing their relations with one another. It is concerned with promoting the public welfare, by conditioning the individual to the acceptance and loyal support of common ideals, ideals that are conceived as having importance not merely for the nation itself, but for civilization, or mankind in general. The state thus engages in public philanthropy, public health, the promotion of science and art, public education, provision of facilities for sport and recreation, and any number of other activities, which reveal its interest in the salvation of the individual, on the one hand, and in the spiritual welfare of the group, as vested with moral responsibility, on the other. Whenever its interests collide with those of other states, it is wont to justify its own way of life by referring to some universal social doctrine, which is analogous to the theological tenets maintained by the churches. It is interested in making "the world safe for democracy," or in ushering in a classless society, or in destroying pluto-democracy, so that a new moral order can be established throughout the earth.

This change from medievalism to modernism, this secularization of religion and religionizing of nationhood, have had both good and bad results. The good effected by the change is the concentration of religion on the need of improving the conditions under which we live, in order to enable men to get the most out of life. The belief that this world is damned, and that there is no hope of improving it, makes men insensitive to the evils that exist. During the Middle Ages, religion did tend to become the opium of the masses. Not only did it train the masses to resign themselves to their suffering, in itself a legitimate use of opium, but it also made those who were not suffering complacent in the enjoyment of their privileges and arrogant and tyrannical in the assertion of those privileges as rights. Democratic nationalism is, therefore, significant not merely politically but also religiously in that it asserts the sacredness of the human soul and its dignity, as a responsible creative moral agent. It regards all men as "endowed by their Creator with . . . unalienable rights . . . among these life, liberty, and the pursuit of happiness." The phrase "endowed by their Creator" was not a conventional cliché but an expression of a profound religious evaluation of human life.

Making nationhood into a religion has also led to evil consequences. In rendering their own prestige sacred and inviolable, the nations have often sacrificed the happiness and dignity of the individual citizen. Like avowedly religious organizations of power, modern states have been intolerant of freedom of expression and jealous of loyalty to international groups. They have been guilty of regimentation and the suppression of the creative differences among men, in order to facilitate domination by those in authority. Moreover, they have used the religion of nationalism to justify domination over other nations; they have launched imperialistic wars in order to bring "civilization," that is, their own brand of civilization, to other peoples. The "law and order" effected by the religion of nationalism, in its sacrifice of the individual to interests that are presumed to be those of the nation as a corporate entity, too often has turned out to be a mirage of order in a desert of disorder. For behind this apparent order are concealed deep and bitter clashes of interest, desperate forces held momentarily in a state of equilibrium so unstable that an insignificant incident would suffice to destroy it and to bring chaos and cataclysm.

The Future of the American Jew, pp. 516–18.

10. Civil Religion in America

The task of American Jewry is to promulgate an indigenous civic religion for the American people that shall act as a unifying influence, uniting all Americans regardless of race, creed, or status, without being authoritative or coercive. That task involves the incorporation into American institutions and practices of those principles in Jewish religion which have a universal import and are therefore transferable to other civilizations.

The universal principles in Jewish religion and their application to American life may be formulated as follows:

1. That God is the God of Israel implies that a people, of which we are a part, should provide the principal experiences on which to base our belief in, or awareness of, God as the power that makes for salvation. Those experiences constitute the substance which should yield the values that give meaning to human life. As Americans, therefore, we should identify those experiences and strivings in American life and history which would not only give organic character to the American people, but also set it on the road to human progress and perfection. To the extent that American experiences and strivings do that, they reveal God as the power that makes for salvation and should be interpreted as such, culturally and educationally.

2. According to the teaching of the Torah and the Prophets, the people of Israel was expected to demonstrate its loyalty to God not merely by worshipping Him, but mainly by practicing justice and righteousness. These are called "the way of the Lord" (Gen 18:19). In the light of that teaching, failure to walk in that way has brought untold suffering on the people of Israel. Unrighteousness is the offspring of pride which takes the form of rebellion against God, or playing the god. Translated into universal terms, that teaching implies that the religion of a people has to find expression principally in the practice of righteousness in its political, economic, and social affairs. That is the divine law for every people. Violation of that law is bound to lead to failure and disaster.

An illustration of the way those principles should be incorporated in American institutional life is afforded by *The Faith of America*.* That book contains programs for the religious observance of American holidays, using for this purpose materials drawn from American literature and historical documents. Each holiday is given a special religious theme. The theme for Lincoln's Birthday, for example, is the ideal of equality and fraternity; for Washington's Birthday, the promise and responsibility of nationhood, and so on with all the other holidays.

Given the wish to survive as a segment of the Jewish people, that wish is bound to seek an outlet in some effort that would give to our persistence as Jews not merely the significance of inertia but rather the lift that comes from being dedicated to a high purpose. That high purpose should be to contribute to the spiritual life of America the kind of civic religion that will place America in the spiritual forefront of the world, as she is now in the political and economic. That high purpose should be to achieve for ourselves a conception of Jewish religion that is as free and creative as poetry, literature, and art, a Jewish religion that is vitally relevant to reality as we know it and live it.

The Greater Judaism in the Making, pp. 477–78.

*The Faith of America: Prayers, Readings, and Songs for the Celebration of American Holidays, compiled by M. M. Kaplan, et. al., New York, 1951.

VIII

Ethics

1. The Ethical Function of Religion

The first thinker was no low-browed, naked savage, just emerged from the wilds, but a much civilized and highly sophisticated dweller in some ancient city. The kind of god or gods that man originally believed in required no furrowing of the brow or painful thinking to be discovered. On the contrary, primitive religion is the product of man's mental feebleness. Being too immature to think out the connection between the various elements in nature and the part they play in making life possible and supplying his needs, he jumped to the conclusion that every object had a spirit of its own which was just as fitful and subject to whims as he was. Hence the elaborate systems of rituals and offerings, and prayers and dances, by which he believed he would cajole these spirits to give him rain, cause the sun to shine, the animals to multiply, and the earth to yield its vegetation. . . . For a long time to come people will use religion in the hope that through it they will be able to ward off illness and to secure prosperity and safety.

This utilitarian function, however, cannot but bring religion into disrepute, for ultimately man will not only acquire greater control over the forces of nature but also realize how inconsistent the scientific control of nature is with the resort to magic and superstition. That is already happening with thousands of the more enlightened. Never having learned that it is possible for religion to have other than a utilitarian function, they conclude that it is bound to disappear with the enlargement of man's sphere of control over his environment. Many, believing themselves sufficiently intellectual, or wishing to be counted among the intellectuals, act out that conclusion.

That religion is as inevitable a part of human civilization as is science or art derives from the fact that, with the progress of civilization, religion ceases to be utilitarian and becomes ethical. This change of function is Judaism's contribution to the spiritual life of mankind. Jewish religion has taught the world that the business of religion is not to help us secure the things we need for our well-being but to get us to use those things righteously once we have secured them. It is undoubtedly much more difficult to know how to utilize, than how to retain, our health. A far greater amount of effort is involved in the righteous use of power and influence than in winning them. The Sage who said it is more difficult to conquer one's spirit than to conquer a stronghold, knew whereof he spoke. Alexander conquered the whole world except Alexander.

It is toward this self-conquest, this control not of the physical but of the human environment, that the Jewish civilization would have religion direct its efforts. When the Greek philosophers grew wise to the folly of employing religion as a means to the control of the physical elements of nature, they abandoned religion and turned to the cultivation of a religionless ethics to guide man in the art of living. When the Prophets denounced the utilitarian use of religion, they transformed and exalted it into a means of cultivating social responsibility.

The Meaning of God in Modern Jewish Religion, pp. 196–98.

2. The Dimension of the Ethical

The study of human life has by this time made it clear that man's deliberate efforts to better his lot and to improve himself lie in more than the one dimension of those vital needs, or vitalities, which man shares with other living beings. As manifestations of physical and mental life, the vital needs are manifestations of power, for life is inherently power. Those needs are governed by nature or necessity; yet in satisfying them, man must reckon with something more than their inherent necessity. Always something asserts itself that clearly lies outside that dimension. So insistent have been those transnatural factors in human life that they have succeeded in winning recognition for themselves as constituting the human differential. All living beings are, to be sure, governed by natural forces or impulses. These may even be the source of those higher developments in man that mark him off from the rest of creation; but only in man do those natural forces or impulses achieve self-consciousness. Self-consciousness introduces a new quality into the content of human life. That new quality impels man to live in other dimensions besides the one of the vitalities or of power. One such dimension is that of the rational, or the universal, and the other is that of the spiritual, or the eternal. The dimension of the rational may be said to give *form* to the content of human life; the dimension of the spiritual may be said to give to it *purpose.*

To the dimension of the rational or the dimension of the universal belong all the interests and values that center around truth, or the knowledge of reality for its own sake, together with all those interests and values which center around moral goodness, or the practice of the right for its own sake. Since in ancient times the development of reason was for the most part limited, except in the case of Hindu and Greek philosophers, to the interests and values of moral goodness, the term "rational" will here be used interchangeably with "ethical," and vice versa. To the dimension of the spiritual, or the eternal, belong the three groups of interests and values that center respectively around (1) personality, or the self as a responsible being, (2) the social group, which is the medium of man's physical and mental life and growth, and which evokes his loyalty, and (3) the totality of things, or cosmos, as divine, or as contributing to man's salvation or self-fulfillment, and as evoking his piety.

The significant fact about any human society, from the most rudimentary to the most civilized, in which the integrative forces are stronger than the disintegrative, is that the rational and the spiritual values not only figure in the mutual relations and expectations of its members but are also regarded as original and autonomous instead of as derived from, or ministering to, the vitalities. To be sure, health, prosperity, and social approval are generally considered rewards for ethical conformity, and for deference to the interests of personality, society, and God; but those rewards are only incidental. In fact, the rationality or spirituality of any act is impugned as soon as it is believed to be motivated by the prospect of reward.

From the foregoing we can realize what is meant by the universality of ethics and religion. The diversities in ethical and religious thought and practice result from the differences in the opportunities to achieve knowledge and social contact with other groups and ways of life. The scope of life possible to a rudimentary society like that of a nomad tribe which wanders from oasis to oasis is far narrower than that possible to an urban community which engages in trade and commerce. That narrowness is bound to be reflected in its ethics and religion. Except when under the influence of some individual or collective passion, human beings normally reckon, according to their lights, with the rational and the spiritual interests. So long as any human group is sufficiently integrated to know itself as a unit and is not subject to extraordinary pressure or influence, it manifests an unmistakable regard for rational and spiritual considerations. Every normal society reflects some sensitiveness to the universal values of reason and to the eternal values of the spirit.

"A Philosophy of Jewish Ethics," in *The Jews*, ed. Louis Finkelstein, pp. 1012–14.

3. Judaism and Ethics

From the standpoint of ethical theory, it may be sufficient to establish the autonomy, the otherness or the different dimensionality, of the moral law of ethical values. But from the standpoint of everyday living and the betterment of human relations, it is necessary to know to which of the needs or vitalities of human life the moral law is to be applied. This involves specifying the particular vital functions which are most prone to moral evil, or to the violation of the moral law. If we divide the vitalities into two main areas, one harboring the physical desires and the other the various strivings and ambitions which function through the mutual relations of human beings, the tendency in certain ages and civilizations, like the Hindu and the medieval Western, has been to regard the physical hungers as man's chief stumbling block. This has been especially true in relation to the sex hunger.

Judaism, on the other hand, may be said to have been the first civilization to insist that the field of human relations is the area most in need of being brought within the dimension of the moral law. The tendency of the strong and the clever to exploit the weak and the simple is, in the estimate of Judaism, the source of man's undoing. To be sure, Judaism abounds in taboo and restrictions intended to restrain the physical hungers from running riot. But whatever provision it makes for such restraint it does essentially in the same spirit as modern society provides for the social health of the community, as a kind of hygienic measure. Only to the extent, however, that human relations are implicated in those physical hungers do those hungers become subject to moral law.

Since the main evil in the area of human relations, which has ever brought in its wake chaos and disaster to human life, is the lust to dominate (directly, when one is strong enough to do so, or indirectly by identifying oneself with the leader or his mob in whom such strength resides), that is the evil against which Judaism principally invokes the moral law. This distinctive note in the ethics of Judaism is quite unmistakable. A summary of the ethical teachings in Israel's Torah might well be the famous scripture in Zechariah: "Not by might nor by power but by My Spirit, saith the Lord of Hosts" (Zech. 4:6), or even the less well known scripture in Samuel: "For not by strength shall man prevail" (1 Sam. 2:9).

"A Philosophy of Jewish Ethics," in *The Jews*, ed. Louis Finkelstein, p. 1019.

4. Challenging Tradition

To be free, men must be able to understand the impact of irrational forces of another kind than those which inhere in nature. They are the irrational forces which are of man's own making. They derive from the authority of the past or from the authority of the multitude. Their power over us proceeds from a disposition of the mind to seek the path of least resistance. There is an inertia of the mind that operates similarly to the law of physical inertia, a tendency to persist in ways that we are used to and to fall in with prevalent currents of thought and action, without questioning whither they are leading us. We thus are in constant danger of being enslaved to ancient superstitions, to inherited social prejudices, to conventional lies, and to specious rationalizations of the mob mind.

To possess inner freedom, the human mind must be able to rouse itself from this inertia, to challenge or question the inherent value of any purpose, ideal, belief, or standard which we are asked to accept merely because it has back of it the prestige of a long tradition or the weight of numbers. This does not mean that man can make himself independent of tradition, or need not reckon with the opinion of his fellows. Man is a social being. His progress depends on his being able to utilize the accumulated culture to which innumerable individuals in all the past generations have contributed and to avail himself of the experience of his contemporaries, particularly of those whose opinions may be more valid than his own, because of better access to the facts on which they are based. But when the pressure of tradition or public opinion imposes itself on the individual to the extent that he feels called upon to abdicate his right to think for himself about anything whatsoever, then tradition or public opinion has become a tyranny. Such abdication of the individual judgment makes for the salvation neither of the individual nor of society. It is a form of slavery which the man who possesses inner freedom will confront with the challenging mind.

The challenging mind sees in enslavement to tradition but another form of enslavement to habit. It is generally recognized that a person may become enslaved by his own habits. Habits are indispensable; habit formation insures the most efficient discharge of necessary functions. But when circumstances make the discharge of this function unnecessary or undesirable, the inability to break away from habit is slavery. The child develops habits of dependence on his parents; if he retains these habits in later life and does not acquire new habits of self-reliance, economic independence, and the emotional capacity to form new family ties, he is a slave to them. Similarly a society develops traditional customs, laws, standards, and conventions which help it to meet the demands of life and contribute to the welfare of all its individual members. But these customs, laws, standards, and conventions originated, at the time of their origin, in response to the needs of that society. As long as they seem to function well, it is good that the individual conform to them rather than yield to mere passing whim or egoistic impulse. But when the traditional culture pattern does not contribute to the welfare of the society and its component individuals, the mind must be free to alter and reconstruct the traditional culture pattern, to seek the development of new and better social habits to meet the changed situation.

We must realize that tradition is social habit multiplied a thousandfold through the reinforcement which each individual receives from every other and from the cumulative strength acquired through repetition by each generation. Beliefs, values, institutions become second nature and maintain themselves by their own momentum long after the purposes which they originally served have been outlived.

In the past, both church and state were able to exercise unlimited despotism, by virtue of the power lent them by tradition. It has become fashionable to ascribe to organized religions the principle of the dignity of the individual. That is not true. The organized traditional religions have always deprecated and frowned down the challenging mind. They have always treated it as dangerous and in need of suppression. In traditional religious circles, free thought is still regarded as synonymous with irreligion and anarchy.

The flame of intellectual freedom, the freedom of the challenging mind, was kindled in ancient Greece and has burned only intermittently and very dimly most of the time. But, even in Greece, Socrates had to pay the price of martyrdom for his intellectual freedom. Socrates, Plato, and Aristotle should be credited with having been the first to foster the inner freedom of the challenging mind. The Stoics managed to keep alive intellectual independence, but the Church extinguished it and brought on the long night of the Middle Ages, until it was rekindled by the Renaissance and the Enlightenment.

Just as humanity, however, was beginning to enjoy its emancipation from bondage to the past, it commenced to forge for itself the chains of an infinitely worse bondage. It became enslaved to the tyranny of the multitude. With the spread of superficial literacy, the invention of numerous new means of communication, and the acquisition of the power to release at will a flood of printed matter, the art of propaganda was developed as a technique for making men slaves. Propaganda has been employed to regiment the human mind and make it think and believe whatever those in power want it to think and believe. Never in the history of mankind was the human being so much in danger of becoming de-individualized and depersonalized. Totalitarianism means the complete subordination of the individual to the mass. There is but one way in which it can be resisted and ultimately defeated. If the individual is not to be sucked into the vortex of the mass, he must consciously retain his selfhood; he must refuse to accept blindly and unquestioningly purposes imposed from without.

The Future of the American Jew, pp. 289–91.

5. Ethics, Symbols, and Rites

The meanings expressed by traditional Jewish symbols and observances must be not merely stated, but stated in terms that are relevant to the needs and interests of living Jews. Explanations of rites and symbols, in the terms in which our fathers explained them, may convey no meaning to Jews of our generation. To say, for example, that the whole complex of rites observed on Yom Kippur has for its purpose to effect atonement for our sins means nothing to us as modern Jews, unless the terms "sin" and "atonement" are given new meanings. Only when these are reinterpreted in a way that reckons with modern psychological and ethical insights, and we are made to understand how the observance of the traditional Yom Kippur rites can help us to redirect our own purposes to advantage, to surmount our personal limitations, to escape frustration and achieve self-fulfillment—only then can we, as modern Jews, fully benefit by their observance.

The Future of the American Jew, pp. 426–27.

6. Exploiting Others: The Original Sin

From time immemorial the problem of sin and suffering has occupied the human mind. Men have felt that human life is not what it ought to be, that it is very different from what God had originally designed for man. Somehow man, in the exercise of his freedom of will, must have taken a wrong step that set him on the wrong track and frustrated God's benign purpose in creating the world. The ancients naturally ascribed this wrong step to the common ancestor of the human race, the first man. The sin of Adam, as told in the biblical myth, is not merely *a* sin but the *original sin*, the archetype from which all sin, the source of all human suffering, springs. That sin is symbolically represented by the eating of the fruit of "the tree of the knowledge of good and evil." What made that act of such transcendent importance, so fatal in all its dire consequences, was that eating of this fruit had the effect of making man "like a god, knowing good and evil."

The sin that is symbolized by man's eating the fruit of the tree of the knowledge of good and evil has nothing to do with man's aspiration to imitate God's ways. It implies the very opposite of that aspiration, namely, the attempt of man to *play the part of a god*, to set himself up as a deity, to usurp God's role of law-giver and to become a law unto himself, to make his own desires the standard of his action, to *taste* for himself the *good* and the *evil* without reference to divine sanctions or to any law that says, "Thou shalt," or "Thou shalt not."

"Being like a god" is thus at the opposite pole of being Godlike, which is what the Torah would have man be. "Be ye holy, for I the Lord thy God am holy" (Lev. 19:2) is given as the sanction for the observance of our religious precepts. Before creating man, God is represented in the Torah as saying, "Let us make man in our image, according to our likeness" (Gen. 1:26). This would seem to imply that man's being Godlike was intended by God and hence could not possibly be resented by Him. Our Sages, too, gave every encouragement to man's imitating God's ways. The injunction "Thou shalt love the Lord thy God and cleave unto Him," they interpreted to mean that man was to "cleave to His attributes," to imitate Him; as God is merciful, so man should be merciful; as God is just, so man should be just.

If we interpret the symbolism of the Eden story in the light of the foregoing contrast, it immediately becomes clearly intelligible. The sin, which is the source of all sins, and which may well be held responsible for the whole gamut of preventable human ills, is the abuse of human freedom by the attempt of men to make their own interests and passions the sole determinants of their behavior. When we consider how mortal men have oppressed and exploited their fellow men, and have ruthlessly disregarded the feelings, the needs, the very lives of the men and women whose vital powers they appropriated to their own uses as though they had indeed created them, it was not farfetched to assume that even death came into the world out of the necessity of thwarting this tendency of men to play the god, and to make havoc of the world in doing so.

The Future of the American Jew, pp. 274–75.

7. Redemptive Love

In contrast with man's cardinal sin, which consists in playing the god, man's cardinal virtue consists in being Godlike. To be Godlike is to exercise that redemptive love which expresses itself as forgiveness in such a way as to elicit penitence from the sinner.

Redemptive love has nothing in common either with erotic love or with possessive love. It not only calls forth the best in others as well as in ourselves, when the love is mutual and no grievance of any kind mars it; it can also break down the wall of evil and wrongdoing that divides men, and reestablish happy and wholesome relations among them. The commandment "Thou shalt love thy neighbor as thyself" (Lev. 19:18) has evidently nothing to do with erotic love, which does not have to be commanded but controlled, nor with possessive love, which can hardly be regarded as love. The only kind of love which does not emerge spontaneously is redemptive love. Though we must assume its presence deep down in our nature at its best, we have to exert our powers of mind and will to bring it forth. That is why it is the subject of divine command.

We are least prone to love our neighbor when he has done us injury, when he has harmed us in our well-being or reputation. The natural course is to allow ourselves to be swept on by the urge of anger, hatred, and the desire for revenge. Comes the divine behest and pulls us back. "Thou shalt not take vengeance nor bear any grudge against the children of thy people, but thou shalt love thy neighbor as thyself" (Lev. 19:18). Whether we should wait with our forgiveness until he who has wronged us repents or should extend it before he has repented is a moot question in Jewish tradition. In the Testament of the Twelve Patriarchs (18:2), one of the apocryphal writings, we are bidden, "If anyone seeketh to do evil unto you, do well unto him and pray for him." This precept is found not only in the unofficial writings. Even in our canonical writings we come across the specific teaching that a man should turn the other cheek to him who has smitten him on the one cheek (Lam. 3:30). But there are no two opinions anywhere in Jewish tradition with regard to retaliation, even where the wrongdoer is in no repentant mood. "They who do not persecute those who persecute them, they who suffer wrong in silence and requite it not, are deemed the friends of God" (Talmud, Yoma 23a).

It may well be that, from the standpoint of punitive justice, we have the right to give vent to our hatred and to retaliate the wrong done to us, particularly when the wrongdoer shows not the slightest evidence of regret or repentance. Even then we should hold ourselves in check. For every time we give way to hatred, we impair our capacity for love. So much is that capacity an integral part of our nature at its best that, when it is weakened or destroyed, we cannot help but experience frustration. Revenge may be sweet, in that it is the gratification of a hereditary biological impulse which we share with the animal world. But it is not part of the essential humanity in our nature. That essential humanity yearns to express itself in outgoing redemptive love. When we defeat love by yielding to an impulse which we share with the subhuman, we cannot be happy.

The Future of the American Jew, pp. 331–32.

8. Equality as a Religious Ideal

The ideal of equality when conceived both as spiritual and as economic equality would mean that all human beings are entitled to experience the dignity of selfhood or personality, the moral character of society, and the reality of God.

To experience the dignity of selfhood means that every individual must be able to feel that the society in which he lives not merely regards him as a means to an end but recognizes him as an end in himself. He must not be treated as a mere cog in the machinery of production but must be given as much of freedom of choice in the way he earns his livelihood and in the way he spends his leisure as is consistent with the similar rights of others and the security of all. As long as he contributes to the productive process in accordance with his abilities, whether it be little or much, he is entitled to be treated with respect, and not be made a tool for the compulsory service of others, who take advantage of his dependence on them.

To experience personal equality in this sense, it is not necessary that all people have equal or identical powers or tasks, or that none must be in any way dependent on others. It is right that the skillful surgeon be permitted to operate and the incompetent forbidden. The fact that I put my life in the surgeon's hands, when I permit him to operate on me, does not make me feel inferior to him, even though I do not possess his powers and am dependent on his skill for my very life. Differences in the circumstances of life or in the physical and mental ability of individuals would not be felt as constituting a serious problem, if every man knew that under no circumstances would he lack the opportunity to feed, clothe, and shelter himself and his dependents by engaging in work of his own choice, to marry and raise a family without the specter of destitution, and to engage in those physical and mental exercises and pursue those cultural and recreational interests that are nearest to his heart.

To experience the moral character of society, we have to be aware that society is neither an organized mob that imposes its will by violence on other social groups or individuals nor a mechanism in which every man's life follows a predetermined pattern, wherein his own choices hardly count for anything. We have to be aware of society as functioning in the spirit of a community. A community might be defined as that form of social organization in which the welfare of each is the concern of all, and the life of the whole is the concern of each. In such a society there would still be differences in authority, based on functional divisions. Traffic regulations would still have to be obeyed, and engineers, rather than hucksters, poets, or clergymen, would direct the building of bridges. But men would, nevertheless, know themselves to be equal, if each one could feel that under no circumstances would he have to be alone, unwanted, unimportant to his fellow men, insecure and forced to fend for himself, unaided against starvation, disease, and all the natural and social ills. Under no circumstances would he be compelled to join the pack in murdering and pillaging other societies. Under the principle of equality, such a society would have to embrace all the men and nations of the earth. . . .

To experience society as moral implies the dependence of society itself on a spiritual power operative not merely in man, but in the cosmos. What mankind has become, and all that it aspires to become, must be achieved in accordance with the conditions of nature. If, therefore, man must learn from nature itself how to subdue nature, not in the sense of using it for his individual survival but of learning from it how to insure the survival and abundant life of all men, that power cannot be limited to man but must interpenetrate nature itself and the whole cosmos.

Whenever men experience their dignity as responsible agents of spiritual power, whenever they can envisage society as the Kingdom of God, they realize what it means for the spirit of the cosmos to emerge out of nature and give it worth and meaning. To realize that is to experience the reality of God. That experience is implicit in whatever is done for the happiness of the individual and the welfare of society. The function of organized religion is to render that experience explicit. By articulating that experience, by encouraging men and communities of men to seek such experience as a conscious purpose, we further the ideal of human equality. On the other hand, by discouraging any honest effort of men to commune with God, the source of life's value for them, we deny them equality of spiritual status. This it is what makes religious freedom so important. It must be conceived as the right of all men to seek to cultivate in themselves, and in such free association as they may choose, the religious experience, the sense of their rapport with all that renders life worthwhile for them as individuals, as members of a particular society or communion, and as human beings sharing in the life of the cosmos.

The claim of any religion, therefore, to be the exclusive custodian of the opportunities of human salvation, to deny validity to the claims of other religions to the experience of the reality of God, or to assume that only through its doctrines and rites can men experience that reality, is vicious, and is a sin against the ideal of equality. The spirit, which is turning human nature away from the proclivity to seek only the survival of the individual or of his own limited social group and is in the process of establishing universal human brotherhood to insure the opportunity of survival to all men, operates within every human being and human society that seeks communion with it. Although some individuals and religious communities may possess more and others less of this spiritual power, none is totally lacking in it, and none has a monopoly of it.

The contempt of one religious tradition for another, the ready assumption of that other's inadequacy, and the effort at religious hegemony are evidences of the naturalistic worship of power, and are inconsistent with the worship of the spirit. Consequently the pragmatic implication of the demand for equality of opportunity to experience the reality of God is the abandonment of all efforts at trying to win people away from one religious communion to another. Any ideal that is of universal significance, that belongs to the worship not of power but of spirit, is capable of adoption by, and adaptation to, any and all religious traditions.

The Future of the American Jew, pp. 324–27.

9. The Status of Women*

The Jewish woman was treated far better than her status would indicate. In this respect, the Jews were no different from any other people. Westermarck** points out that even among primitive peoples, where the woman is in bondage to her male relations, either to a father, husband, or brother, she is seldom made to experience the logical consequences of her position. The husband, for example, cannot punish or divorce his wife without the consent of the tribe. Husbands, as a rule, are fond of their wives, and wives are loyal and affectionate to their husbands. Among the Guinea Indians, woman is legally held to be the property of

---

*The traditional sources upon which this section is based are to be found in the footnotes of the original text.—eds.

**Edward Westermarck, *The Origin and Development of Moral Ideas* (London, 1912).

man in as literal a sense as is his dog: he may even sell her, if he chooses. Yet, even among them, the woman manages to exercise considerable influence. In general it is true that among savages the married woman, though subject to her husband's authority, often occupies a respected position in the family and the community. All this, however, does not mitigate the evil of inferior status which the woman occupied in ancient society. A happy lot often goes together with a status of subjection. Thousands of slaves in the South of the United States deplored their emancipation. They undoubtedly enjoyed greater security and were accorded much kindlier treatment than have fallen to the lot of the Negro since the Civil War has made him a free man. But, from the standpoint of human values, that can hardly serve as a reason for regarding slavery as ethical.

It is this confusion between lot and status which is responsible for the usual misunderstanding of the well-known chapter in the Book of Proverbs about "the woman of valor." That chapter is mistakenly regarded as placing the woman on a high pedestal. It does nothing of the kind. It is flattery paid by a parasitic husband to the hard-working wife who slaves for him. She works from early dawn to late night, buys and cultivates her fields, attends to all the needs of her family, dispenses alms, and renders service, and all for what? That her husband might have no lack of gain and spend his time with his cronies in the city gate, where they squat all day in idleness and smoke their narghiles.

Whatever the woman's lot may have been in past Jewish life, traditional Jewish law undoubtedly treated her as a lower type of human being than man. In Jewish law, the woman is on the same plane with minors, slaves, and people of unsound mind. Like them she is exempted from all observances which are intended for fixed times, with very few exceptions. She is exempt from such *mitzvot* as [reciting the] *sh'ma, tefillin* [phylacteries], *tzitzit* [fringes], *shofar,* and *sukkah.* She is not counted in a quorum necessary for public prayer, nor is she considered worthy of being included in the *mezumman** for the recital of the benedictions after a meal. If, as an expression of pious devotion, she should write a Torah scroll, it would be unfit for use in public worship. Together with minors and slaves, women are exempt from the study of the Torah. The father is under no obligation to teach his daughter Torah, nor is the mother expected to teach her son. She is permitted, not commanded, to study Torah, and that permission is extended only to the written, not to the oral Torah. It is a generally accepted principle in rabbinic literature that the reward for performing a duty which is optional is far below that for the performance of a duty which is obliga-

---

*When three or more males above the age of thirteen have eaten together, they join in the "Grace after Meals."—eds.

tory. Hence, the woman who does take advantage of the permission to study the written Torah must not expect any too great reward. The father who teaches his daughter Torah is regarded as though he taught her frivolity. Although this last statement was the opinion of Rabbi Eliezer and not that of Ben Azzai, the fact is that it reflects the prevailing attitude of our forebears.

It is not only in matters religious, however, that the woman is made to feel her inequality, but principally in matters juridical. The woman is not qualified to act as witness, to say nothing of her acting as judge. Exception is made in the case of a woman testifying in behalf of another whose right to remarry is in question. Maimonides, in quoting that law in his Code, finds it necessary to tell the reader not to be surprised at this concession. The reason her testimony is accepted is that the truth is bound to come out in the end anyhow. Even a slave's testimony would be accepted under those circumstances. Moreover, the woman holds an inferior status in the law of inheritance. The provision made for the sustenance and marrying of daughters at the expense of their father's estate was not derived from the principle of inheritance but was dictated by the fear of the social consequences of their being left without some means of support.

But it is in the marriage relationship chiefly where the woman's inferior status is fraught with tragic consequences to her. In traditional Jewish law, the marriage relationship is practically on the same plane as the relationship between master and slave. The man, in marrying the woman, acquires her or gains possession of her. The technical term in Jewish law is *kinyan*. The term *kiddushin* [which is derived from the word *kadosh*, holy] for the marriage act has nothing of the connotation of sacredness about it, all the fine preachments to the contrary notwithstanding. The fact that the husband must perform the threefold marital duties toward his wife in no way raises her status much above that of a menial. This is evident from the law which prescribes that every woman must perform for her husband the five following services: spin and weave, wash his hands and face, pour the wine, prepare the bed, and wait on him. These services are obligatory no matter how much wealth the woman brings to him at marriage. If she refuses, says Maimonides in his Code, she may be compelled by the use of the rod.

"The Sages have commanded," writes Maimonides, "that the husband should love and honor her more than himself and should not intimidate her unduly. He should speak gently with her; he should not be irascible or cranky. On the other hand, they have also commanded the woman to honor her husband implicitly. She should always stand in awe of him. She should do his bidding and consider him as though he were a prince or a king. She should comply with all his wishes and remove from his presence whatever annoys him." The homiletic statement that a woman's place is in the home, Maimonides formulated into law. According to him, the husband should prevent his wife from being seen too frequently outdoors. About once or twice a month is all that she should be permitted to leave her house. Maimonides declares that it is the husband's duty to be distrustful of the wife's fidelity though he advises the husband not to carry such an attitude too far.

According to Jewish law, whatever the wife earns or happens to find, as well as the income derived from possessions she brings to him at marriage, belongs to her husband. Even what she earns by working overtime belongs to her husband. If she dies during his lifetime, he alone can inherit from her. After his marriage, no promise to waive this right is binding upon him.

The woman experiences the worst effects of her status when she can no longer continue to live with her husband. It is then that his mastery asserts itself. He alone has the power of divorce. According to traditional law, he can divorce her arbitrarily without her consent or refuse to grant her a divorce, no matter how much she would welcome it. The reform instituted by Rabbenu Gershom, which necessitates her consent, has not been universally respected and can be circumvented easily, since the husband can threaten to desert his wife and thus deprive her of the right to remarry. On the other hand, the wife cannot divorce her husband under any circumstances. It is true that there are a number of specified conditions under which the Jewish court may compel the husband to divorce his wife. In the first place, those conditions are far from including the more personal reasons for incompatibility, and secondly, if the husband leaves the jurisdiction of the Jewish court, the woman is left without redress. Unfortunately our spiritual leaders, instead of taking steps to change the ancient law, try to explain it away. "While, in form, the husband executed the divorce," writes Louis M. Epstein,* "in essence Talmudic law recognizes the woman's right to divorce her husband, or to be more exact, to institute divorce action. And if her petition is granted, the court forces the husband to issue the bill of divorce." This statement is typical of the kind of apologetics which have all too long led us to evade the issue, instead of attacking it frontally.

Another instance of the ill-effects of the woman's inequality is apparent in the case of the childless widow whose deceased husband is survived by one or more brothers. The childless widow cannot remarry unless she obtains a release (*halitzah*) from her husband's brother. This situation can be, and all too often is, exploited by an unscrupulous brother-in-law to extort money. But even where extortion is not resorted to, unfortunate developments may hinder her remarrying, as when, for example, the deceased husband is survived by a brother who is only an

---

*Louis M. Epstein, *The Jewish Marriage Contract* (1927), p. 203.

infant. Under these circumstances, the woman has to wait thirteen years, until the infant becomes of age to grant a release, before she is permitted to remarry.

The purpose in calling attention to these laws is not to convey the impression that the status of the Jewish woman was worse than that of the woman in any other ancient civilization. The fact is that in many respects it was much better than that of the woman under Roman or Greek civilization. In pre-Christian Germanic law, the man could with impunity sell, give away, lend, and even kill his wife. In Christianity, St. Paul's teaching that it is the duty of the woman to be subservient to her husband has been regarded as authoritative. As late as the thirteenth century, we find that, in Germany, the husband was advised to chasten his wife only with a rod, as comported with the dignity of an honorable man. Toward the end of the sixteenth century, the Church was still discussing the question whether the woman was a human being in the full sense of the term.

There can be no question that the Jews possessed a more wholesome sex morality and a more adequate appreciation of the family institution than other peoples. This fact by itself was sufficient to mitigate the evils resulting from the inferior status of the woman. Nothing, however, can be gained by glib attempts to misrepresent what actually was, in the past, the recognized law. "The testimony of Jewish scholars, whose utterances have been so extensively cited," says an apologist,* "lends support to the conclusion that woman was not accorded by Jewish law a position essentially inferior to man." This is not true. The very statement by George Foot Moore quoted in proof of this generalization contradicts it. "It is interesting," says Moore, "to note that the tendency of courts and custom has been to protect the woman. The law could not be abrogated, but ways to minimize its ill effects as society changed were adopted." This is different from the statement that her position was not inferior to that of the man.

The important point to remember is that modern civilizations are gradually recognizing the need of granting woman complete equality with man. It cannot be long before the woman will enjoy all the rights that go with full-fledged personality. This fact is enough to constitute a challenge to us Jews. The question we must be prepared to answer is: What will Judaism do to abolish the woman's judicial, civic, and religious disabilities?

Already during the first decades of the era of Jewish Emancipation the Jewish woman became aware that she was accorded a more dignified status outside Jewish life. This explains why many talented Jewish women not only began to lose interest in Jewish life, but actually turned

*Emily Solis-Cohen, *Woman in Jewish Law and Life* (New York, 1932), p. 63.

against it. Women of the type of Henrietta Herz, Dorothy Mendelssohn, and Rachel Levin felt that it was too circumscribed. If we do not want our talented women to follow their example, we must find in Judaism a place for their powers. This cannot come about, unless all taint of inferiority will be removed from the status of the Jewish woman.

The Future of the American Jew, pp. 404–409.

10. Rejecting the Chosen People Idea

Despite the tendency in certain quarters to consider ideas as mere by-products of the interplay of blind social and economic forces and to regard reason as a mere rationalization of instinctive passions and desires, we Jews must insist on clear and forthright thought as indispensable. We must strive to overcome the inertia which keeps us chained to a thought-world entirely alien to the modern spirit. There is as much difference between our universe of discourse and that in which our fathers lived before the Emancipation, as between the modern mind-picture of the physical universe and the one which prevailed until Copernicus proved that the earth moves around the sun. Just as, in ancient times, men thought that the earth was the center of the universe, and that their own homes, being equidistant on all sides from the horizon, were the center of the earth, so our fathers, in premodern times, regarded the drama of human life as exhausting the whole meaning of creation, and the Jewish people as the hero in that drama, with all other nations merely the supporting cast.

The idea of Israel as the chosen people, must, therefore, be understood as belonging to a thought-world which we no longer inhabit. It fits in with a set of ideas that were congruous and rational enough in their day. But it can no longer help us to understand relations, or to orient ourselves to conditions, as they exist today. The very notion that a people can for all time be the elect of God implies an epic or dramatic conception of history, a history predetermined in form and aim. Nowadays for any people to call itself "chosen" is to be guilty of self-infatuation. It is paradoxical for the Jewish people to be collectively guilty of self-infatuation, when individually so many Jews are guilty of self-hate. The skeptical attitude of the average Jew toward the doctrine of the chosen people may be sensed in the Yiddish folk-rendering of the classic phrase "Thou hast chosen us from all peoples." That rendering is *"Vos hostu gevolt hobn fun di Yidn?"*—"What didst Thou want of the Jews?"

Emancipation has undermined the status of the Jews as a nation. Enlightenment or rationalism has undermined the status of Jews as a *kenesset* or an *ecclesia*. The traditional basis for the belief that Israel was God's chosen people was the assumption that the miraculous events recorded in the Torah concerning the Patriarchs and their descendants in Egypt represented factual truth. By far the most significant of these miraculous events was God's self-revelation to Israel on Mount Sinai. It was as unthinkable to question the truth of those events as to question the reality of one's own body. Under those circumstances, Jews could not possibly regard themselves as other than the most privileged of all peoples. Those circumstances, however, no longer obtain with the majority of modern-minded men and women. The modern-minded Jew cannot consider the miraculous events recorded in the Torah and in the rest of the Bible as other than legendary. He, therefore, cannot accept them as evidence of the traditional Jewish doctrine that Israel is God's chosen people. The attempt to supply other evidence is itself a departure from tradition. Such an attempt might be justified if at least the new evidence were convincing. But is it convincing?

Unable to accept literally the traditional version of the doctrine of the chosen people, the religious wing of the early *Maskilim* [or proponents of Enlightenment], the first Reformers, and the middle group who designated themselves as the Historical School reinterpreted that doctrine to mean one or all of the following propositions, which are set forth in Kaufmann Kohler's *Jewish Theology* (1918) as justifying the claim of the Jews to being a chosen people:

1. Jews possess hereditary traits which qualify them to be superior to the rest of the world in the realm of the religious and the ethical.

2. Their ancestors were the first to achieve those religious and ethical conceptions and ideals which will, in the end, become the common possession of mankind and help them to achieve salvation.

3. Jews possess the truest form of the religious and ethical ideals of mankind.

4. Jews are entrusted with the task of communicating those ideals to the rest of the world.

First, the proposition that Jews possess unusual hereditary traits which entitle them to be God's elect is based on a series of unproved generalizations concerning certain qualities as being characteristic only of Jews, and on biological assumptions concerning heredity which are entirely unwarranted. It is one thing for an ancient Sage to express his love for his people by describing them as unique in the possession of the traits of chastity, benevolence, and compassion. But it is quite another thing for a modern person seriously to assert that, because Jewish life has manifested these traits, Jews alone are inherently qualified to grasp and promulgate the truth of religion. We expect a greater regard for objective fact than is evidenced by such sweeping statements about hereditary Jewish traits.

If Jews were to adopt the foregoing reinterpretation of the doctrine of election, they would, by implication, assent to the most pernicious theory of racial heredity yet advanced to justify racial inequality and the right of a master race to dominate all the rest of mankind. The truth is that historical circumstances, as well as geographic environment and social institutions, are greater determinants of national traits than heredity. Moreover, to represent divine election merely as confirming naturally inherited traits is to identify it virtually with natural selection. It is but one step from such identification to the identification of God with the process by which the physically weak are weeded out. We know all too well from current experience how such a concept of God is only another name for the apotheosis of the will to power.

Secondly, for Jews to claim sole credit for having given mankind those religious and ethical concepts which hold out the promise of a better world smacks of arrogance. The Greek philosophers, the Stoics in the Roman period, the humanists of the Renaissance, and the rationalists of the eighteenth century have made highly significant contributions to spiritual and moral truth. The religious philosophies of the Hindus antedate all others, and are experiencing a remarkable revival in our day. Even if Jews were the first to enunciate the great moral and spiritual teachings, it would be immodest of them to boast about it. That would not make them better or superior to the rest of the world in any sense whatever. The first-born has no right to claim that he is better or more beloved than the other children. Special privileges no longer attach to primogeniture.

It is said that to express at this late date dislike of what sounds like pretension is merely to yield to "the conventions of Anglo-Saxon taste." Since when is humility a virtue prized by the Anglo-Saxon rather than the Jewish tradition? Our Torah praises Moses for his meekness. It records the prayer of Moses that he be blotted out of God's book, if only his people might enjoy God's grace. It tells of his refusing to be disturbed by the news that Eldad and Medad were prophesying in the camp and his exclaiming in response, "Would that all the Lord's people were prophets!" (Num. 11:29). Can we imagine Moses thanking God that He had not made him like the rest of Israel but had made him the chosen vehicle for conveying God's message to his spiritually inferior brethren?

Thirdly, for Jews to maintain that they possess the truest form of truth would be understandable if they still believed that the teachings of their religion are immutable and infallible. However, with the modern dynamic conception of Jewish belief and practice being accepted by those of light and leading among them, the only meaning such claim can have is that Jews generally have managed to advance a bit ahead of every new development of spiritual truth. No one, however, who knows how far behind the best thinkers of their day some of our greatest Jewish spiritual leaders have been at times can subscribe to this reinterpretation. Spinoza, who truly did forge ahead of his contemporaries, was excommunicated.

The very assumption of a predetermined and permanent superiority, no matter in what respect, does not lend itself to reinterpretation. Our purpose in reinterpreting traditional values should be to retain and emphasize those elements in them which are compatible with our own highest ethical standards. Among those ethical standards, to which any traditional value must necessarily conform if it is to continue functioning in our lives, is that conception of human worth and individual dignity which regards as immoral any classification of human beings into superior and inferior. This does not mean that we must shut our eyes to the fact that human beings are unequal in their gifts and attainments. What it means is that we should not assume *a priori* that a particular race, group, or people is endowed, by nature or by God, with any gift which entitles it to regard itself, *ipso facto*, as superior. By no kind of dialectics is it possible to remove the odium of comparison from any reinterpretation of an idea which makes invidious distinctions between one people and another.

Finally, the fourth proposition confuses the doctrine of Israel's *election*, as expressed in the overwhelming majority of biblical allusions which deal with Israel's relation to God, with the doctrine of Israel's *mission*, which is the subject of less than a dozen passages in the second part of Isaiah. There is not the slightest implication in the multitude of references to Israel as a chosen people that it is expected to fulfill the mission of making God known to the nations.

As for the few unmistakable allusions to the mission of Israel, the manner in which the mission is to be discharged has very little in common with what we usually associate with missionary activity, or even with exemplary conduct. The light which Israel is to be unto the nations is portrayed by the Prophet as radiating from Israel's brilliant career as a nation in its own land, dispensing justice and maintaining peace in the name of its God. The establishment of the ideal Kingdom of God in the Land of Israel is what the Prophet hoped would lead the rulers of the world and their nations to acknowledge the God of Israel as sovereign (Isa. 2:2–4; Mic. 4:1–3).

There are many apologists for the doctrine who cling to the assertion of divine election, but compromise on its implied claims. They even confess to an awareness of the distaste which the assertion of divine election provokes in many modern-minded people. They seem to understand and even to admit that "extolling God for 'not having made us like other peoples' is grating." Nevertheless, they maintain that, properly interpreted, the doctrine still remains valid and should not be discarded.

Though the belief expresses a certain national pride, or a sense of national privilege, "it carries with it also a sense of consecration and responsibility." No one can question the fact that the belief of being divinely elect has long been associated in the Jewish mind with consecration and responsibility. However, we cannot ignore the other implications of that belief, especially those which are often sharply stressed, as in the *Alenu* and the *Havdalah* prayers. In the latter, the invidiousness of the distinction between Israel and the nations is emphasized by being compared with the distinction between light and darkness. It is that invidiousness which is highly objectionable and should be eliminated from our religion.

There are some who argue that the chosen-people idea is not out of harmony with our modern universe of discourse. They reject the supernaturalist version of the revelation of the Torah on which tradition bases belief in the election of the Jewish people. For them that belief rests rather on the evidence of history that at least the Western world is indebted to Israel for its fundamental religious ideas and institutions, as are also those peoples and individuals in the East who have been converted to Christianity or to Mohammedanism. This fact seems to them to indicate that the Jews are committed by their history to the purpose of converting the world to belief in the unity of God, with all the ethical implications of that belief. "Those who today believe in the election of Israel," writes Dr. Bernard J. Bamberger, "are those who regard Judaism as a universal religion, as *the* universal religion, with a message for all men."*

Though none would dispute the spiritual indebtedness of the Western world to Israel, the inference from that indebtedness that Israel was chosen by God to be His messenger to mankind is nevertheless a grating *non sequitur*. When a delegation of Chicago ministers visited Abraham Lincoln to urge the abolition of slavery, one of their number told him that it was God's will that he free the slaves. To which Lincoln replied: "If it is, as you say, a message from your Divine Master, is it not odd that the only channel He could send it by was the roundabout route by way of that awful wicked city of Chicago?" The Jewish people may not be awfully wicked, but one may still ask: "If God has a message for all mankind, is it not odd that the only channel through which He could send it should be the roundabout route via Zion?" To say that many of the most significant religious ideas of the Western world are of Jewish origin does not answer that question. For all we know, Lincoln might have gotten some very good suggestions from Chicagoans. But Lincoln

*Bernard J. Bamberger, "Are the Jews a Chosen People?" in *Reconstructionist* 11:16.

rebuked the arrogance which assumed that he himself had less access to divine guidance than the Chicago ministers, and his rebuke was justified. The assumption by an individual or group that it is the chosen and indispensable vehicle of God's grace to others is arrogance, no matter how euphemistically one phrases the claim to being chosen.

Moreover, if Israel's having influenced the world religiously in the past proves that the Israelites are God's chosen people, what inference are we to draw from the fact that Israel is today *not* influencing the religions of other peoples, but rather being influenced by them? Who can read the works of such men as Sholem Asch and Franz Werfel, to name two of the most distinguished Jewish writers, by way of example, without perceiving the profound influence that Christianity has had on many Jews? Does that prove that the Christian Church has been chosen and Israel rejected? Would we not resent such an inference? It has been well said that "Ideals remain real only when one continues to realize them." If that is true, then the doctrine of the chosen people, whatever validity it may have had in the past, is today utterly unreal.

The Future of the American Jew, pp. 211–19.

11. The Vocation of the Jewish People

Jewish survival depends entirely upon our achieving a moral realism which, on the one hand, will wean us away from the futile compensatory mechanism of imagined superiority and, on the other, will enable us to find the basis for intrinsic worth of Jewish life in the daily round of contemporary living. The only kind of Jewish survival that would constitute a creative adjustment to the world as it is today is one in which the two elements of our tradition would continue to function, namely, Jewish peoplehood and Jewish religion. But what peoplehood and religion represent today must be stated in different terms from those which were current in the past.

The essence of Jewish peoplehood can no longer be identified either with political unity or with religious uniformity. Political unity will have to be confined to Jews living in their own homeland. Uniformity will have to be replaced by a fundamentally common spirit. Likewise, the essence of Jewish religion can no longer be made to depend upon the factual truth of the supernatural events which are recorded in the Torah and on the presumable conclusion that they prove the election of Israel. Jewish religion will have to be based on what objective study has shown to be the function of a religion in the life of a people. That function is so to inspire and direct the energies of a people as to help its individual men and women to achieve their destiny as human beings, or to make the best use of their lives.

The place previously occupied in the Jewish consciousness by the doctrine of election will have to be filled by the doctrine of vocation. The whole course of Jewish history has been so dominated by religious motivation that Jews cannot be true to themselves, as a people, without stressing the religious character of Judaism. Jewish religion would have Jewish civilization make for the enhancement not only of Jewish life but of the life of mankind and thus help to render manifest the cosmic purpose of human life. Jewish religion expects the Jew to live the civilization of his people in a spirit of commitment and dedication. To live thus is to live with a sense of vocation or calling, without involving ourselves in any of the invidious distinctions implied in the doctrine of election, and yet to fulfill the legitimate spiritual wants which that doctrine sought to satisfy.

It is generally assumed that the idea of "vocation" is a Christian, particularly a Protestant, idea. As a matter of fact, that idea is no less Jewish than it is Christian. Thus we read in the Talmud: "A familiar saying in the mouth of the Sages of Yavneh was this: 'I (who study Torah) am a creature (of God); my work is in the city, his in the field; I rise early to my work, he rises early to his. Just as he cannot excel in my work, so I cannot excel in his.' Perhaps thou wilt say: I do much and he does little (for the Torah). But we have learned, 'He who offers much and he who offers little are equal, provided that each direct his heart to heaven' " (Berakhot 17a). Judaism should extend the significance of vocation to include nations as well as individuals. No nation is chosen, or elected, or superior to any other, but every nation should discover its vocation or calling, as a source of religious experience, and as a medium of salvation to those who share its life.

It has been suggested that for an individual to experience the presence of God in his life as a divine calling, he has to meet the following conditions: He has to be engaged in doing needful work, work that calls into use his best powers and encourages their development, and, finally, that enables him to contribute his share to the welfare of mankind. If Jews wish to feel a sense of vocation, all they need to do is to apply themselves to those tasks which would be most likely to meet for the Jewish people the foregoing three requirements.

If we Jews would accept that, or some similar program, as our vocation, we would not need to have our morale bolstered up by such a spiritual anachronism as extolling God "for not having made us like the other nations." Instead, we would find our calling as a people so absorbing, so satisfying, and so thrilling that we would have every reason in the world to thank God for having manifested His love to us, as He does to all men and nations who have found their true vocation, and for having rendered us worthy to be identified with His great and holy name.

It may be argued that not all vocations are of equal importance to society. The role which the President of the United States has to fill is far more crucial than that of some janitor of a "Five and Ten." It is not belittling either Mr. Jones or his vocation, if we regard the President's task as infinitely more crucial.

Granted. And granted, too, that Israel's role in the history of mankind is also a crucial one. That would still not justify inclusion in the liturgy of prayers praising God for making Israel's role more crucial. What would Americans have said if, on his accession to office, a President would pray, "I thank Thee, Lord, that Thou hast not made my vocation that of the janitor John Jones, but hast chosen me from among all Americans to lead the nation and mankind to peace"? A truly religious soul never reacts in that way to the fact of his being given a crucially important vocation. He is rather humbled by that fact and disposed to question his own qualifications, accepting as a grave and burdensome responsibility the tasks to which, in loyalty, he feels dedicated.

All these considerations make it clear that, whether we apply rational or pragmatic criteria, the traditional formula concerning Israel's divine election is objectionable. Rationally, it has no place in the realm of discourse from which belief in the supernatural revelation of religious truth has been excluded. Pragmatically, it is objectionable, as barring the way to peace and harmony among religions, and as making for self-righteousness and cant. All the genuine values that once attached themselves to this belief can be maintained by substituting for it the doctrine of "vocation." What more important calling could a people have than to promulgate, by its way of life, the truth of the universal presence of God in all religions, and the universal obligation of every man to use his traditional *sancta* for glorifying not merely his own people or church, but mankind as a whole?

The Future of the American Jew, pp. 228–30.

12. The Meaning of Religious Tolerance

From the psychological point of view, organized religions are integral to particular civilizations and cannot be understood apart from them. They always express the collective personality of a particular society. They are as nontransferable and incommunicable as is individual personality. What they mean to their own members and what they mean to others can never be the same, any more than I can mean to you what I mean to myself. Their differences are not merely quantitative variations in the degree of truth that each contains in its tradition, but each is a unique manifestation of the divine, just as each human being is such a unique manifestation. The whole concept of superiority, therefore, falls to the ground. It is meaningless, because there is no common standard of measurement and because the meaning of religion is involved in its relationship to all other phases of the civilization which has produced it and cannot be abstracted from this context without damage. We can no more separate a religion from a civilization than we can separate a whirl-pool from a river.

When we speak of our religion as the truth, we forget that "truth" is an abstract noun derived from the adjective "true," and that what may be true for certain people in certain situations is not necessarily true for others in other situations. Thus, if a devout Christian tells me that he finds in the adoration of the personality of Jesus all the inspiration that he requires for living a life that satisfies his spiritual needs, I cannot as a Jew say this attitude is not true, although I am so conditioned that I could not possibly find it true in my own experience. On the other hand, if I say to him that I can find in the Torah literature of the Jew the reflection of an attitude toward life more satisfying than any I could find in the New Testament or elsewhere, I, too, am speaking the truth, and my religion is as true as his. But, since his religion is not a part of the Jewish civilization that has conditioned my thinking and feeling, and my religion is not a part of the Christian civilization which has conditioned his, comparison between the two is meaningless. Each exists in its own right and has no need to justify itself to its own members or to others by any assertion of superiority.

Judaism in Transition, pp. 281–82.

IX

Jewish Education

1. The Aims and Objectives of Jewish Education

The aim of Jewish education may be defined thus: to develop in the rising generation a desire and a capacity (1) to participate in Jewish life, (2) to understand and appreciate the Hebrew language and literature, (3) to put into practice Jewish patterns of conduct both ethical and religious, (4) to appreciate and adopt Jewish sanctions and aspirations, and (5) to stimulate artistic creativity in the expression of Jewish values. It is almost superfluous to add that all of these objectives presuppose a type of Jewish life which is completely integrated into a progressive and dynamic American life. In view of the high ethical and spiritual implications of the Jewish civilization, an American Jewish child who has the advantage of a Jewish training of the proper kind has his sympathies broadened, his tastes refined, and his striving socialized.

No whit less important than reckoning with the perpetuation of Jewish life and culture is to reckon with the well-being and growth of the individual child. The Jewish educative process must start with the actual experiences of the child as he lives them in the present and lead him constantly so to reorganize and reinterpret his experiences that he comes to identify his own good with the good of society in general and do so in a manner that will indicate growth in mind and character. To achieve this end the child must be given increasing control over his own experience so that he will himself be able to shape and direct it toward aims freely and intelligently chosen. Restated from the standpoint of the child, the following should be the objectives of Jewish education:

1. *To give insight* into the meaning of spiritual values and their application to different types of experience, religious, moral, social, and political; Jewish life as a developing civilization; the spiritual character of that civilization; the relationships of Jewish to other civilizations in the past; the course that Jewish life must henceforth take in the different countries of the world, and especially in America.

2. *To foster an attitude* of respect toward human personality as such; tolerance toward other groups, races, faiths; intellectual honesty, open-

mindedness, and responsibility; social- and international-mindedness; loyalty to and participation in Jewish life in this and other countries.

3. *To train appreciation* of individual and group creativity in the values of civilization; Jewish creativity in religion, ethics, language and literature, mores, laws and folkways, and the arts.

4. *To inculcate ideals* of justice and kindness in our social and economic relationships; peace and tolerance; a just, thriving, creative Jewish homeland in Palestine, a creative Jewish life in America.

5. *To condition habits* of reflective thinking; purposive experiencing; using leisure to develop personality; affiliation with the synagogue or *bet am;* celebrating Jewish Sabbaths, festivals, etc.; observing Jewish customs and ceremonies; reading Hebrew books and periodicals, Anglo-Jewish books, Anglo-Jewish press, Yiddish press, Bible, Talmud, etc.; contributing to the upbuilding of Palestine; helping to support social-service and educational institutions; attending Hebrew and Anglo-Jewish theaters, concerts, etc.; patronizing Jewish artistic endeavors; buying Jewish books, works of art, etc.

6. *To impart knowledge* of the Hebrew language; Jewish history; the outstanding selections from the Bible, the Talmud, and subsequent Jewish writings; history and meaning of Jewish customs and ceremonials, religious beliefs, ethical ideals; current Jewish problems, institutions, endeavors; Jewish arts and crafts, home furnishing, cooking, etc.

Judaism as a Civilization, pp. 482, 486–87.

2. Linking Culture and Ethics

The right of the Jews to lead a normal and unhampered religious life must clearly be recognized as the only measure that is consistent with true liberty. The religious schools which they establish will be able to develop in the child a Jewish consciousness, understanding by that term his becoming so integrated with the House of Israel that he conceives for it a loyalty which gives meaning to his life and value to his personality. Of course, the Jewish consciousness which the religious school should foster in our youth must be brought into practical relation with the social environment in which we Jews find ourselves. Unless, by means of it, our children will make better citizens of the state, unless it will fit them spiritually for the larger world in which they must live, unless it will give them worth and character, it cannot endure. But the important fact to note about the true function of the Jewish religious school is that it must aim at results like these by means of the loyalty and inspiration it fosters in the child through having his life bound up intimately with the life of the Jewish people. A Jewish school falls short of its purpose if it does not cultivate in the child that power of social imagination whereby he might be enabled to live over in his own soul the most fruitful and ennobling experiences of Israel, past, present, and future.

With a deeper insight into the social significance of religious education, the function of the school should be something else than that of storytelling. Whatever moral and spiritual influence it wants to exert upon the life of the child, it must do so by making the child feel himself a part of a social environment that expects him to live up to its ideals. Adjustment to environment and not to abstract principles should be the aim of any elementary training, religious or secular. Right conduct is the product of a well-organized social imagination. According to this principle the task that devolves upon the Jewish religious school is to cultivate in the child a sense of warm intimacy with the Jewish people, with its life and its institutions, to create within him a sense of exaltation in those experiences of his people which have constituted for the human race the very footprints of God, and to implant within him a high ambition to contribute his share toward the perpetuation and enrichment of its spirit.

"The Function of the Jewish School," in
The Jewish Teacher 1:1 (Jan. 1916), pp. 11–12.

3. The Training of Character

If religious education is to be effective in character training, as we today understand good character, it must make radical changes in its content and method. Instead, for example, of discouraging the questioning of traditional beliefs and teachings, it should encourage the honest expression of doubt and the critical evaluation of the group culture, past and present. Loyalty to the group must be taught as residing not in the acceptance of traditional beliefs and practices, but in devotion to the common ethical purposes of the group. Education should foster that kind of group unity which respects differences. It should teach the pupil to appreciate the standpoint of others, without necessarily abandoning his own. It should value truth above dogma and righteousness above conformity.

Moreover, in addition to helping the individual to think independently and honestly about his ethical relations, it should give him practice in ethical conduct. This can be done only by putting him in a position of social responsibility. That is one of the great advantages which camps afford. When Jewish children live together, work together, and play together in a juvenile community in which they are made to feel themselves part of the historic Jewish people, they get to know what Judaism, as a way of life, really means. They have to hold up their end of responsibility for common projects and are judged by their "peers," children of their own group, on their personal relations to their fellows and to the group as a whole.

With a little more thought, similar situations of personal responsibility in initiating and carrying through group projects can be created in the religious school. In this way it would train the child's character, by guiding him in the self-directed pursuit of ethical goals.

Questions Jews Ask, pp. 359–60.

4. Jewish Spiritual Values

It is possible to indicate the difference which a genuine and active belief in God can, and frequently does, make in people's lives. It is to that difference that any instruction which is intended to render the Bible significant in our lives must be related. That difference expresses itself, among other things, as: holiness, humility, gratitude, and faith.

The teacher's task consists, accordingly, in utilizing the biblical content to imbue the pupil with the spirit of holiness, humility, gratitude, and faith. He could not very well carry out that task efficiently without communicating to the pupil a vivid sense of the reality of God. In what follows we shall attempt to give some examples of how these spiritual attitudes are the very soul of biblical teaching, and how they are integrally related to what the name of God has always meant to those whose religion is more than skin deep:

1. Holiness as a state of mind, or spiritual attitude, is awareness of being related or dedicated to that which renders life significant and saves it from frustration. Whatever, therefore, is related or dedicated to God is holy, in that it calls forth that awareness. Together with the awareness of the reality of the Jewish people, the Bible emphasizes awareness of being dedicated to God, as the state of mind which that people is expected to foster. . . .

2. The humility which has God as its point of reference and which should be utilized to give vivid reality to the God-experience is a far deeper and more inclusive character trait than is humility toward our fellow men. Unlike the attitude of holiness which is illustrated in various

situations through narrative, laws, and exhortations, the humility which man must experience as part of his awareness of God is seldom the direct theme in any of the biblical subject matter. We learn how important is this type of humility through the repeated emphasis in the Bible on the sin of pride. That sin is illustrated in the Bible as frequently as is the virtue of holiness. The sin of pride consists in that arrogant self-sufficiency which leads man to deny his dependence on, and submission to, a higher power than himself. He who is guilty of that sinful attitude expresses it by defying all law. He plays the god, and he is a law unto himself. For a time he may pursue his evil course and achieve his vaulting ambition, but in the end his power is broken, and he is thrust from his high pedestal. . . .

3. Gratitude, which is the appreciation of the blessings we enjoy, has its point of reference in God. That means that we are aware of being indebted for all those blessings to the entire life process. Whatever in religion has to do with worship is intended to express and to foster the feeling of gratitude. The entire sacrificial cult, the motivating purpose of which was to convey awareness of communion with God, fostered gratitude. All songs in praise of God that are contained in the Pentateuch, the historical works, and the prophetic writings, and almost the entire collection of Psalms, are evocations of pious gratitude. Of all the states of mind which come near to experiencing vividly the reality of God, a feeling of gratitude with its overtones of serenity and dependence on a transcendent source of power is perhaps the one which most approximates that experience. Since gratitude is so closely associated with worship, everything in the Bible that has anything to do with worship, whether in the form of narrative or of legal and ethical prescription, should be carefully studied.

4. Finally, we have the attitude of faith, which is a direct affirmation of a transcendent power that impels and sustains man in his striving for self-fulfillment. The occasions for the exercise of faith are those in which circumstances seem to negate the existence of such a power. When misfortune befalls us, when we suffer in our own persons or witness the sufferings of others, life tends to become meaningless, and we are apt to fall into despair. That is the time for the evocation of the courage to carry on. To the extent that we succeed in evoking such courage within ourselves, we have a direct experience of the transcendent power which we identify as God.

The Future of the American Jew,
pp. 459–61.

5. The Value of Jewish Tradition

The value of Jewish tradition to the modern Jew is not dependent on its assertion of superiority over other traditions. Those traditions should not be considered its rivals, since they cannot function for the Jewish people, and the Jewish tradition cannot function for other peoples or fellowships. Jewish tradition should be transmitted as a cluster of human values existing in their own right. Anyone who keeps a diary would not like to see it destroyed, though it may not compare in literary and historical worth with that of Samuel Pepys. He values it because it is his own, because it reveals his own individuality. Whether good, bad, or indifferent from a moralistic standpoint, the Jewish tradition—with its heroisms and events, its laws, struggles, tragedies, defeats, dreams, and yearnings—constitutes the actual experiences of the people. Jews should want their children to weave these experiences into their own world, to appropriate them as an integral part of their own consciousness. Once communicated in this spirit, the Jewish tradition would fill a deep psychological need. The most obscure peoples find the drama of their history, the courage of their own heroes, and the inspiration of their poets enough reason for cherishing their tradition. Apart from its relevance for Jews, the intrinsic worth of the Jewish tradition offers abundant reason for its cultivation.

The modern interpretation of the Jewish tradition should focus on universal loyalty and responsibility as a means of developing ethical character. "So be loyal to your own cause," wrote the philosopher Josiah Royce, "as thereby to serve the advancement of the cause of universal loyalty." Just as loyalty to one's own home expresses itself in protecting family life from corrupting and disintegrating influences, so loyalty to one's fellowship and civilization should encompass all institutions that further human civilization and promote human welfare.

The Religion of Ethical Nationhood, pp. 182–83.

6. Jewish Cultural Values

The main purpose of all Jewish schools is to stress those values of the Jewish heritage which serve as a bond of unity and brotherhood. These values may be classified as follows: (1) the three-thousand-year history of Israel, (2) Eretz Yisrael as its common and continuous aspiration, (3) a vast literature recording Jewish spiritual life, (4) Hebrew as the original and resurrected vernacular of the Jewish people, (5) the Messianic goal of a warless world united by the will to social justice and ethical nationhood, (6) faith in the spiritual or transcendental meaning of human life, and (7) the Jewish calendar with its Sabbaths and festivals as dedicated to the activation of all the values inherent in the six foregoing items.

The Religion of Ethical Nationhood, p. 174.

7. Hebrew and Yiddish in Jewish Education

Outside the State of Israel the Hebrew language should not be the sole means of imparting a Jewish education. On the other hand, no Jewish education can be deemed adequate which fails to impart facility in the understanding of the Bible, prayer book, and other Jewish literature in the original, and which does not enable the individual Jew to maintain contact through the Hebrew language with the inner life of Israel.

Our life as Jews is unthinkable without our cultural and spiritual heritage. The Yiddish language and culture are an important part of that heritage. If we will not retain them as part of that heritage, we will eliminate from it a most valuable segment. In that literature and culture are preserved the following values produced by centuries of Jewish life in Eastern Europe: (1) the folk spirit resulting from the use of Yiddish as the vernacular of the principal centers of Jewish life during that period, (2) the wealth of the pietistic Hassidic lore that has inspired so much of modern Jewish poetry, fiction, and drama, even beyond Hassidic circles, (3) much of the social idealism manifest in the literature of Jewish socialism, trade unionism, and Labor Zionism. Jewry can ill afford to consign the culture embodying these values to oblivion.

Questions Jews Ask, pp. 357, 376.

8. Jewish Peoplehood and the Teaching of the Bible

Since the basic purpose in teaching the Bible is to give the pupil an awareness of the reality of his people, it is necessary to reinstate the primacy of the Pentateuch in the Bible-study curriculum. The three aspects of the Pentateuch that should be reckoned with from the standpoint of that purpose are: the narrative, the legal, and the one which stresses the significance of Eretz Yisrael. Two of the aspects, the legal and the one that has to do with Eretz Yisrael, should be utilized as a means of developing in the mind of the pupil a sense of the reality of Israel; and the narrative, a consciousness of his destiny as a member of the Jewish people.

A way must be found whereby both of these objectives—consciousness of Israel's reality and of her destiny—can be liberated from the acceptance of the narratives as historic fact, or of the laws as supernaturally revealed and therefore as eternally binding. This liberation should be effected while the pupil is undergoing his Jewish training. Otherwise, he is likely to repudiate the facts of Israel's reality and destiny, as soon as he discovers that the narratives are largely nonhistorical or fictional, and that Israel's ancient laws could not have originated as described in the Torah.

Yet neither the reality nor the destiny of the Jewish people can have any meaning unless they are associated with Eretz Yisrael. So large does that Land loom in the Torah that it is, indeed, appropriate to regard the Torah as a legal document, whereby the God of history has deeded the Land to the Jewish people. It would not at all be amiss if the entire Torah material that bears on Eretz Yisrael were interpreted from the point of view of Israel's relation to its Land. Surely in our day, when the reclamation of Eretz Yisrael as our national home is the one purpose that spells the revival of the spirit of Israel, teaching the Torah from that point of view would knit that Land with contemporary Jewish life.

The historical books of the Bible should be taught as carrying forward the main themes of the Torah, which deal with Israel's destiny. There the conditional character of Israel's hold on the Land is especially highlighted. Attention should be focused on Israel's long struggle for survival against external and internal forces of destruction. Only at the end of that struggle did Israel achieve that profound understanding of what God expected of man which rendered its religion and way of life of universal significance. The prophetic books reveal the inner conflict.

They define the main issues about which that conflict raged: idolatry, lack of confidence in the God of Israel, exploitation of the weak by the strong, and self-indulgence. From the standpoint of national self-awareness, not the Prophetic books as such, but the fact of their having been canonized and given the status akin to that of Torah, has set the standard for national self-scrutiny and self-criticism. That standard is of universal import. It will have to be adopted ultimately not only by individuals but by nations, if mankind is to survive.

The Future of the American Jew,
pp. 458–59.

9. Jewish Education and the Arts

Art possesses the magic whereby it is able to express the seemingly ineffable and to communicate what is ordinarily regarded as incommunicable. The distinctive and individual, when expressed in artistic form, acquire universal significance. In their art, peoples reveal themselves to each other at their best and learn to respect and reverence each other.

The Future of the American Jew,
p. 357.

. . . The element of artistic creativity cannot be left completely to spontaneous achievement. It is a plant that must be carefully and tenderly nurtured. Far from being recognized as an indispensable element of Jewish education and living, a few schools grant it the tolerance extended to an extracurricular fad. The very significance of Judaism as a civilization would be lost if artistic creativity in the expression of Jewish values were treated as something secondary in the program of American Jewish life. To give to this objective the place that it deserves in a program of Jewish education, it is necessary to extend the field of artistic creativity. Not only religious but other human values, not only those derived from the past of the Jewish people but those drawn from contemporary Jewish life, must find expression in art forms. Furthermore, the gamut of artistic expression must be widened to include poetry and song, music, drama, dance, painting, sculpture, and architecture. When Judaism has acquired the potency of multiple appeal, not even extreme diversity of belief will threaten its integrity.

Judaism as a Civilization, p. 486.

10. Emphasizing Adolescent and Adult Education

Lacking the motivating environment of an integrated Jewish community, and lacking educational material of intrinsic interest to the Jewish child, the concerned Jewish adult orbits in a vicious circle. In the absence of relevant Jewish educational material the Jewish curriculum is devoid of interest. The children's lack of interest "justifies" parents in withdrawing their children from schools and in withholding their moral and financial support. Their negativism discourages the creation of new educational material and techniques which might have served the present needs of the Jewish child. At what point can this vicious circle be broken?

Obviously not at the point of the child's participation in the educational process. The social situation is beyond his comprehension and the content of the Jewish instruction does not appeal to his present interest. Adults, however, are in a position to appreciate the new need for Jewish education. Common sense indicates that the emphasis be put on the education of the Jewish adolescent and adult rather than on that of the child. Not that Jews should discontinue their present effort to maintain and conduct schools for Jewish children. But they must recognize that no serious advance can be made in the Jewish education of their children unless and until they inaugurate an extensive movement for the Jewish education of the adult.

A well-planned and vigorously executed program for adult Jewish education would break through the vicious circle described above. Adults would want their children as well as themselves to possess the sort of Jewish knowledge that would make for self-respect. They would therefore encourage their children to take advantage of the best available facilities for Jewish instruction and would interest themselves in the effort to improve the quality of that instruction. Finally, they would experience the need for themselves and for their children of a functioning, status-conferring Jewish community, so that Jewish education would not be a thing detached and remote from all other vital interests but would be integrated into the communal life of the Jewish people. And, having experienced this need, they would seek to satisfy it by helping to effect the necessary reorganization of American Jewry.

The Religion of Ethical Nationhood,
pp. 186–87.

11. Study in the Synagogue

Throughout the written and oral tradition the study of Torah is regarded as of far higher spiritual rank than worship and prayer. Whereas worship and prayer are directed toward the attainment of peace of mind, the study of Torah can set in motion all the moral influences that go into the molding of character and the shaping of society. Hence Torah study is stressed again and again as directly commanded by God; the duty of prayer is treated, on the whole, as a rabbinic ordinance.

The Religion of Ethical Nationhood, p. 175.

12. Jewish Education and the Survival of Humanity

We have to approach the problem of education as a problem in engaging in an art, a problem which Aristotle sought to solve by indicating as a necessary procedure the awareness of the purpose, the resources, the form, and the implementation. This procedure, if followed in Jewish education on all levels, would call for the following:

1. The purpose of Jewish education is far more complex than it could ever have been in the past. There are so many more serious crises in human life than was the case in the past that we dare not ignore. Erich Fromm writes the following in the Epilogue to his book *The Crisis of Psychoanalysis**: "The real crisis today is one that is unique in human history: it is the crisis of life itself. . . . We are confronted with the probability that within fifty years—and perhaps much sooner—life on this earth will have ceased to exist; not only because of nuclear, chemical and biological warfare (and every year technological progress makes weapons that are more devastating) but also because of technological 'progress' making the soil, the water and the air unfit for the sustenance of life."

It should therefore be the primary purpose of all education, that is to be more than a means to making a living, to get people to want only what they absolutely need physically, socially, and spiritually, neither more nor less. All greeds and superflous needs are bound to lead to the dread fulfillment of Fromm's warning. The subject of ecology and its implications must be an integral part of Jewish education. Together with

*(New York, 1970), p. 159.

it, the elimination of war, ethical nationhood, and individual freedom must constitute the aim of Jewish education on all levels from the most elementary to the most advanced, as a lifelong process.

2. The resources on which to draw the subject matter of Jewish education should be the study of Judaism as an evolving religious civilization in the light of the most advanced thinking and practical experience, insofar as they throw light on the immediate present. The dominant spirit in the use of the resources should not be that of historicism but that of pragmatism.

3. The form of Jewish education should not be that of faith but of wisdom, in conformity with the demands of reason and intelligence. The identification of religion with unquestioning faith in tradition is unwarranted as far as the Bible is concerned. The term *emunah* in the Bible does not mean faith; it means faithfulness, and it is attributed to God.

4. The implementation calls for social engineering in the interests of social democracy and religious pluralism.

"Jewish Consciousness," in *Reconstructionist* 38:6 (Sept. 22, 1972), p. 11.

X

Worship and Ritual

1. Worship and Righteousness

No notion has been so prevalent and so misleading as the one that the mere act of worship has a spiritualizing effect on the human being.* Before worship can have any genuine spiritual influence upon us, before it can reveal God to us, we must qualify ourselves by an arduous discipline in deeds of self-control, honesty, courage, and kindness. When we come to the synagogue, after having tried our utmost to deal fairly with our neighbor, to suppress our evil impulses, and have made an effort to meet our responsibilities as human beings, then worship can yield its measure of spiritual strength and give us a sense of inward peace. Communion with God is a reward of holy and righteous living.

Does this imply that the synagogue has no place for sinners, or that those who have gone astray morally have no right to participate in religious worship? There must be no shrinking from the logical consequences of the principle here laid down. The only condition on which that principle would allow a sinner to enter the synagogue, in the hope of benefiting by its services, would be that he repent in his heart before he takes the name of God upon his lips. "For transgressions that are between man and his fellow the Day of Atonement effects atonement only if he has appeased his fellow" (Mishnah Yoma 8:9).

The Meaning of God in Modern Jewish Religion, p. 262.

*Kaplan distinguishes between worship and prayer. Worship is a public or private act of commitment to God. Prayer is a form of worship that includes petitioning God. Other forms of worship include association with others, thanksgiving, praise, aspiration, confession of sins, and statements of commitment (see Henry N. Wieman, *Encyclopedia of Religion*, ed. V. Ferm [New York, 1945], pp. 602, 830–31). In Judaism, study is a primary form of worship (see Nathan Isaacs, "Study as a Form of Worship," in *Great Jewish Ideas*, ed. A. E. Millgram [Washington, D.C., 1964].—eds.

2. God and Prayer

Modern scientific and philosophic thought regards all reality not as something static but as energy in action. When we say that God is Process, we select, out of the infinite processes in the universe, that complex of forces and relationships which makes for the highest fulfillment of man as a human being and identify it by the term "God." In exactly the same way, we select, among all the forces and relationships that enter into the life of the individual, those which make for his highest fulfillment and identify them by the term "person." God and person are thus correlative terms, the meaning of each being relative to and dependent on that of the other, like parent and child, teacher and pupil, citizen and state. God is the Process by which the universe produces persons, and persons are the processes by which God is manifest in the individual. Neither term has meaning without the other. So to conceive of God is to regard Him as personal, in the sense that He manifests Himself in our personality, in every effort of ours to live up to our responsibilities as human beings. At the same time He is not a person, since He cannot be compared with a human person, any more than the human person can be compared with one of his momentary acts.

In the light of this understanding of the correlation of the human person and God we can understand the function of prayer. Prayer aims at deriving, from the Process that constitutes God, the power that would strengthen the forces and relationships by which we fulfill ourselves as persons. We cannot help being aware of our dependence on the Process which we identify as God, namely, on all that makes for goodness, truth, and beauty in the world, for our success in achieving a mature, effective, and well-adjusted personality, and we naturally articulate that need in prayer.

But in what terms can we address God? We cannot do so in terms of scientific or philosophical abstractions, like process or energy, any more than we ordinarily use such terms in thinking about ourselves. Nobody would think of saying: Those processes in relation to my body which make for my personality are hungry. One would say quite simply: I am hungry. Similarly one would not address one's neighbor in terms of all the processes which make him the person that he is; one would address him simply as *you*. For similar reasons, we address God in prayer as *Thou*.

Questions Jews Ask, pp. 103–104.

3. Praying and Thinking

To say "I believe in praying" sounds to me as absurd as to say "I believe in thinking." The question whether prayer is effective is only a special form of the question whether thought is effective. And just as we make use of the best thoughts of others in order to channel our own thinking into the surest and most beneficial effectiveness, so should we make use of the most noble and sincere prayers of others to channel our own prayers into a life of the greatest nobility and sincerity. This is why I like to pray and why I frequently resort to the prayers of those who could speak their mind in the language of prayer. Unfortunately, we Jews have limited prayer to the deadening routine of reciting the few meager passages which go to make up our official prayer book.

From an unpublished manuscript.

4. Public Worship

There is a tendency nowadays to treat all religious ritual, and especially prayer, as the concern of the individual. This tendency should not be taken too seriously. Worship is too deeply rooted in the social nature of the human being to be easily discarded. So long as a people will have holidays and festivals to commemorate the events in its career, to recall its victories and to confirm its strivings, the institution of public worship will remain. Public worship is a means of giving a people that collective consciousness which unifies its life and integrates all of its individuals into an organized totality. Though its form may change, it is certain that before long it will be reinstated in all normally functioning civilizations. . . .

Public worship is far from incompatible with the modern outlook on life. It has far more exalted uses than that of setting in motion forces that might fulfill one's private desires. Those uses go together with a conception of God which precludes the magical consequences of offering praises addressed to Him. Likewise, the authoritarian aspect of ritualism is no longer tenable, for it can no longer be believed that, in order to be effective, worship must take on the form laid down by authority, and that the least departure from it is heresy and rebellion. A certain element of uniformity is necessary, because it is the very purpose of worship to arouse a feeling of common consciousness. But to make uniformity an indispensable requisite of worship negates spontaneous self-expression. Least of all should stereotyped liturgical formulas which have ceased to call forth any emotional response usurp the place of new formulations of spiritual yearnings.

Public worship meets two essential needs of human nature: the need for selecting and retaining those aspects of reality that make life significant, and the need for identifying oneself with a community which aspires to make life significant. Public worship meets this twofold need, because it affirms this meaning of life and the primacy of its moral and spiritual values, and because it gives reality, purpose, and self-consciousness to the collective spirit of a people. The usual objection to the traditional liturgy is that it abounds in endless praises of the Deity. But even that objection can easily be overruled. Only a philistine literalism can miss the poetic beauty and majesty of the traditional type of hymnologies. Primitive man, no doubt, resorted to praising his deity as a means of eliciting favors from him. But in the higher civilizations, when the pious sang praises to God they gave utterance to the ineffable delight they derived from communion with Him. The modern equivalent of that experience is a glimpse into life's unity, creativity, and worthwhileness. To articulate that experience in the midst of a worshipping throng is a spiritual necessity of the normal man. He needs it as a means of affirming the meaning of life and of renewing his spirit.

Judaism as a Civilization, pp. 346–47.

5. The Significance and Abuse of Ritual

The participation in a common ritual helps to cement the we-feeling of the group. Having lost significance as a means of forcing spirits or gods to do the will of human beings, rituals that may have been magical in origin acquire symbolic significance. A talisman designed to keep evil spirits from attacking one's person or one's home becomes a symbol like *tefillin* or *mezuzah*, expressive of consecration of the individual or the home to the service of God and His law of righteousness. All the arts, all the cultural media by which men communicate ideas and emotions, depend on symbols. Religion cannot dispense with them. And those symbols that require action are particularly effective, because they involve simultaneously so many of our senses and emotional responses.

There is, however, an ever-present danger of abusing ritual. An unenlightened use of ritual may lead to superstitious belief in its magical efficacy, as when people read Psalms as a means of healing the sick. But a more dangerous abuse, perhaps, comes from its very power as a symbol. A ritual may be associated symbolically with false values. The ritual of burning an effigy of Haman on Purim, which is practiced in some countries on that occasion, could be a source of evil if used to arouse hostility to the gentile community. Moreover, even when associated symbolically with valid ideals, rituals can be abused by the tendency to assume that the performance of the symbolic rite is itself a virtuous act, whether it impels one to serve the ethical ideal it symbolizes or not. The meticulous observance of ritual is always a temptation to self-righteousness.

Nevertheless, as with religion in general, so with its ritual aspect, it would be folly to dispense with it because of its possible abuse. Human culture cannot dispense with symbolic forms for conveying spiritual values. Though those forms are insufficient to achieve spiritual results, they are indispensable. They need, however, to be rendered relevant to the highest needs of those who make use of them.

Questions Jews Ask, pp. 226–27.

6. Religious Observances Are Folkways

It is of vital importance to have a significant term besides *mitzvot* for those customs which have been referred to as "commandments pertaining to the relations between man and God." A term is needed that would indicate a different approach from that with which we come to positive law or jurisprudence. The term "folkways" meets that requirement. In the traditional literature, the term *minhag* denotes a ritual practice for which there does not seem to be any basis in the authoritative writings, and which by the mere reason of its being in vogue exercises a claim on conformity. It is never applied to the customary practices which are prescribed in the Torah, because it lacks the connotation of being as imperative as those practices. It therefore comes nearest to expressing what is conveyed by the term "folkways."

If we were henceforth to designate all "commandments pertaining to the relations between man and God" as *minhagim* or "folkways," we would accomplish a twofold purpose. First, we would convey the thought that they should not be dealt with in a legalistic spirit, a spirit that often gives rise to quibbling and pettifogging. They should be dealt with as the very stuff of Jewish life, which should be experienced with spontaneity and joy, and which can be modified as circumstances require. Secondly, we would convey the implication that not only should as many "commandments" or folkways as possible be retained and developed, but that Jewish life should be stimulated to evolve new and additional folkways. Folkways are the social practices by which a people externalizes the reality of its collective being. The more alive the collective being, the more it abounds in affirmative folkways. Of negative folkways, Judaism has plenty, but of affirmative folkways calculated to render Jewish life interesting and contentful, it has at present far too few. . . .

It is evident, of course, that not all Jewish folkways are equally important. Evaluation will be simpler if we classify them as religious or cultural, according to the interest about which they center. In the religious folkways, the main purpose is to emphasize the cosmic relationship implied in religious experience. Institutions like the Sabbath, the festivals, and worship are intended for that purpose. The cultural folkways are the customs which emphasize the common life and interests of the group. The Hebrew language, the Jewish calendar, the wearing of the *talit* at services belong to cultural folkways, insofar as they express the folk spirit. In actual life both cultural and religious elements are interwoven in the same folkway. Religious folkways are those in which the religious mood predominates; cultural folkways, those in which the folk spirit is emphasized.

Judaism as a Civilization, pp. 431–33.

7. Reconstructing Ritual

If the changes proposed for Jewish ritual are intended to give it vitality and freshness, there is no need to fear that such changes will ever lead to a radical break with tradition. Reconstructionism does not wish to give a *coup de grâce* to important rites which, in our day, tend to be neglected. On the contrary, it wishes so to modify them that they would be likely to be revived. To reconstruct means to reaffirm, reachieve, reestablish.

One or two illustrations may serve to make this clear. It has been proposed, for example, that Jews permit themselves to ride to the synagogue to attend services on Sabbaths and holidays. Rigid conformity with the traditional rule against riding would keep many of them from attending public worship on those days. Only by relaxing the rule prohibiting riding is it possible to reinstate public worship on the Sabbath and holidays as a hallowing influence on Jewish life.

Or take the proposal to call up women to the reading of the Torah. That is an innovation, and hence a departure from traditional practice. It is justified, however, because it adds to the significance of the Torah reading. As long as women had no share in public life, it was no derogation of their status as persons to exclude them from taking part in the reading from the Torah. But in our day, to exclude women from such participation is to treat them as inferior. Here, too, the departure from traditional usage prevents us from committing what is now regarded as a moral wrong, but also tends to strengthen rather than weaken a traditional value, that of reverence for the Torah.

Thus, this rule can be set down by which the danger expressed in the question may be avoided: Only such ritual changes as tend to render religion both ethical and spiritual should be made.

On the whole, we live in an age in which we often have to fall back upon a principle recognized in Jewish tradition itself. Our Sages interpret the verse *"Et la-asot la-adonai heferu torateka"* in a way which may be paraphrased as follows: There are times when, for the sake of God, it is necessary to suspend His Law.

Where deviation is necessary because of conditions beyond one's control, two considerations should be kept in mind: One, an effort should be made to find a way of retaining at least some part or element of the traditional practice; the other, some new practice should be instituted that might serve as a substitute for the one that cannot be observed.

Questions Jews Ask, pp. 236–37, 239.

8. Democracy and Ritual Observance

The attempt to apply the principle of democracy to the area of ritual practice is without precedent, and beset by many difficulties. We must expect much fumbling, before we succeed in beating out a path. On the one hand, as modern-minded men, we cannot conceive of ritual practice as having a theurgic or magical efficacy. At best it can only be a form of religious self-expression. It is unthinkable to resort to sanctions to compel conformity with ritual practices that do not honestly express one's own personal convictions. On the other hand, to treat ritual as if it were a private affair is to fail to appreciate its very significance. A salute to the flag would be meaningless if everyone designed his own flag. Ritual arises from and is directed toward awareness of social unity and communion. Is there a middle course between, on the one hand, unjust and futile effort to impose ritual uniformity and, on the other, complete anarchy, ranging from an excess to the complete abolition of ritual?

The fact that ritual answers an intrinsic need of human nature leads us to believe that it ought to be possible to come upon such a course. Even Jews who are far removed from the traditional way of life are not averse, on principle, to ritual. They would welcome ritual that is endowed with beauty and significance. However, to try to impose on all Jews a regimen of uniform religious observance is out of the question. It should, nevertheless, be possible for like-minded groups to define their own minimum standards of ritual observance, which they would agree to accept, and conformity to which would thus be self-imposed.

The *modus vivendi* here envisaged certainly would not result in that uniformity of Jewish ritual observance which prevailed in the past. But it would do away with the present amorphous and anarchic character of Jewish life. It would make Jews realize that to belong to a Jewish religious organization of any kind imposed more important obligations than merely paying one's dues. It would tend to foster religious self-expression without which religion is starved from inanition.

The Future of the American Jew, p. 398.

9. The Symbolic Significance of Ritual

The chances of retrieving Jewish ritual practices are greater if we learn to approach them from a socio-psychological, instead of a theological, standpoint. Viewed empirically, religious symbols are objects displayed, or actions performed, as a means of evoking helpful attitudes, ideas, and values pertaining to God. Symbols are inherently a means of communication. If they are religious in character, they act as a means of communication concerning states of mind pertaining to God which are regarded as helpful by a number of people. Those people, by virtue of their common approval of what those symbols mean, constitute a religious fellowship or community. Symbols, therefore, perform for them the additional function of articulating their collective mind or soul. Such is the collective mind of a people, a church, or a religious fellowship. And, finally, all relationship to God is assumed by those who wish to abide in it to be essential to their salvation, or fulfillment, as human beings. The religious symbol, therefore, by making them aware of that relationship, functions normally as a means to their salvation. Thus the three realities to which religious symbolism points are: divinity, community, and salvation.

God, not merely as a metaphysical being, but as the object of worship and prayer, is the power that makes for salvation of man through the community which organizes its entire social order around the purpose of man's salvation. In the symbolic significance of a ritual practice, God should be conceived as the source of all moral and spiritual values. That makes an important difference in the way those values are regarded. Detached from their source in God, and from their function as means to salvation of man, all moral and spiritual values are apt to be, in the final analysis, the expression of the will of the ruling classes and their servitors. Related, however, to God as the power that makes for man's salvation, they constitute groping attempts of human nature to approximate those ways of human living which are certain to perpetuate the human race and to help it fulfill its highest potentialities.

The normal procedure, therefore, in the process of reinterpretation of the traditional realities referred to by the religious symbolism is to note, in the first place, what the religious community does for the individual. It provides him with a social heritage of language, habits of thought and action, and a sense of values—all of which contributes to the process of his humanization. For that alone the human being should feel indebted to the community into which he is born and whose ways of life shape his character. He should behold in that community the agency through which God, as the power that impels man to become fully human, actually manifests Himself. That attitude toward one's community is perfectly natural and understandable and can well be fostered without resort to the belief in its divine chosenness, or in its being a *corpus mysticum*. Given, therefore, a genuine feeling of oneness with a community, whatever supernatural notions have been associated with its place in mankind can easily be reinterpreted into terms which lift that sense of oneness to the level of moral and spiritual responsibility.

Secondly, a far more difficult and more urgent problem is that of knowing to what end we should direct and foster the inner drive to fulfill ourselves as human beings. Religious ritual, freed of supernaturalism and interpreted symbolically, can help to keep alive that drive. Even if it cannot advance the knowledge of what that self-fulfillment consists in and how it can be achieved, it can at least intensify the desire to attain that knowledge. That is how we can come to know God in the way it is possible for man to know Him—as the power that makes for salvation.

Judaism Without Supernaturalism, pp. 49–50, 52–53.

10. Ritual Prohibitions and Ritual Acts

A necessary corollary of the criterion that Jewish ritual must enable the individual to experience Jewish life as worthwhile is a reversal of the relative importance which, in the popular mind and in the traditional codes, attaches to prohibitions and affirmative injunctions. From the legalistic viewpoint, the violation of a prohibition is a sin of commission, while the neglect of an affirmative injunction is only a sin of omission, and consequently less reprehensible. But the moment we get away from the legalistic approach and treat Jewish observances as religious folkways designed to insure the enhancement of the value of Jewish life, the affirmative injunctions assume the more important role. For, in the realm of ritual usage, *desisting* from a specific act seldom carries with it the feeling of satisfaction that comes with the actual *performance* of a ceremony. The formidable list of traditional *don'ts* has served to alienate from Jewish religious life a large number of Jews who could not see in what way they, or anybody else, benefited by these prohibitions.

A word of caution against discarding prohibitions is, however, in order. A guide for usage should attempt to preserve, with respect to any practice, the atmosphere—often indescribable in words—with which it has been traditionally surrounded. Frequently the atmosphere that has been part of a traditional custom can be preserved, or revived, only by giving heed to the prohibitions traditionally associated with its observance. The most beautiful Seder service would, for most Jews, be irremediably spoiled by a failure to reckon with the prohibition of leavened food on the Passover. Even the individual who personally finds no value in a prohibition that is widely observed by Jews should conform to it in public, wherever his failure to conform would be offensive to the religious sensibilities of a large number of Jews.

The Future of the American Jew, pp. 423–24.

11. Ritual and Legalism

Ever since modern science and technology have enabled man to achieve progressive control of the forces of nature, he has been veering away from traditional religion. The average person has almost no understanding of the fundamental difference between religion and magic. Hence he seldom treats religious symbols as symbols which are intended to direct his thinking and to bring his emotions and his will under control, to help him achieve his full humanity.

The so-called conflict between religion and science is actually a conflict only between religion, conceived as theurgy,* and science, conceived as a method based upon experience and experiment. There can be no quarrel between religion conceived as a source of values and meanings, and science, as a description of objective reality. It will take a long time, however, before those who have become alienated from religion will come to realize that their alienation is based on misunderstanding. In the meantime, as far as Jewish religion is concerned, the resistance to it on the part of Jewish secularists will continue as long as the religious practices in it will savor of their original theurgy, by reason of the halakic or legalistic spirit in which they are still observed—or not observed—by both the Orthodox and the Conservative groups. That legalistic spirit is avowedly in keeping with the belief in the supernatural origin of those religious practices. If, however, they are to be retained—and there is great spiritual value to their retention—they have to be dissociated from all residues of theurgy and supernaturalism.

Judaism Without Supernaturalism, pp. 48–49.

12. The Dietary Laws as Folkways

In the next stage of the Jewish civilization, the distinction between animals that divide the hoof and chew the cud and those that do not, or between *kosher* and *trefa*, or between fish which have scales and fins and those which have not, will not be observed as dietary "laws" commanded by God, or as mystic symbols of what man must do to qualify himself to enter into communion with God. But these distinctions should be maintained as traditional folkways which add a specifically Jewish atmosphere to the home. Such observances should not be regarded as intended to help one earn salvation in the here or in the hereafter, nor to produce a marked effect upon one's character. Maimonides' argument that the forbidden foods have a physiological effect which is prejudicial to the mind or spirit is scarcely worth considering. Equally untenable are the so-called hygienic reasons which are ad-

*For an explanation of theurgy, see p. 70.

vanced in defense of the dietary laws. Such arguments are not only contradicted by experience; they have the additional disadvantage of counteracting the spiritual effect which those practices were wont to exercise. By giving them a utilitarian purpose, their function as a means of turning the mind to God is bound to be obscured. Such justifications are gratuitous from the ancient point of view and unacceptable from the modern point of view. But if Jews are not to exaggerate the importance of the dietary practices, neither should they underestimate the effect those practices can have in making a home Jewish. If the dietary folkways are capable of striking a spiritual note in the home atmosphere, Jews cannot afford to disregard them.

Once these practices lose their character as laws and become folkways, Jews will be able to exercise better judgment as to the manner of their observance. There need not be the feeling of sin in case of occasional remissness, nor the self-complacency which results from scrupulous observance. Moreover, since the main purpose of these practices is to add Jewish atmosphere to the home, there is no reason for suffering the inconvenience and self-deprivation which result from a rigid adherence outside the home. From the standpoint urged here it would not be amiss for a Jew to eat freely in the house of a Gentile and to refrain from eating *trefa* in the house of a fellow Jew. By this means, dietary practices would no longer foster the aloofness of the Jew, which, however justified in the past, is totally unwarranted in our day. As for the fear that social intercourse between Jews and Gentiles may lead to the disintegration of Judaism, the reply is obvious: if Judaism is inherently so weak that it requires the artificial barriers of social aloofness fostered by dietary laws for its maintenance, the very need for maintaining it is gone. It is true that increased social contact with the Gentiles will prove a challenge to Judaism's inherent strength, but that challenge cannot be met by a defensive retreat.

Judaism as a Civilization, pp. 440–41.

13. New Meaning for the Rite of Yom Kippur

The *purpose* of Jewish existence is to be a people in the image of God. The *meaning* of Jewish existence is to foster in ourselves as Jews, and to awaken in the rest of the world, a sense of moral responsibility in action. . . .

We act irresponsibly, in the first place, when we do not belong to some spiritual group that exists for the purpose of fostering moral and religious values. And we act irresponsibly when we do not persuade such groups to give primacy to the task of arousing the conscience of mankind to the imperative need of putting an end to all international and civil wars. . . .

The threat of global war and total annihilation of the human race is no longer a mere nightmare. It is an ominous reality at our very doorsteps, from which the most ingeniously contrived air-raid shelters will not save us.

The moral responsibility of forestalling that dread possibility devolves on all of us individually and collectively. We dare not escape that responsibility by taking refuge in the claim of individual powerlessness. . . .

We Jews have a Day of Atonement for fasting and prayer, for the forgiveness of sins and the resolve to improve morally and spiritually. If we are to take ourselves and our religion seriously, we should observe the Day of Atonement primarily as a day of protest against the waging of war, and of appeal to all other spiritual bodies also to dedicate a day for fasting and prayer for like protest. Then will those in the seats of authority among the nations of the world be impelled to give heed, and use their power, to render the earth safe for mankind.

The Purpose and Meaning of Jewish Existence, pp. 318–19.

14. Observations

Religious worship, like everything else in life, should be three-dimensional: It should entertain, instruct, and inspire; and it should maintain the proper balance among these three functions.

A true prayer is one the very utterance of which is partly its own fulfillment.

Thanksgiving implies appreciation of the benefits we enjoy.

It is an excellent antidote to the propensity to make unwarranted or neurotic demands upon the world.

Hence the devout recital of *Hamotzi* and *Birkat Hamazon* is good therapy.

In Jewish religion all authoritative prayers, whether of petition or for forgiveness, are bifocal, with God and Israel as their foci.

From this human standpoint they are we-centered and not I-centered.

They fulfill a spiritual function by infusing the ego with God-and-we-awareness.

There can be no question that good medical care is more likely to cure the sick than prayer.

Can we then dispense with prayer when one is sick?

No. We need prayer to remind us that good medical care is the way to obtain God's help for the sick, and to thank God for showing us that way.

But why bring God in? Why is not good medical care enough?

Because it cannot solve the problem of what a person should do with his health.

People whose religion begins and ends with worship and ritual practices are like soldiers forever maneuvering but never getting into action.

Not So Random Thoughts, pp. 204–10.

XI

Reconstructionist Judaism

1. Jews in Need of a
   New Approach

The differences between the world from which the Jew has emerged and that in which he now lives are so sharp and manifold that they almost baffle description. The Jew shared with the rest of the ancient world the universal belief that salvation meant the attainment of bliss in the hereafter as a result of having lived according to the will of God in this life. Consequently he was free from all self-questioning and doubt. He was sure of his privileged position in the scheme of divine redemption. But all such conceptions together with the reasoning upon which they are based are alien to the modern world. In the short time that the Jew has lived in the modern world, these conceptions have become almost unintelligible to him. He thus finds himself deprived of what had been the principal justification for his loyalty to Judaism.

The only adequate substitute for other-worldly salvation which formerly motivated the loyalty of the Jew to his social heritage is a creative Judaism. This means that Judaism must be so reconstructed as to elicit from him the best that is in him. It must be so conditioned as to enlarge his mental horizon, deepen his sympathies, imbue him with hope, and enable him to leave the world better for his having lived in it.

The Jews who are likely to assume the task of thus conditioning Judaism are they who cannot do without it and yet cannot do with it as it is. As a rule, they are those with whom Judaism is a habit. Coming from intensely Jewish homes, they have had Judaism bred into their very bones. Jewish modes of self-expression and association with fellow Jews are as indispensable to them as the very air they breathe. They would like to observe Jewish rites, but so many of those rites appear to them ill adapted to the conditions and needs of our day. They are affiliated with congregations, but they are bored by the services. They take an active part in Jewish organization, but are revolted by the futility, waste, and lack of sincerity. They cannot help feeling that many an opportunity for reaching into the soul of the Jew, improving his character, and eliciting his powers for good is thoughtlessly neglected. Anachronisms abound where cogency and relevance could prevail. Much that might be rendered beautiful and appealing is allowed to remain stale and flat. The teachers and scholars, instead of following the example of Moses, the teacher of all teachers, who went down to the people, ensconce themselves in the ivory tower of abstract learning.

Others, again, cannot do without Judaism because it is a nostalgia with them. It haunts them and gives them no rest. But as it is constituted at present, it offers no field for the expression of their innermost selves. Such Jews may never have seen anything Jewish in their homes, but some atavistic yearning or childhood memory has awakened within them. Now they want to become reunited with their people. If they are of a romantic temperament they may idealize their people's failings. Otherwise they may be repelled by the petrifaction of many of its lauded traditions and institutions and the aimlessness of most of its collective activities.

Judaism as a Civilization, pp. 511–12.

2. Judaism in Need of a New Approach

It is a far cry from the simple Judaism of the past to the intricate program called for by Judaism as a civilization. Accustomed to think of Judaism as a form of truth, whether divinely revealed or humanly achieved, we conclude that complexity is a sign of artificiality. It is therefore necessary to recall that Judaism as a civilization is not a form of truth, but a form of life. The higher the organism is in the scale of life, the more intricate and complex its structure. To survive, Judaism must become complex. It must absorb some of the very forces and tendencies that threaten it, effect new syntheses on higher levels of national life, and enter upon a career which will set up new goals in the evolution of civilizations.

In sum, those who look to Judaism in its present state to provide them with a ready-made scheme of salvation in this world, or in the next, are bound to be disappointed. The Jew will have to save Judaism before Judaism will be in a position to save the Jew. The Jew is so circumstanced now that the only way he can achieve salvation is by replenishing the "wells of salvation" which have run dry. He must rediscover, reinterpret, and reconstruct the civilization of his people. To do that he must be willing to live up to a program that spells nothing less than a maximum of Jewishness. True to his historic tradition he should throw in his lot with all movements to further social justice and universal peace, and bring to bear upon them the inspiration of his history and religion. Such a program calls for a degree of honesty that abhors all forms of self-delusion, for a temper that reaches out to new consummations, for the type of courage that is not deterred by uncharted regions. If this be the spirit in which Jews will accept from the past the mandate to keep Judaism alive, and from the present the guidance dictated by its profoundest needs, the contemporary crisis in Jewish life will prove to be the birth-throes of a new era in the civilization of the Jewish people.

Judaism as a Civilization, pp. 521–22.

3. Making Jewish Religion Acceptable

The difference between Jewish religion and all others does not consist so much in the uniqueness of its conception of God, as in the uniqueness of its *sancta*.* Loyalty to Judaism need, therefore, involve no pretensions to religious superiority. Jewish religion differs from the other religions not in being unlike them, for they too, have *sancta* that help them to salvation or self-fulfillment, but in being *other*, in having *sancta* that are the products of Jewish historic experience and not of the historic experience of other branches of human society. We are faithful to Jewish religion, not because we have chosen it as the best of all religions, but because it is ours, the only religion we have, an inseparable part of our collective personality as a people. If some of us find that religion unacceptable in the form in which it has come down from the past, there is nothing but inertia to stop us from making it acceptable.

The Future of the American Jew, p. 47.

4. Reconstructionism and Jewish Tradition

The main concern of the Jewish Reconstructionist movement is to transform Jewish life from a liability, which so many Jews think it is, into an asset, which so few Jews conceive it possible to be. Far too many Jews

*The events, places, objects, institutions, and heroes to which a religion ascribes superlative importance or sanctity.—eds.

who have never heard of [Heinrich] Heine or read anything by him have adopted as their life slogan what he intended only as a gibe when he said that Judaism was not a religion but a misfortune. Were that description of Judaism true, then Judaism would be bankrupt. And if Judaism were bankrupt, then the Jew would be a man without a tradition. That is even worse than being a man without a country. For a man without a country is a man without a present, from the standpoint of citizenship, while a man without a tradition is a man without a past, without a future, and without a present, from the standpoint of being fully human.

What Reconstructionism seeks to do with the Jewish tradition is often misunderstood. Its effort to have that tradition function as an asset rather than as a burden is misinterpreted by those who use the Reconstructionist movement as an alibi for dropping traditional observances, not because they call for extraordinary sacrifice, but because they emphasize one's Jewishness. Actually, our movement is intended so to invigorate the Jew that he would not feel weighed down by his responsibilities as a human being, as a citizen, and as a Jew. Moreover, it wants to render being a Jew as natural as breathing. Such invigoration and naturalness will come to the Jew if he can be made to experience the worthwhileness of Jewish life, if through that life he can be enhanced as a human person, and if all whose lives touch his can be enhanced in equal measure.

For a tradition, or a way of life, to be an asset, instead of a burden or a liability, it has to do two things: one, impel us to be and do our best, and two, imbue us with sufficient courage to endure the worst that may befall us. Until about a century and a half ago, no Jew doubted for one moment that his tradition and the Jewish way of life could do just these two things for him. Since then, that assumption has been challenged. The entire world outlook of modern man—and most Jews insist on being among the first to adopt everything modern—has led to their questioning the authenticity of the tradition and of the historical basis of its teachings about God, man, and the world. In addition, the traditional way of life was predicated on the self-segregated and isolationist status of the Jewish community. That status has become absolutely untenable in the modern world which demands free intercourse and exchange of ideas and experiences, as indispensable to intellectual and moral growth as well as to the general peace.

Judaism Without Supernaturalism, pp. 207–208.

5. The Reconstructionist Understanding of Judaism

If we are to interweave our own historic way of life with the life which we must share with our neighbors, we have to rethink our beliefs, reorganize our institutions, and develop new means of self-expression as Jews. Since our problem is to keep alive that which differentiates us Jews as a group from the rest of the world, it is of the utmost importance to have a definition that corresponds with fact. It is certainly not true to fact that religion, or a particular set of beliefs about God, with practices related to these beliefs, is all that distinguishes the Jews as a group from non-Jews. If Judaism is to mean that which unites Jews into an identifiable and distinct group, then it is a religious civilization. As such, Judaism is the ensemble of the following organically interrelated elements of culture: a feeling of belonging to a historic and indivisible people, rootage in a common land, a continuing history, a living language and literature, and common mores, laws, and arts, with religion as the integrating and soul-giving factor of all those elements.

The peoplehood, the culture, and the religion of the Jews are one and inseparable. Their mutual relationship may be compared to that which exists among the three dimensions of the physical body. They correspond to the three concepts referred to in the popular dictum: Israel, the Torah, and the Holy One, blessed be He, are one (cf. *Zohar* 5:73b). In this statement, "Israel" represents peoplehood; "Torah," or Israel's way of life, represents culture; and "the Holy One" represents religion. The purpose in pronouncing them one is to stress the fact that none of the three terms can even be understood except in relation to the other two. Jewish religion, Jewish peoplehood, and Jewish culture are all aspects of the same reality, and each is meaningless apart from its relation to the totality of Jewish life.

The Future of the American Jew, pp. 35–36.

6. Reconstructionism and Reason

It is not true that Reconstructionism is based on reason, in the sense that Reconstructionism ignores the substance of human life, which consists of sensate experience, will, and emotion. To claim that Reconstructionism fails to reckon with all or any of these nonrational aspects of human life is certainly not warranted. The function of reason is to help us organize our life, which is full of conflicts and tensions. A normal life calls for both rest and exercise, society and solitude, self-assertion and self-control, realism and idealism, competition and cooperation. To resolve these conflicts by assigning the proper place to each of the many contradictory responses to vital human needs, reason is necessary. It, alone, can indicate how we can fit each of them into a unitary pattern of living that does justice to all of them.

Reconstructionism, therefore, though not based on reason, attempts to make the best possible use of reason in bringing order and meaning into Jewish life. We depend on reason to help us adjust the needs of Jews as individuals to their need for perpetuating Jewish life, to reconcile the natural right of Jews to differ from one another in theology and ritual with the need for their working together for common aims, to harmonize the legitimate claims of the American community on the American Jew with the claims of world Jewry and its historical homeland, Eretz Yisrael. Without recourse to reason to resolve these conflicts and many others like them, Jewish life is bound to deteriorate, and eventually to be lost. That is why Reconstructionism regards the maximum use of reason as indispensable to the survival of Jewry and of Jewish religion.

Surely, the fact that reason is "applicable to any religion" does not detract from its importance for Jewish religion. On the contrary, since reason is needed to bring order into the life of every individual and every group, we are the more justified in relying on it to bring order into our personal and communal life as Jews. When we consult a physician about our health, do we not act on the assumption that, since the science of medicine can cure others, it can similarly bring us healing? By the same logic, if reason can help other religions to survive, we should be all the more confident that it can help Jewish religion to do so. . . .

A misunderstanding of what we should expect of a religion assumes that the worth of a religion depends on its revealing some truths about God and man which no other religion does. On the basis of that assumption, it would be irreligious for Judaism to submit to the dictates of universal reason. But that assumption misconceives the role of religion in any human society. That role is to enable its adherents to live the good life. Since reason is undoubtedly essential in enabling us to live the good life, we Jews should use it to help us lead a good Jewish life. In that sense, Reconstructionism regards reason as indispensable in interpreting and applying Jewish religion.

Questions Jews Ask, pp. 453–54.

7. Reconstructionism and Change

The criterion which is to determine whether a suggested change is beneficial or detrimental to Judaism is the extent to which it helps Judaism to retain its continuity, its individuality, and its organic character.

The continuity of Judaism is maintained so long as the knowledge of Israel's past functions as an integral part of the Jew's personal memory, and is accompanied by some visible form or action symbolic of that fact. An organism has been defined as "an object which develops and maintains a unified pattern of response to changing situations." Unless, therefore, we can insure some degree of continuity between the past and the future of Jewish life by means of "a unified pattern of response to changing situations," the very notion of the Jewish people as a social organism is absurd.

The individuality of Judaism is maintained so long as the newly instituted custom, sanction, idea, or ideal helps to keep alive the element of otherness in the Jewish civilization. Not separatism must henceforth be the principle of living as a Jew, but otherness. Separatism is the antithesis of cooperation and results in an ingrown and clannish remoteness which leads to cultural and spiritual stagnation. Otherness thrives best when accompanied by active cooperation and interaction with neighboring cultures and civilizations, and achieves an individuality which is of universal significance.

The organic character is maintained so long as all the elements that constitute the civilization play a role in the life of the Jew. Any attempt to live or transmit only certain elements in Judaism to the neglect of others is bound to end in failure, since in Judaism as a civilization the normal functioning of each element is bound up with and conditioned by the normal functioning of every other. Even though it may not be possible in the Diaspora to foster each element to its full extent, there is a minimum below which it must not be allowed to fall, lest all the other elements of the civilization be jeopardized.

Judaism as a Civilization, pp. 514–15.

8. Historical Consciousness and Historical Conscience

What do we mean when we speak of "unconscious evolution"? We do not mean that those who participated in making the adjustment of Jewish tradition to the changing conditions of life were acting automatically without any conscious purpose in what they were doing. Our Sages were not automata. They were intelligent human beings, using their wits in solving the problems that confronted them. When, for example, they first interpreted the biblical law "an eye for an eye" as referring to money damages, they could not have been unaware that they were instituting a change in the legal practice of their day. The very fact that they discussed the matter is evidence of their awareness. To call that change "unconscious," in the sense that it did not involve a conscious choice between alternatives, is absurd.

What is meant by "unconscious evolution" is that those who proposed the change in practice believed that they were not amending the law, but giving a correct interpretation of its original intent. They assumed that somehow, in the course of time, the law had come to be interpreted wrongly, and they were restoring its true meaning. They could believe that to be true because they lacked the historic sense. The development of a historical perspective is a very recent phenomenon. Had the rabbis of the Talmud possessed it, they would have realized the radical difference between their own ideas of justice and those of an earlier age. This lack of historical consciousness is all that can be correctly referred to when we say that, in the past, the evolution of Jewish law was unconscious.

Nowadays, however, we have not only a historical consciousness but also a historical conscience. That inevitably prevents us from arbitrarily reading into an ancient tradition whatever we happen to think true or just. When, therefore, we find ourselves without corroboration, or precedent, in tradition for what we regard as true or just, we must seek to give effect to it, even though that involves a deliberate departure from traditional norms. To refuse to do so would be to turn our back on truth and justice. To do so is what we mean by "conscious" change.

For example, there can be no question that, in traditional Jewish law and ritual, women did not enjoy equal status with men, in respect to marriage and divorce, inheritance, the right to give evidence in court, etc. Since we cannot honestly assume that the laws as formulated in the traditional codes meant women to enjoy that equality, we must, if we believe in the equality of the sexes, make the necessary changes in law and custom as a conscious and deliberate amendment to earlier standards. This is an example of a planned reconstruction of Jewish law and Jewish life.

Questions Jews Ask, pp. 435–37.

9. Reconstructionism and Deliberate Planning

The quality and quantity of life that spell Judaism must be rediscovered and reemphasized. It must be recognized as nothing less than a civilization. It must figure in the consciousness of the Jew as the *tout ensemble* of all that is included in a civilization, the social framework of national unity centering in a particular land, a continuing history, a living language and literature, religious folkways, mores, laws, and art. . . .

For Judaism to become creative once again, it must assimilate the best in contemporary civilizations. In the past this process of assimilating cultural elements from the environment was carried on unconsciously. Henceforth that process will have to be carried on in deliberate and planned fashion. Therein Judaism will, no doubt, have to depart from its own tradition. But conscious and purposeful planning is coming to be part of the very life process of society. No civilization, culture, economy, or religion that is content to drift aimlessly has the slightest chance of surviving. It is in the spirit, therefore, of adopting the best in other civilizations and cooperating with them, and not in the spirit of yielding to their superior force or prestige, that Judaism should enter upon what will constitute a fourth stage in its development.

Judaism as a Civilization, pp. 513–14.

10. Jewish Renewal and Jewish Unity

We [Jews] must now renew ourselves by spelling out, in terms of contemporary social and economic needs, the purpose to which we have been dedicated from our very beginnings as a people. . . . We should accept that the substance of divinity is the process of cosmic interdependence which is implied in the doctrine of God's oneness. God functions as the power that makes for the fulfillment of human life through man's sense of moral responsibility. This is the only reliable source of authentic justice verifiable by everyday experience.

The Jewish concept of authentic justice deprecates the political state which is based on "rugged individualism," with its corollary of international irresponsibility, manifest as either isolationism or imperialism. It advocates the . . . state which attempts to synthesize individualism and collectivism with international and intranational responsibility. Such a . . . welfare state is founded on the cosmic law of universal interdependence, whereby every human being can fulfill his highest potentialities. . . .

Renewal, in [the Reconstructionist approach to] Jewish ecumenism, means a reunification enabling Jews to experience the living reality of the Jewish people as an organic, vitally functioning fellowship. This would happen despite the variety of the nations among which Jews are dispersed and into which they are often culturally integrated. Jewish ecumenism spells coexistence of all Jewish groups. It is only the Orthodox who are likely to refuse to "coexist." But the Jewish people can manage to exist without them, if need be, as it managed to exist without the Sadducees and, later, without the Karaites.

"Reconstructionism Is Ecumenical," in *The Jewish Spectator* (Feb. 1965), pp. 13–14.

11. A Movement to Revitalize Judaism

Reconstructionism is a movement to revitalize Judaism. It does to Judaism what Copernicus did to astronomy: it shifts the center of gravity of Jewish life from Jewish religion to Jewish peoplehood. It does to Judaism what Darwin did to biology: it affirms that Judaism has undergone evolution in response to the changes it has encountered in the world about it. It does to Judaism what Whitehead did to philosophy: it gives Judaism "concreteness and adequacy." In formulating a modern scientific ideology based on the assumption that Judaism is an evolving religious civilization, Reconstructionism is habituating Jewish life to the scientific climate of opinion of our day.

Reconstructionism focuses attention on what is wrong with Jewish life and on what has to be done to set it right. It follows Lincoln's well-known advice, "If we could first know where we are and whither we are tending, we could better judge what to do, and how to do it." On the basis of such knowledge, Reconstructionism tries to give both driving force and direction to a sprawling amorphous social amalgam known as world Jewry.

Reconstructionism is based on an adequate ideology, in that it views Judaism synoptically, scientifically, and functionally. It is synoptic, in that it sees Judaism as a multidimensional way of life; it is scientific, in that it sees Judaism as subject to the laws of human nature and society; it is functional, in that it calls upon us to improve the Jewish situation by reconstituting the Jewish people, reinterpreting the traditional conception of God, and replenishing Jewish culture.

In brief, Reconstructionism aims to render Judaism authentic, relevant, and morally and spiritually uplifting for the modern Jew.

"The Aims of Reconstructionism" [Reconstructionist Pamphlet Series]

12. The Ideology of Reconstructionism

1. Judaism is nothing less than a civilization. It consists of the group life of a people identified with a particular land, having a continuous history, a religion in common, a language and a literature of its own, and folkways, mores, law codes, and arts of its own.

2. Judaism as a religious civilization has been evolving in response to the changes in the world about it. It has passed through three stages in its evolution and is now on the threshold of a fourth stage.

3. Jewish religion is that aspect of Judaism which enables the Jew to utilize every event, act, and experience of Jewish life as a means of coming to know and worship God as the power in the universe that impels and helps him to achieve salvation, or to make the most of life.

4. As a civilization, Judaism is the product of more than a millennium of autonomous national life of our ancestors in Eretz Yisrael, and approximately two millennia of Diaspora life outside Eretz Yisrael. With the establishment of the State of Israel, the Jewish people is now in need of being reconstituted on new structural lines.

5. Outside Eretz Yisrael, Judaism can function in the life of the Jew only as a secondary civilization, the primary one being that of the country of which he is a citizen. Outside Eretz Yisrael, Jews have to live in two civilizations.

6. As a secondary civilization outside Eretz Yisrael, Judaism can flourish only through the medium of local organic communities, ethically

functioning Jewish religion, and social and cultural intercourse with the Jews in Israel.

7. The revitalization of Jewish religion, both in Israel and in the Diaspora, is indispensable as a means of giving purpose and direction to the rebirth of the Jewish people.

8. For the Jewish religion to be revitalized, it has to evolve a conception of God and the salvation of man which, by virtue of its greater approximation to reality than any of the conceptions thus far advanced, is bound to be more effective than they have been in impelling man to think and act with a sense of moral responsibility.

9. Jews outside Eretz Yisrael, whose primary civilization is that of the country they live in, owe it to their Jewish religion to foster the spiritual significance of the memorable heroes, events, texts, and places of their country's civilization. They can thus fulfill their own religious vocation as well as express their loyalty to their country in terms of universal spiritual values.

"The Aims of Reconstructionism" [Reconstructionist Pamphlet Series]

13. Observations

A people can live as long as it can reconstruct its life to meet changing conditions.

Men say the future isn't what it used to be.
    Neither is the past.
    Both are in need of reconstruction if we are to have a livable present.

Much of our traditional record of the past is myth, and much of our past is without record. That is why we are in need of reconstructing our past.

Reconstructionism seeks to put gates through the fences that divide Jews into sects.

Reconstructionism tries to say old things in a new way and new things in an old way.

Reconstructionism, far from claiming to have said the last word concerning Judaism, religion, ethics, or salvation, stresses the importance of saying the first correct word in each instance.

In describing what makes human beings fully human, the philosopher R. B. Perry states: "They not only possess adaptation but acquire it. They exhibit not only organization and adaptation but reorganization and readaptation."

Reconstructionism is thus the application to the Jewish people of that which makes human beings fully human.

Traditional Judaism was sick:
   Came the Orthodox doctors and prescribed more prayer and *mitzvot*.
   Came the Reform doctors and advised the amputation of nationhood.
   Came the secularist doctors and advised the amputation of religion.
   Came the Conservative doctors and said that all that traditional Judaism needed was a change of climate of opinion.
   Came the Reconstructionist doctors and pointed out that what Judaism needed was neither prayer nor surgery, but mental therapy. It needed first to rid itself of delusions of grandeur that alternate with a sense of guilt and inferiority. And then it needed to acquire both a sense of reality and a faith in its own capacity to meet life on its own terms.

The Orthodox conception of the ideal Jewish life is to swim against the stream.
   The Reform view is that Jewish life can be lived by swimming with the stream.
   The Reconstructionist view is that Jewish life is a matter of swimming across the stream.

The difference between Judaism as a religion and Judaism as a civilization is the difference between a *point* of reference and a *frame* of reference.

Construct or reconstruct; don't merely conserve or reform.

Not So Random Thoughts, pp. 293–96.

Bibliography

I. Books and Selected Essays and Articles by Mordecai M. Kaplan*

A. Books

Basic Values in Jewish Religion. New York, 1957.

The Daily Prayer Book (with Jack Cohen, Ira Eisenstein, Eugene Kohn, and Ludwig Nadelmann). New York, 1963.

Dat Ha-umiyut Hamusarit (Hebrew translation of *The Religion of Ethical Nationhood*). Jerusalem, 1975.

Erkey Hayahadut Vehithadshutam (Hebrew translation of *The Meaning of God in Modern Jewish Religion*). Jerusalem, 1938.

The Faith of America (with J. Paul Williams and Eugene Kohn). New York, 1951.

The Festival Prayerbook (with Jack J. Cohen, Eugene Kohn, and Ludwig Nadelmann). New York, 1958.

The Future of the American Jew. New York, 1949.

The Greater Judaism in the Making. New York, 1960.

Ha-emunah Vehamusar. (*Faith and Ethics.* In Hebrew.) Jerusalem, 1954.

High Holiday Prayer Book (with Eugene Kohn and Ira Eisenstein). New York, 1948.

Higher Jewish Education and the Future of the American Jew. Los Angeles, 1963.

If Not Now, When? (with Arthur A. Cohen). New York, 1973.

The Jewish Reconstructionist Papers (ed. M. M. Kaplan). New York, 1936.

Judaism as a Civilization. New York, 1934.

Judaism in Transition. New York, 1936.

Judaism Without Supernaturalism. New York, 1958.

Know How to Answer. New York, 1951.

Lehidush Peney Hatsionut (Hebrew translation of *A New Zionism.*) Jerusalem, 1959.

The Meaning of God in Modern Jewish Religion. New York, 1936.

*A complete bibliography of the writings of Mordecai M. Kaplan may be found in *The American Judaism of Mordecai M. Kaplan* (New York, 1990), ed. Emanuel S. Goldsmith, Mel Scult, and Robert M. Seltzer.

A New Approach to the Problem of Judaism. New York, 1924. (Reprinted as *A New Approach to Jewish Life.* New York, 1973.)

The New Haggadah for the Pesah Seder (with Eugene Kohn and Ira Eisenstein). New York, 1941 (rev. 1942, 1978).

A New Zionism. New York, 1955 (2nd enlarged ed. New York, 1959).

Not So Random Thoughts. New York, 1966.

The Purpose and Meaning of Jewish Existence. Philadelphia, 1964.

Questions Jews Ask. New York, 1956 (rev. 1966).

The Religion of Ethical Nationhood. New York, 1970.

The Sabbath Prayer Book (with Eugene Kohn and Ira Eisenstein). New York, 1945.

Di Tsukunft fun der Yidisher Religye. (*The Future of the Jewish Religion.* In Yiddish.) New York, 1938.

B. Selected Essays and Articles

"The Aims of Reconstructionism." In the Reconstructionist Pamphlet Series. N.d. [1966].

"Answer." In *The Condition of Jewish Belief,* ed. Editors of *Commentary,* 117–23. New York, 1966.

"Between Two Worlds." In *Varieties of Jewish Belief,* ed. I. Eisenstein, 133–46. New York, 1966.

"The Contribution of Judaism to World Ethics." In *The Jews: Their History, Culture and Religion,* ed. L. Finkelstein, 1: 680–712. New York, 1949.

"Escaping Judaism—Sin or Neurosis?" In *Reconstructionist* 27, no. 12 (October 20, 1961): 6–12.

"The Evolution of the Idea of God in Jewish Religion." In *The Seventy-Fifth Anniversary Volume of the Jewish Quarterly Review,* ed. A. A. Neuman and S. Zeitlin, 332–46. Philadelphia, 1967.

"The Function of the Religious School." In *The Jewish Teacher* 1, no. 1 (January 1916): 5–13.

"The Future of Judaism." In *The Menorah Journal* 2, no. 3 (June 1916): 160–72.

"How Man Comes to Know God." In *Proceedings of the Rabbinical Assembly of America, 1941–1944.* Vol. 8, ed. A. H. Neulander, 256–71. New York, 1944.

"How to Live Creatively as a Jew." In *Moments of Personal Discovery,* ed. R. M. MacIver, 93–104. New York, 1952.

"The Influences That Have Shaped My Life." In *Reconstructionist* 8, no. 10 (June 26, 1942): 27–36.

"Interdependence of Religion and Science." In *Shiv'im: Essays and Studies in Honor of Ira Eisenstein,* ed. R. A. Brauner, 15–20. Philadelphia, 1977.

"Jewish Consciousness." In *Reconstructionist* 38, no. 6 (September 22, 1972): 7–11.

"Judaism." In *Modern Trends in World Religions,* ed. A. E. Haydon, 15–24, 179–88. Chicago, 1934.

"Lessons of Catholic Ecumenism." In *The Jewish Spectator* (January 1965): 8–10.

"The Meaning of God for the Contemporary Jew." In *Tradition and Contemporary Experience,* ed. A. Jospe, 62–76. New York, 1970.

"Naturalism as a Source of Morality and Religion." In *Reconstructionist* 29, no. 1 (February 22, 1963): 6–11; no. 2 (March 8, 1963): 11–16.

"Our God as Our Collective Conscience." *Reconstructionist* 41, no. 1 (February 1975): 13–16.

"Our Religious Vocation." In *Reconstructionist* 27, no. 20 (February 9, 1962): 5–13.

"The Pragmatic Theology of the Hebrew Bible." In *Reconstructionist* 43, no. 6 (September 1977): 7–12.

"A Program for Labor Zionists." In *Jewish Frontier Anthology, 1945–1967*, 495–504. New York, 1967.

"A Program for the Reconstruction of Judaism." In *The Menorah Journal* 6, no. 4 (August 1920): 181–96.

"The Reconstitution of the Jewish People." In *Reconstructionist* 27, no. 19 (January 26, 1962): 5–14.

"Reconstructionism." In *Religion in the Twentieth Century*, ed. V. Ferm, 431–45. New York, 1948. (Paperback reprint: *Living Schools of Religion*. New York, 1958.)

"Reconstructionism Is Ecumenical." In *The Jewish Spectator* (February 1965): 12–14.

"Religion in a New Key." In *Reconstructionist* 26, no.1 (February 19, 1960): 15–18.

"The Religious Creed of Nationalism: After Sixty Years." In *Reconstructionist* 35, no. 13 (December 12, 1969): 7–13.

"Response." In *Jewish Identity*, ed. B. Litvin, 232–35. New York, 1965.

"The Revelation of God in the Human Spirit." In *Reconstructionist* 34, no. 8 (May 30, 1958): 7–12; no. 9 (June 14, 1958): 12–15.

"The Supremacy of the Torah." In *Reconstructionist* 30, no. 7 (May 15, 1964): 7–17. (Published originally in *Students Annual of the Jewish Theological Seminary of America:* 180–92. New York, 1914.)

"Toward a Philosophy of Cultural Integration." In *Approaches to Group Understanding*, ed. L. Bryson, L. Finkelstein, and R. M. MacIver, 589–625. New York, 1947.

"Toward the Formulation of Guiding Principles for the Conservative Movement." In *Tradition and Change*, ed. M. Waxman, 289–312. New York, 1958.

"The Truth About Reconstructionism." In *Commentary* 1, no. 2 (December 1945): 50–59.

"Unity and Diversity in the Conservative Movement." In *Tradition and Change*, ed. M. Waxman, 211–28. New York, 1958.

"The Unsolved Problem of Evil." In *Reconstructionist* 29, no. 7 (May 17, 1963): 6–11; no. 8 (May 31, 1963): 11–16.

"Wage Peace Or . . ." In *Proceedings of the Rabbinical Assembly, 1963*, ed. J. Harlow, 47–56. New York, 1963.

"What Is Judaism? In *The Menorah Journal* 1, no. 5 (December 1915): 309–18.

"What Is Our Human Destiny? In *Judaism* 2, no. 3 (July 1953): 195–203.

"When Is a Religion Authentic?" In *Reconstructionist* 30, no. 11 (1964–65): 9–18; no. 12: 20–26.

II. Selected Books, Essays and Articles about Mordecai M. Kaplan

A. Books

Agus, Jacob B. *Guideposts in Modern Judaism*, 125–33, 388–414. New York, 1954.
———. *The Jewish Quest*, 46, 72, 233. New York, 1983.
———. *Modern Philosophies of Judaism*, 284–385. New York, 1941.
Ahlstrom, Sidney E. *A Religious History of the American People*, 978–79. New Haven, 1972.
Alper, Michael. *Reconstructing Jewish Education*, 281–322. New York, 1957.
Ben-Horin, Meir. *Common Faith—Uncommon People*. New York, 1970.
Berkovits, Eliezer. *Major Themes in Modern Philosophies of Judaism*, 149–91. New York, 1974.
Blau, Joseph L. *Judaism in America*, 66–69, 105–7. Chicago, 1976.
———. *Modern Varieties of Judaism*, 167–85. New York, 1966.
———. *The Story of Jewish Philosophy*, 305–12. New York, 1962.
Borowitz, Eugene B. *Choices in Modern Jewish Thought*, 98–120. New York, 1983.
———. *A New Jewish Theology in the Making*, 99–122. New York, 1968.
Cohen, Arthur A. *The Natural and the Supernatural Jew*, 203–19. New York, 1962.
Cohen, Jack J. *The Case for Religious Naturalism*. New York, 1958.
———. *Jewish Education in Democratic Society*, New York, 1964.
Cohen, Naomi W. *American Jews and the Zionist Idea*, 39–40, 126–28. New York, 1975.
Dushkin, Alexander M. *Living Bridges*. Jerusalem, 1975.
Eisen, Arnold M. *The Chosen People in America*, 73–98. Bloomington, Ind., 1983.
Eisenstein, Ira. *Creative Judaism*. New York, 1953.
———. *Judaism Under Freedom*. New York, 1956.
———. *What We Mean by Religion*. New York, 1948.
———, and Eugene Kohn, eds. *Mordecai M. Kaplan: An Evaluation*. New York, 1952.
Glazer, Nathan. *American Judaism*. Chicago, 1972.
Goldsmith, Emanuel S. *Modern Trends in Jewish Religion*. Washington, D.C., 1965.
Goodman, Saul L. *Traditsye un Banayung* (Yiddish), 177–91. New York, 1967.
Gordis, Robert. *Judaism for the Modern Age*, 168–72. New York, 1955.
Hertzberg, Arthur. *The Zionist Idea*, 534–44. New York, 1959.
Kaplan, Benjamin. *The Jew and His Family*, 190–95. Baton Rouge, La., 1967.
Katz, Steven T. *Post-Holocaust Dialogues*. New York, 1983.
Kaufman, William E. *Contemporary Jewish Philosophies*, 175–216. New York, 1976.
Klein, Isaac. *A Guide to Jewish Religious Practice*. New York, 1979.
Kohn, Eugene. *The Future of Judaism in America*. New York, 1934.
———. *Good to Be a Jew*. New York, 1959.
———. *Religion and Humanity*. New York, 1953. (Paperback reprint: *Religious Humanism*. New York, 1963.)
Levinthal, Israel H. *Point of View*, 83–103. New York, 1958.
Libowitz, Richard. *Mordecai Kaplan and the Development of Reconstructionism*. New York, 1984.

Liebman, Charles S. *The Ambivalent American Jew*, 73–77. Philadelphia, 1973.
Martin, Bernard. *A History of Judaism*, 2:415–20. New York, 1974.
Miller, Alan W. *God of Daniel S.* New York, 1969.
Noveck, Simon. *Contemporary Jewish Thought*, 327–68. New York, 1963.
Parzen, Herbert. *Architects of Conservative Judaism*, 189–206. New York, 1964.
Plaut, W. Gunther. *The Growth of Reform Judaism.* New York, 1965.
Raphael, Mark Lee. *Profiles in American Judaism.* New York, 1984.
Rosenberg, Stuart E. *America Is Different*, 190–92, 200–204. New York, 1964.
———. *The Real Jewish World.* New York, 1984.
Rosenblum, Herbert. *Conservative Judaism.* New York, 1983.
Rosenthal, Gilbert S. *Four Paths to One God*, 213–56. New York, 1973.
Rudavsky, David. *Modern Jewish Religious Movements.* New York, 1979.
Schulweis, Harold M. *Evil and the Morality of God.* Cincinnati, 1984.
Schweid, Eliezer. *Hayahadut Vehatarbut Hahilonit* (Hebrew), 143–46. Tel Aviv, 1981.
Seltzer, Robert M. *Jewish People, Jewish Thought*, 748–52. New York, 1980.
Sklare, Marshall. *Conservative Judaism: An American Religious Movement.* Glencoe, Ill., 1955.
Steinberg, Milton. *Anatomy of Faith*, 174–84, 246–53. New York, 1960.
———. *The Making of the Modern Jew*, 306–12. New York, 1952.
———. *A Partisan Guide to the Jewish Problem*, 174–99. Indianapolis, 1945.
Trepp, Leo. *The Complete Book of Jewish Observance.* New York, 1980.
———. *A History of the Jewish Experience*, 397–403. New York, 1973.
———. *Judaism: Development and Life*, 203–8. North Scituate, Mass., 1974.
Urofsky, Melvin I. *We Are One!*, 245–49, 295–97. Garden City, N.Y., 1978.

B. Essays and Articles

Ackerman, Walter I. "On the Making of Jews." In *Judaism* 30, no. 1 (Winter 1981): 87–95.
Agus, Jacob B. "God in Kaplan's Thought." In *Judaism* 30, no. 1 (Winter 1981): 30–35.
———. "*The Religion of Ethical Nationhood:* A Review." In *Conservative Judaism* 34, no. 4 (March–April 1981): 28–33.
Alpert, Rebecca T. "A Defense of Kaplan's Doctrine of Vocation." In *Reconstructionist* 50, no. 1 (September 1984): 25–27.
Angoff, Charles. "Dr. Mordecai Kaplan: A Tribute from a Writer." In *Reconstructionist* 22, no. 5 (April 20, 1956): 14–18.
Ben-Horin, Meir. "Correlativity in Mordecai M. Kaplan's Theology." In *CCAR Journal* 23, no. 3 (Summer 1976): 25–37.
———. "Kaplan and Buber—Tensions and Harmonies." In *Jewish Civilization: Essays and Studies* 1, ed. R.A. Brauner, 227–84. Philadelphia, 1979.
———. "Kaplan's Hypothesis of Faith." In *Judaism* 30, no. 1 (Winter 1981): 36–44.
———. "Salvation in Mordecai M. Kaplan's Theology." In *Journal of Reform Judaism* 26, no. 1 (Winter 1979): 1–16.
Berkovits, Eliezer. "Judaism—A Civilization." In *Judaism* 30, no. 1 (Summer 1981): 53–58.

Blumenfeld, Samuel M. "Mordecai M. Kaplan: Ahad Ha'am of American Jewry." In *Reconstructionist* 22, no. 5 (April 20, 1956): 8–13.

Cohen, Jack J. "Exile and Redemption in Modern Jewish Theology." In *Diaspora: Exile and the Jewish Condition*, ed. E. Levine, 49–60. New York, 1983.

———. "Torat Ha-Reconstructionism." In *Hagut Ivrit Be-America*, vol. 2 (Hebrew), ed. M. Zahori, A. Tartakover, H. Ormian, 392–99. Tel Aviv, 1973.

Eisenstein, Ira. "Mordecai M. Kaplan." In *Great Jewish Thinkers of the Twentieth Century*, ed. S. Noveck, 253–97. Washington, D.C., 1963.

———. "Mordecai M. Kaplan and the Halakhah." In *Jewish Civilization: Essays and Studies*, ed. R. A. Brauner, 2:145–54. Philadelphia, 1981.

———. "More Myths about Kaplan." In *Reconstructionist* 46, no. 5 (July–August 1981): 17–21.

———. "Myths about Mordecai Kaplan." In *Judaism* 30, no. 1 (Winter 1981): 67–71.

Finkelstein, Louis. "Dr. Kaplan's *Greater Judaism*." In *Reconstructionist* 27, no. 3 (March 24, 1961): 21–24.

Goldsmith, Emanuel S. "Judaism, Israel and Diaspora Zionism." In *Jewish Frontier* 42, no. 7 (September 1975): 21–24.

———. "Reconstructing Jewish Worship." In the Reconstructionist Pamphlet Series. N.d. [1966].

———. "Reconstructionist Judaism." In *National Jewish Monthly* 79, no. 10 (June 1965): 4–5, 36.

———. "A Reconstructionist Views Christianity." In the Reconstructionist Pamphlet Series. N.d. [1966].

———. "Why Jewish Survival? An Answer by Mordecai Kaplan." In *Jewish Heritage* 8, no. 1 (Summer 1965): 23–27.

Hartman, David. "The Breakdown of Tradition and the Quest for Renewal: Reflections on Three Jewish Responses to Modernity. Part II: Mordecai Kaplan." *Forum* 38 (Summer 1980): 43–64.

Hertzberg, Arthur. "Introduction." In *Judaism as a Civilization*, by Mordecai M. Kaplan, xix–xxxv. Philadelphia and New York, 1981.

———. "Kaplan on the Promise of America." In *Reconstructionist* 50, no. 3 (December 1984): 13–16.

Hirsh, Richard. "Mordecai Kaplan's Understanding of Religion and the Issue of Cosmology." In *Jewish Civilization: Essays and Studies*, ed. R. A. Brauner, 2:205–19. Philadelphia, 1981.

Jospe, Raphael. "Secularism and Religion in the American Jewish Community." In *Jewish Civilization: Essays and Studies*, ed. R. A. Brauner, 1:285–300. Philadelphia, 1979.

Kaufman, William E. "Buber's and Kaplan's Critiques of Normative Judaism." In *Reconstructionist* 45, no. 5 (July 1979): 7–16.

———. "The Contemporary Relevance of Mordecai M. Kaplan's Philosophy." In *Conservative Judaism* 34, no. 4 (March–April 1981): 11–16.

———. "Mordecai M. Kaplan, Process Philosophy and the Problem of Evil." In *Reconstructionist* 47, no. 5 (July–August 1981): 26–31.

———. "The Transnatural Theology of Mordecai M. Kaplan." In *Judaism* 30, no. 1 (Winter 1981): 45–52.

Kessner, Carole. "Kaplan on Women in Jewish Life." In *Reconstructionist* 47, no. 5 (July–August 1981): 38–44.

Klatzker, David. "The Ecumenical Kaplan." In *Reconstructionist* 47, no. 5 (July–August 1981): 7–16.

Kling, Simcha. "*The Meaning of God:* A Review." In *Conservative Judaism* 34, no. 4 (March–April 1981): 24–27.

Kripke, Myer S. "*Judaism as a Civilization*—Its Enduring Impact." In *Conservative Judaism* 34, no. 4 (March–April 1981): 17–23.

Libowitz, Richard. "Mordecai M. Kaplan as Redactor." In *Reconstructionist* 45, no. 4 (June 1979): 7–13.

Liebman, Charles S. "Reconstructionism in American Jewish Life." In *American Jewish Year Book* 71 (1970): 3–99. New York, 1970.

Meyer, Michael A. "Beyond Particularism." In *Commentary* 51, no. 3 (March 1971): 71–75.

Miller, Alan W. "Reconstructionism." In *Currents and Trends in Contemporary Jewish Thought*, ed. B. Efron, 62–76. New York, 1965.

Morris, Henry. "Mordecai Kaplan's Criticisms of Maimonides' Interpretations." In *Shiv'im: Essays and Studies in Honor of Ira Eisenstein*, ed. R. A. Brauner, 269–76. Philadelphia, 1977.

Rosenthal, Gilbert S. "The Clash of Modern Ideologies of Judaism." In *Great Schisms in Jewish History*, ed. R. Jospe and S. M. Wagner, 199–253. New York, 1981.

Samuelson, Norbert M. "Can Democracy and Capitalism Be Jewish Values? Mordecai Kaplan's Political Philosophy." In *Modern Judaism* 3, no. 2 (May 1983): 189–215.

Schulweis, Harold. "The Temper of Reconstructionism." In *Jewish Life in America*, ed. T. Friedman and R. Gordis, 74–84. New York, 1955.

Schwarz, Sidney H. "Reconstructionism and Conservative Judaism." In *Judaism* 33, no. 2 (Spring 1984): 171–78.

Scult, Mel. "Halakhah and Authority in the Early Kaplan." In *Jewish Civilization: Essays and Studies*, ed. R. A. Brauner, 2:101–20. Philadelphia, 1981.

———. "Mordecai M. Kaplan: Challenges and Conflicts in the Twenties." In *American Jewish Historical Quarterly* 66, no. 3 (March 1977): 401–16.

———. "Mordecai Kaplan's Reinterpretation of the Torah." In *Conservative Judaism* 33, no.1 (Fall 1979): 63–67.

———. "The Sociologist as Theologian: The Fundamental Assumptions of Mordecai Kaplan's Thought." In *Judaism* 25, no. 3 (Summer 1976): 345–52.

———. "A Tribute to Mordecai Kaplan at 100." In *Jewish Book Annual* 38, 106–16. New York, 1980.

Siegel, Seymour. "Kaplan and Jewish Law." In *Judaism* 30, no. 1 (Winter 1981): 59–66.

———. "Mordecai M. Kaplan in Retrospect." In *Commentary* 74, no. 1 (July 1982): 58–61.

Tabak, Samuel. "Ahad Ha-Amist Elements in M. M. Kaplan's Philosophy of Judaism." In *Philip W. Lown: A Jubilee Volume*, ed. J. Pilch, 104–30. New York, 1967.

Weiss-Rosmarin, Trude. "Mordecai M. Kaplan." In *Jewish Heritage Reader*, ed. M. Adler and L. Edelman, 235–41. New York, 1965.

Index